ROYAL HISTORICAL SOCIETY

STUDIES IN HISTORY

New Series

GLADSTONE AND DANTE
VICTORIAN STATESMAN, MEDIEVAL POET

GLADSTONE AND DANTE
VICTORIAN STATESMAN, MEDIEVAL POET

Anne Isba

THE ROYAL HISTORICAL SOCIETY
THE BOYDELL PRESS

First published 2006

A Royal Historical Society publication
Published by The Boydell Press
an imprint of Boydell & Brewer Ltd
PO Box 9, Woodbridge, Suffolk IP12 3DF, UK
and of Boydell & Brewer Inc.
668 Mt Hope Avenue, Rochester, NY 14620, USA
website: www.boydellandbrewer.com

ISBN 0 86193 277 3

ISSN 0269–2244

A CIP catalogue record for this book is available
from the British Library

This book is printed on acid-free paper

t Britain by
dmin, Cornwall

Contents

List of Illustrations

Photographic acknowledgements

The jacket images are reproduced by courtesy of the National Portrait Gallery and the Conway Library, Courtauld Institue; fig. 1 by kind permission of *Punch* Ltd; plate 4 by courtesy of the Birmingham Museums and Art Gallery; plate 5 by courtesy of the Beerbohm Estate; and plate 6 by kind permission of the Aberdeen Art Gallery.

FOR BEN, RACHEL AND MIRIAM

Acknowledgements

Writing this book was helped greatly by scholarships provided by Somerville College, Oxford, and St Deiniol's Library, Hawarden; these enabled me to devote substantial periods of time to studying Gladstone's own annotated editions of the *Commedia* and other Dante-related works at the library. I am most grateful to the Fellows of Somerville College and the Trustees of St Deiniol's for this support.

Among the many librarians, archivists and curatorial staff who have helped in my research, I should like to thank in particular those at the Taylor Institute, the Courtauld Institute, the Royal Academy, the Birmingham City Museums and Art Gallery, the Aberdeen Art Gallery, Manchester Central Archive Office, the Manchester Language and Literature Library, the Sidney Jones Library at Liverpool University and the Liverpool Public Record Office. Most of all, however, I should like to express my gratitude for their cheerful and unfailing support to the staff of the Flintshire Record Office, Hawarden, and of St Deiniol's Library. My thanks are also due to Sir William Gladstone and Mr Charles Gladstone for permitting access to William Gladstone's private study, the 'Temple of Peace' at Hawarden Castle, and for allowing me to quote extensively from family papers. I am grateful also to the Oxford University Press for permission to quote extensively from the Gladstone *Diaries*. Staff at antiquarian booksellers, Bernard Quaritch, tracked down editions of the Gladstone translations that they had originally published, and I thank them for their sporting spirit.

Dr Valerio Lucchesi of Corpus Christi College, Oxford, secretary of the Oxford Dante Society, kindly provided a critical analysis of Gladstone's translations of extracts from the *Commedia*. Dr Eugenio Biagini of Robinson College, Cambridge, generously suggested improvements to the text of the thesis upon which this book is based, and encouraged me on the path to publication, as did Professor David Bebbington of Stirling University, whose additional insights into the mind of Gladstone were most helpful. For the Royal Historical Society, Professor Miles Taylor of the University of York, and Christine Linehan have been kind and patient editors in helping to shape the narrative into a presentable form.

Friends and family – who know more about Gladstone and Dante than they ever hoped to – kept the momentum going, as did two particular friends from St Deiniol's: Dr Mark Nixon and the Venerable William Pritchard, a seasoned Gladstone enthusiast, who generously shared with me not only his wealth of knowledge about Gladstone's private life but also his copy of the *Diaries* on indefinite loan, without which my research would have been much more onerous.

My greatest debt by far, however, is to Professor David Vincent. Now at the Open University, and previously at the University of Keele, Professor Vincent was my doctoral supervisor for the research on which this book is based. Gladstone had his Dante; Dante had his Virgil. For my own *dottore's* guidance along the way I remain extremely grateful.

Anne Isba
December 2005

Abbreviations

Introduction

At first sight, the figures that decorate the memorial tomb of William Ewart Gladstone (1809–98) at St Deiniol's Church, Hawarden, seem strange bedfellows (*see* plates 1 and 2). Two are conventional enough: a guardian angel stands at the prow of a Homeric ship of souls at the head of the monument, and an early Christian saint at one corner. But a bronze bas-relief on the front displays a pair of adulterous lovers from medieval Italy. At two of the other corners stand a Jewish king and a pagan Greek philosopher. They are not the obvious choice for a memorial to a life-long, God-fearing High Anglican statesman, even a pan-European one. Yet they all have a common link. St Augustine, the lovers Paolo and Francesca da Rimini, King David, Aristotle the philosopher, the winged angel, Homer and a ship of souls – all feature prominently in the dramatic work of the figure standing at the fourth corner of the tomb, by Gladstone's feet. They are all characters in the *Commedia*[1] of the thirteenth-century poet, philosopher, politician and theologian, Dante Alighieri (1265–1321).[2]

Gladstone did not, as far as we know, specify the design of his memorial before his death on Ascension Day 1898.[3] It was commissioned by the Gladstone family, from William Blake Richmond, eighteen months later, after the death of Gladstone's wife Catherine. Richmond was a family friend of long standing. His father had painted members of the Gladstone family earlier in the century.[4] He was himself called to Hawarden, the Glynne family seat that became the Gladstone home, immediately on Gladstone's death in order to sketch the Grand Old Man laid out in his study.[5] Richmond understood what Gladstone would have wanted.[6] He explained his choice of figures for the memorial tomb to Gladstone's daughter, Mary Drew:

---

1   Dante simply called his work the *Commedia*. It was Giovanni Boccaccio, a near-contemporary and the first incumbent of the chair of Dante Studies, established at Florence to atone for the city's mistreatment of the poet, who added the epithet 'divine'. Dante's original is used here.
2   David appears six times in the *Commedia*, Aristotle four, Augustine three and Homer twice. There is one appearance by the pilot angel guiding the ships of souls across Purgatory, although there are many other angel appearances overall.
3   Although William and Catherine had already discussed funeral arrangements, the details remain unknown.
4   Personal communication from the Venerable William Pritchard, former archdeacon of Montgomery, February 2001.
5   The sketch was dedicated to Sister Kate Pitts, who had nursed Gladstone in his final decline.
6   In 1903 Richmond had already exhibited a painting of Paolo and Francesca at The New Gallery which opened in London in 1888. The whereabouts of this picture are unknown.

1

The personages were chosen as fruitful types of manhood from whom Mr Gladstone gleaned much, whose work he loved, whose genius was ever the study of his spare hours as well as in a sense they were his master spirits . . . the story of Paolo and Francesca was a favourite with Mr Gladstone who thought its treatment by Dante . . . was one of the most touching as well as one of the most noble and restrained efforts of genius to be found in any language.[7]

Richmond's memorial was built by John Douglas and follows the style of the Arts and Crafts movement, as does much of Hawarden Church.[8] It was dedicated in 1906, six years after the death of Catherine, whose marble image lies next to that of her husband.[9] William and Catherine's mortal remains are buried in Westminster Abbey, rather than at Hawarden. But the Hawarden church monument is the intimate memorial established by those that knew and loved Gladstone best, and Dante one of the dominant presences they chose to decorate his spiritual resting-place.

Next door to Hawarden Church stands St Deiniol's Library, Gladstone's gift to the nation. Its west face is also adorned with a figure of Dante, high up on the wall of the library wing (see plate 3). Across the park at Hawarden Castle, in Gladstone's private study library, his 'Temple of Peace', there are two more figures of Dante: a life-size bronze bust on prominent display on a book cabinet, and a smaller one on the mantelpiece. Together, these concrete images of Dante represent a powerful visible reminder of the medieval Florentine poet's enduring influence in Gladstone's life.

Lord John Morley, Gladstone's friend, colleague and first official biographer, wrote: 'What interests the world in Mr Gladstone is even more what he was than what he did.'[10] Dante is part of who Gladstone was. To understand his interest in Dante is to understand better the man himself. The basic fact – but only that – of Gladstone's enthusiasm for Dante has been public knowledge ever since Morley's biography was published in 1903. This was partly because, at that time, Morley alone had sight of Gladstone's diaries, in which he records how Dante's *Commedia* provided him with a guide, a companion and a canon for living. But it was partly also because Morley shared and discussed with Gladstone his enthusiasm for Dante, and the poet's symbolic importance at what was a crucial time in Italian and European history.

Young Gladstone first became aware of Dante at Eton, through his close friend Arthur Hallam. It was after Hallam's untimely death that Gladstone began to tackle the *Commedia* seriously. Tracking his reading of the poem

---

[7] William Blake Richmond to Gladstone's daughter Mary Drew, quoted in Simon Reynolds, *William Blake Richmond: an artist's life*, Norwich 1995, 293.
[8] The stained glass windows, for example, include designs by William Morris, Edward Burne-Jones and Henry Holiday.
[9] The materials used in the construction of the monument are also of Italian provenance: the figures of Gladstone and his wife are of Carrara marble, the tomb of Siena marble and the plinth of Rosso Antico marble.
[10] John Morley, *Life of Gladstone*, London 1908, i. 2.

through the *Diaries* highlights the way in which Gladstone's personal circumstances at various times predisposed him to embrace with such enthusiasm the ethos of the *Commedia*, and explains how his Dante studies were sustained over the course of a lifetime.

Gladstone was not alone in his enthusiasm for Dante. Throughout the nineteenth century Dante was a popular image in Britain in both art and literature, particularly for the Pre-Raphaelites and especially in the context of the Risorgimento. The Florentine poet and his work played an important part in conditioning the nineteenth-century British view of Italy, comparable perhaps with the late twentieth-century perception of eastern Europe on the brink of a new age of freedom. But there coexisted two very different elements in the popular Victorian appropriation of Dante and the story he told. There was the perception of Dante as the *persona* he presented in his own poetry, and little more; and there was the respect for Dante as a real and multi-faceted person in history. It was this latter view of Dante, as person rather than just *persona*, that set apart Gladstone's appreciation of him from that of many of his contemporaries.

Gladstone's many, and frequently lengthy, visits to Italy were often undertaken in a spirit of exile; he would instinctively head there, for example, when out of office, thus reversing Dante's fate of having to leave Florence when sacked. During these trips, Gladstone's love and understanding of the country and Florence's most famous poet-in-exile grew in parallel with his political maturity as a liberal statesman.

In two crucial areas of life – women and religion – the attitudes of Gladstone and Dante were very close. This is another reason why the *Commedia* provided an important and enduring source of support and inspiration to Gladstone. Gladstone had a deep affinity with many aspects of the medieval tradition of courtly love. This tradition, specifically as it relates to female virtue as the interface between human and divine love, permeates Dante's *Commedia*. Belief in the feminine ideal is evident in all areas of Gladstone's life: even his work among prostitutes, aimed at restoring fallen women to the virtuous status he believed to be naturally theirs.

On the question of popes, the papacy and the respective authority of Church and State, Gladstone and Dante also had much in common. They shared a deep distrust of the papacy, though for different reasons. The idea that the temporal and spiritual were equal but opposite spheres which should mutually support, but not encroach on, each other became important to them both in different ways. And, finally, they shared with good Christians the concept that the world is a place of spiritual exile, and life a pilgrimage back to God.

Gladstone wrote on most things that interested him. Dante was no exception. His literary output on the poet covers sixty years from 1834 until shortly before his death. His published translations of three passages from the *Commedia* – plus some critical assessments of them – are in an anthology compiled with his brother-in-law George Lyttelton. He also, in retirement, undertook a painstaking evaluation of whether Dante ever studied at Oxford, an exercise variously described as a *tour de force* or a *jeu d'esprit*.

Gladstone and Dante shared many personal characteristics, which must have endeared the medieval Florentine poet to the nineteenth-century British statesman. Perhaps this, above all, provides a clue to an overall understanding of Gladstone the man. For it is indisputable that Dante provided Gladstone with a 'coping mechanism' such that, after a difficult day in parliament, he would write in his diary that he read a little Dante 'for quiet'.

For Dante, the massive task he gave himself, during political exile from Florence, of writing the *Commedia* was, amongst other things, what would nowadays be called therapy. For Gladstone, the act of reading the *Commedia* provided a similar source of comfort, perhaps in its own way also a form of therapy. It was different from Gladstone's other ways of handling stress: his attempts at rescuing fallen women, rearranging his book collections, felling trees or diary-writing. It was a different, but parallel, form of escape from the tension and anxieties that accompanied him throughout his life. In Dante, Gladstone may have found a nourishment he lacked elsewhere, and been reinforced in his belief that to strive to submit one's personal will, however imperfectly, to what appeared to be God's purpose would, in the end, receive its just reward.

The volumes of commentaries about the life and work of Gladstone and Dante are equally vast. There is a striking difference, however, in each man's own output. Gladstone's is almost unquantifiable. In private as well as public life, there was hardly a subject on which he was not prepared to express his views in writing, from Homer to horticulture. Some 750 boxes of official papers still wait to be evaluated at the British Library. Not all his private correspondence and documents relating to his family life, the Gladstone-Glynne manuscripts, stored at St Deiniol's and accessed through the Flintshire Record Office, have yet been evaluated. The original diaries have returned to Lambeth Palace.

Dante's output, by contrast, is relatively limited. There is the three-part *Commedia*; the *Vita nuova*, a book of youthful love poems linked by a prose commentary on the nature of poetry, which proved a rich source of inspiration for the Pre-Raphaelites; and there are a few minor works. These include another poetry collection, the *Canzoniere*; the partial *Convivio*, an imaginary banquet of learning and science; the *De vulgari eloquentia*, a treatise in Latin on the Italian vernacular; thirteen letters in Latin, the most significant of which were written to the Holy Roman Emperor Henry VII in whom Dante placed his forlorn hopes for the unification of Italy; and the *De monarchia* which states, in the most complete manner, Dante's views on the perfect government of human society, the issue of papal and imperial power and the need for a universal empire as the sole guarantor of justice and liberty.

Gladstone's diary entries show that he read most of these subsidiary works, in addition to his reading of the *Commedia*. He read the *Vita nuova* on Christmas Day 1855, *De vulgari eloquentia* on 2 January 1861 and *De monarchia* the same week. In later years he also read several other works and commentaries relating to Dante. These include Longfellow's translation of *Purgatory* (18 February 1864), *Dante e la libertà moderna* (30 December 1875), samples of a new translation by Dean Edward Plumptre of Wells Cathedral (2 January 1883), three works by the Swiss Dante scholar Scartazzini (on various dates in 1887 and 1888) and a translation by Comoldi around the same time. In 1888 he also read commentaries on Dante by Carducci (29 January) and Hettinger (11 February); on 25 March the same year he began Boccaccio's *Vita di Dante*, which may have helped persuade him that Dante studied at Oxford. In 1892 he read another commentary on the *Commedia* and *Canzoniere* by Dean Plumptre (3 May), also quoted in his essay on Dante at Oxford, which was published the same year. The next year Gladstone read a new publication entitled *Dante and Swedenborg* by F. Sewall (24 January 1893) and a new translation of *Purgatorio* by W. Shadwell with an introduction by Walter Pater. While his reading of the *Commedia* itself was less in later years – and this may be because he had, by then, committed most of it to memory, his reading around Dante never ceased. Gladstone's last mention of Dante in print appeared just months before his death in an appreciation of his 'earliest near friend', the late Arthur Hallam, which appeared in the *Daily Telegraph* of 5 June 1897, less than a year before he died.[11] Since it was Hallam who had first introduced Gladstone to Dante, the wheel had come full circle.

Even though, by the end of his life, Gladstone had read almost all of Dante's minor works as well as the *Commedia*, it is the influence of Dante's major work that was significant. By the time he began reading the lesser works, his *Diaries* show that Gladstone had been studying the *Commedia* for over twenty years. Moreover the ideas contained in Dante's subsidiary writings are consistent with the *Commedia* – his 'universal volume' – in which they achieve their consummate poetic expression.

It is more difficult to chart the extent of Gladstone's casual reading of Dante, or his discussions about the poet with other scholars. The *Diaries* note only his formal reading programmes, and then only their start date, and not his informal reading. As an old man, Gladstone told Morley that he only read Dante in the parliamentary recess, in order to have a 'large draught' of him.[12] However, it seems not unlikely that in earlier years Gladstone, like Ruskin, may have kept the *Commedia* to hand to dip into as one of the many

---

11 Paget Toynbee, *Dante in English literature from Chaucer to Cary*, London 1909, i. 417. Toynbee mentions Gladstone's having had a letter or article about Dante published in the *Manchester Evening News* in January 1898, a few months before he died and post-dating the Hallam memoir. British Library searches have established that there was no such item on the date specified by Toynbee, either in the *Manchester Evening News* or the *Manchester Guardian*. There was, however, an unattributed article on the letters of Dante Gabriel Rossetti in the *Manchester Guardian*, although it was so poorly reproduced as to be largely unreadable. This had no connection with Gladstone, but may have led to the confusion.
12 Morley, *Gladstone*, ii. 593.

'five-minute' books that were kept around his homes. Also, while certain diary references specify that, on meeting an acquaintance who was interested in Dante, the poet came up for discussion – as with the German theologian Ignaz von Döllinger – others do not. For example, on three occasions in as many weeks in July 1876, as well as on one occasion ten years earlier, the *Diaries* mention that Gladstone met the duke of Sermoneta socially.[13] What they do not mention is that the 14th duke was better known as Michelangelo Caetani, one of the foremost Italian Dante scholars of the day. It seems unlikely that during their meetings the *Commedia* was not touched upon. Dean Plumptre, Anthony Panizzi of the British Museum and James Lacaita, who was Gladstone's amanuensis at the time of the Naples episode, were also close acquaintances and Dante scholars. But the sparse nature of Gladstone's entries in the *Diaries* means that only very occasionally is the substance of any discussions on the subject of Dante revealed.[14]

His diaries represent Gladstone's account to God for the use of his time, an approach he owed to the influence of his older sister, Anne:[15] 'From childhood his sister Anne had brought him up to believe that waste [of time] was sinful and that at the Last Day he would be called to a reckoning of how he had spent every minute accorded him.'[16] This attitude is reminiscent of Virgil's to Dante. 'Pensa che questo dì mai non raggiorna' ('Remember that today never dawns again'), Dante recalls Virgil telling him in *Purgatorio*, adding, 'Io era bel del suo ammonir uso/ pur di non perder tempo' ('I was well accustomed to his admonition never to lose time').[17] But this approach to journal-writing also means that Gladstone's diaries read more as lists than analyses. Where they refer to Gladstone's often intense study of Dante, they give little mention of his response to that study. 'Recommenced with great anticipations of delight the Divina Commedia';[18] or, 'Finished the Divina Commedia – again. Each time it is an event in life, and suggests very much.'[19] These are as expansive as it gets. Happily, H. C. G. Matthew, the editor of the diaries, supplements Gladstone's daily journal material with additional information taken from his travel journals, providing a detailed narrative of some of his time in Italy, when much of his serious Dante study programmes were undertaken.[20]

---

[13] W. E. Gladstone, *Diaries*, ed. M. R. D. Foot (vols i–ii) and H. C. G. Matthew (vols iii–xiv), Oxford 1968–94, ix, entries for 3, 8, 24 July 1876. The entry for 25 Sept. 1884 indicates that Gladstone also read Michelangelo Caetani's *Tre chiose . . . nella Divina Comedia di Dante Alighieri; Three explanatory notes . . . in the Divine Comedy of Dante Alighieri*, n.p. 1876.
[14] *Gladstone diaries*, i, p. xxxvi.
[15] Ibid. i, p. xix.
[16] Ibid. i, pp. xl–xli.
[17] *DC, Purgatorio*, canto 12, 84–6.
[18] *Gladstone diaries*, ii, entry for 11 Nov. 1836.
[19] Ibid. vi, entry for 20 Jan. 1867.
[20] Gladstone's travel-writing seems to have been well-regarded. His description of the

Morley and other biographers

Before the publication of the *Diaries*, the only important source of public information on Gladstone's life was the biography commissioned by the family from Morley.[21] Gladstone approved the choice, having taken a favourable view of Morley's biography of Cobden. Gladstone was a trustee of Cobden's manuscripts and had consequently been considerably involved in Morley's work which he described as 'one more added to the not very long list of real biographies'.[22] Morley stressed that, in any life of Gladstone,

> His lifelong enthusiasm for Dante should on no account . . . be left out. In [him] it was something very different from casual dilettantism or the accident of a scholar's taste. He was alive to the grandeur of Goethe's words: *Im Ganzen, Guten, Schönen, resolut zu leben*, 'In wholeness, goodness, truth, strenuously to live'. But it was in Dante – active politician . . . as well as poet – that he found this unity of thought and coherence of life, not only illuminated by a sublime imagination, but directly associated with theology, philosophy, politics, history, sentiment, duty. Here are all the elements and interests that lie about the roots of a man, and of the civilisation of the world.[23]

One of the disadvantages of Morley as a biographer, from the point of view of Gladstone's study of Dante, is that Morley was an agnostic. For that reason he declined on principle to be a pall-bearer at Gladstone's funeral at Westminster Abbey, despite the prestigious participation of the future Edward VII and his son.[24] Paradoxically, Morley's agnosticism was one reason why he was chosen as a biographer by the family. They had no wish for Gladstone's spiritual life to be disclosed at this early stage. However, since Dante provided for Gladstone a spiritual inspiration that had its basis in the Christian ethic, Morley's biography leaves a large gap.

Moreover, if the obstacle facing any life-writing is the difficulty of achieving objectivity, this is particularly true of Victorian biography with its clear allocation of information to either the personal or the public realm. This was not necessarily hypocrisy or self-delusion, rather a question of preserving and protecting private life from outside scrutiny to a degree unimaginable today. Edmond Gosse, an approximate contemporary of

ascent of Etna was published in Murray's guide to Sicily, according to *The Gladstone papers*, ed. A. Tilney Bassett, London 1930, 33.

21 Morley was appointed Irish Secretary in 1886 in Gladstone's third government. He had no experience but brought a 'supple and, on the whole, sympathetic intellect, and a wide range of contacts, radical, Irish and journalistic': H. C. G. Matthew, *Gladstone*, Oxford 1997, 493.

22 Ibid. 528.

23 Morley, *Gladstone*, i. 150.

24 'The absence of John Morley from the list reflected, perhaps, family sensitivity to his agnosticism': Matthew, *Gladstone*, 528.

Morley, exemplifies the dilemma faced by a nineteenth-century biographer with an instinct for a more realistic type of life-writing. Gosse was so exercised by the prevalent hagiographic approach to biography that, in respect of two of his subjects, he wrote two separate biographies for each. Gosse's father Philip was immortalised by Edmund in a formal biography published in 1890. In 1907 Edmund published anonymously an alternative version of his perception of his life with his father, *Father and Son*, a book which, by entering the private realm, flouted the traditions of polite life-writing. Ten years later Gosse published a biography of the illustrious contemporary poet Algernon Swinburne. At the same time, in order to counter-balance this with a more truthful account of Swinburne's amoral life, Gosse also compiled a *Confidential paper on Swinburne's moral irregularities*. Until quite recently this was 'reserved from public use' at the British Museum. Gosse's problem with the duality of Victorian representation of famous people is expressed in his review of Lytton Strachey's *Eminent Victorians*, one of the major works to break away from the traditional biographical eulogy. Gosse, who has been described as trying to preserve social decorum while seeking existential truth, wrote that the fault of Victorian biographers lay, 'not in their praise, which was much of it deserved, but in their deliberate attempt in the interest of what was Nice and Proper – gods of the Victorian Age – to conceal what any conventional person might think of as not quite becoming'.[25]

This was the context of life-writing at the turn of the century when Morley was writing his biography of Gladstone. Morley had asked to see Gladstone's journal:

> He saw it; skimmed through it; and for reasons of overwhelming weight in their day, suppressed most of what he found. What Morley did with the diary – both what he put in his book, and what he left out – played a part in forming the book's character, from which in turn the modern received view of Gladstone derives.[26]

Weightier matters than Gladstone's enthusiasm for Dante will have governed decisions on inclusion or exclusion. But the fact remains that with no-one else (but for one exception discussed below) having access to Gladstone's journal until it began to be published as the *Diaries* in 1968, the extent of Gladstone's interest in the poet remained uninvestigated.

It may have been that Morley felt overburdened by the sheer volume of material at his disposal. The Gladstone family archivist, Tilney Bassett, wrote that 'Lord Morley once stated that his heart failed him on two occasions. One was his entry into Dublin Castle; and the other was the first sight of the Gladstone papers at Hawarden.'[27] Morley had to work through a quarter of a

---

[25] Edmund Gosse, *Some diversions of a man of letters*, London 1919, 321.
[26] *Gladstone diaries*, i, p. xxv.
[27] *Gladstone papers*, 1.

million documents. 'Sheer quantity overwhelmed him, and he took no trouble, when he quoted any of them, to quote correctly.' As a result, the biography's 'reliability in detail does not match its impressive tone'.[28]

Since Morley had at least glanced at the Gladstone journals, there are more Dante references in Morley's work than in other early biographical material. These include work by Williamson, Wemyss Reid, Tilney Bassett, Magnus, Feuchtwanger[29] and others whose books fill the gap until the full extent of Gladstone's Dante scholarship became clear when the *Diaries* were published. The few early biographers who mention Gladstone's interest in Dante at all – and most do not – invariably take their lead from Morley. The reference most frequently borrowed from him is to Gladstone's four dead 'doctors' – Dante, Aristotle, Augustine and Bishop Butler – from whom he claimed to have learned more than from any living teachers.

Even Paget Toynbee, the prolific and pre-eminent Victorian Dante expert, resorts to quoting Morley's lengthy explanation of Dante's importance to Gladstone as Gladstone's (rather than Morley's) main contribution to an appreciation of Dante in English art and literature, but adding in his own words that: 'In the study of Dante, few, even of Italians, were so well versed as Gladstone.'[30] Toynbee was the Oxford scholar responsible for putting Gladstone's name forward for honorary membership of the elite Oxford Dante Society in 1876. It was also he who, in an essay on Oxford and Dante, pointed out two errors in Gladstone's work on that same subject. It seems reasonable, therefore, to assume that if Toynbee were prepared to find fault with Gladstone in one context, a favourable comment by him on Gladstone's Dante scholarship in another could also be relied on for critical distance.

Returning to Morley and the same stock phrases from his biography that recur, attributed or not, in other people's, there are two notable exceptions. The first is the journalist Thomas Wemyss Reid. His 1899 biography of Gladstone includes a brief commentary on Gladstone's 1861 translations of three Dante passages – including a reproduction of part of the English version – together with a view on the 'Dante at Oxford' question. This implies that he may have been party to private information confirming the significance to Gladstone of the Dante issue. The second, more significant, exception is John Hammond in his work, *Gladstone and the Irish nation*. Hammond, seeking to explain Gladstone's popular appeal in comparison with more obvious nineteenth-century candidates such as Shaftesbury and Chamberlain, states that it was Dante, together with Homer, that determined Gladstone's liberal approach to politics.

There is interesting background to Hammond's confident assertion.

---

28 *Gladstone diaries*, i, p. xxvii.
29 David Williamson, *William Ewart Gladstone: statesman and scholar*, London 1898; T. Wemyss Reid, *Life of William Ewart Gladstone*, London 1899; *Gladstone papers*; Philip Magnus, *Gladstone: a biography*, London 1954; E. J. Feuchtwanger, *Gladstone*, London 1975.
30 Toynbee, *Dante in English literature*, ii. 601.

Morley apart, he alone of the early biographers was permitted to read an abridged family copy of Gladstone's diaries while his children were still alive. (The originals were confined to Lambeth Palace until M. R. D. Foot, a student of Hammond, and H. C. G. Matthew, a student of Foot, were commissioned by the family to begin editing them for publication.) Hammond was given access to this on condition that he reveal the privilege to no-one else.[31]

Even after the publication of the diaries and realisation of the extent of Gladstone's life-long interest in Dante, Gladstone's more recent biographers – Richard Shannon and Roy Jenkins, to name but the most prominent and prestigious after Matthew[32] – have still tended to draw primarily on those same Dante references received from Morley. Two commentators who have investigated the Gladstone–Dante relationship more closely are Owen Chadwick and Alison Milbank. Chadwick, in his essay 'Young Gladstone in Italy', given as a lecture at St Deiniol's Library,[33] brings together several strands of Gladstone's early interest in Dante, although in a limited way, since at the time of writing in 1978 not all volumes of the *Diaries* had been published. Milbank's *Dante and the Victorians*,[34] the only sustained attempt to address the subject, places Gladstone in the overall context of nineteenth-century Britain, but briefly, and primarily from a theological viewpoint.

Above all, however, mention must be made of Eugenio Biagini's short biography of Gladstone. In just three concise paragraphs it articulates in a most straightforward and useful manner the importance of Dante to Gladstone in three key areas – his Christianised Aristotelianism, pan-Europeanism and idealisation of women.[35]

As he became more proficient in Italian, Gladstone was increasingly captivated by the aesthetics of Dante's language, in particular its eloquent, evocative compression and compactness, or what T. S. Eliot describes as an 'economy of words'.[36] It was also to his reading of Dante that Gladstone attributed any gift for poetry that he had: 'I think a poetical faculty did develop itself in me between twenty and thirty, due perhaps to having read Dante with a real devotion and absorption.'[37]

---

[31] *Gladstone diaries*, i, p. ixxv. Matthew adds that 'much of the force of Hammond's *Gladstone and the Irish nation*, described by Michael Foot as "the most formidable and incisive piece of original research yet published on the history of England or Ireland in the second half of the nineteenth century" derived from his sight of this document which – truncated as it was – gave him new insights into Gladstone's character and methods'.

[32] Richard Shannon, *Gladstone: Peel's inheritor, 1809–1865*, and *Gladstone: heroic minister, 1865–1898*, London 1999. See also Roy Jenkins, *Gladstone*, London 1995.

[33] The lecture was later published in the *Journal of Ecclesiastical History* xxx (1979), 245–59.

[34] Alison Milbank, *Dante and the Victorians*, Manchester 1998, 172–4.

[35] Eugenio Biagini, *Gladstone*, Basingstoke 2000, 11–12.

[36] T. S. Eliot, *Dante*, London 1929, 32.

[37] *Gladstone papers*, 34.

But there is an enormous gap between understanding Dante and being able to render him in another language. Dorothy Sayers, perhaps the best-read Dante translator, examined the problems in detail in the introduction to the first volume of her own version of the *Commedia*.[38] Gladstone described the Dante translation process as trying to separate the 'bone from the marrow'.[39] T. S. Eliot commented that Dante's poetry 'is often expressed with such a force that the elucidation of three lines needs a paragraph'.[40]

So, what degree of artistic competence Gladstone managed to achieve – or could hope to achieve – in his own translations is debatable. What is important, however, is not the aesthetic quality of his or any other renderings of the *Commedia*, but the resonance of the ideas and the ethos contained within it, and the degree to which those ideas and that ethos formed, informed and reinforced Gladstone's own ideas about life, both here and in the hereafter.

---

[38] Dante Alighieri, *The Divine Comedy: Hell*, trans. and intro. Dorothy Sayers, Harmondsworth 1987, i. 45–65.
[39] W. E. Gladstone, 'Lord John Russell's translation of Dante's Francesca da Rimini', *English Review* (Apr. 1844), 1–16.
[40] Eliot, *Dante*, 17.

1

From First Encounter to Serious Scholarship

Towards the end of his life, Gladstone wrote to his Italian friend and Dante scholar Gianbattista Giuliani that Dante was for him 'a solemn master . . . These are not empty words. The reading of Dante is not merely a pleasure, a tour de force, or a lesson; it is a vigorous discipline for the heart, the intellect, the whole man'.[1]

In an earlier letter to his Oxford friend Henry – later Cardinal – Manning, Gladstone called Dante one of four 'doctors' or teachers who had a profound influence on him.[2] The original dictionary definition of 'doctor' is still 'teacher', as is its Italian equivalent. Writing to yet another friend, Sir Francis Doyle, in 1880, Gladstone said:

> I was born with smaller natural endowments than you and I also had a narrower early training. But my life has certainly been remarkable for the mass of continuous and searching experience it has brought for me ever since I began to pass out of boyhood. I have been feeling my way; owing little to living teachers, but enormously to four dead ones.

Morley identifies these four dead doctors as Dante, Augustine, Aristotle and the eighteenth-century theologian Bishop Joseph Butler.[3] Gladstone was clear – despite Chadwick's insistence to the contrary[4] – that these four doctors did more than just provide food for thought, or spiritual nourishment. He insisted that, although they were of prime importance to 'the speculative man . . . would they were such to the practical, too'.[5]

What initially triggered Gladstone's interest in the Florentine poet? How did that interest develop to such a degree that Gladstone saw Dante as his 'doctor' or teacher? Dante reached a peak of popularity throughout Europe in the nineteenth century. But Gladstone's devotion to his 'doctor' was different from the common enthusiasm for a dead poet whose centuries-old aspirations

---

1   This is quoted in Morley, *Gladstone*, i. 151.
2   Ibid. i. 155n. Morley identifies the other three as Augustine, Aristotle and Bishop Joseph Butler. Augustine and Aristotle also figure on Gladstone's memorial tomb at Hawarden (King David making up the fourth in place of Butler), and on the front of St Deiniol's Library.
3   Ibid. i. 154.
4   Chadwick, 'Young Gladstone', 246. Chadwick insists that, for Gladstone, Dante was exclusively a devotional aid.
5   Morley, *Gladstone*, i. 155n.

for his country were at last being realised in the new Italy of the Risorgimento.

The concept of a 'doctor' or 'dottore', a guide leading his disciple through the pilgrim's progress of life, is taken directly from Virgil's role in the *Commedia*, and represents an appropriation from Dante that seems unique to Gladstone. In the *Commedia* it is Virgil, the 'poets' poet' of the Middle Ages, the symbol of human reason, chronicler of the foundation of the Roman Empire and supposed prophet of Christianity, who leads Dante through Hell and Purgatory until the time comes to hand the task over to Beatrice – representing theology, the Church and divine grace – for the rest of the journey to God. As early as canto 5 of *Inferno*, Dante is calling Virgil 'dottore', an epithet repeated many times in various forms in the course of *Inferno* and *Purgatorio*.[6]

The idea of a select group of four doctors or teachers is also taken directly from the early part of the *Commedia*. In Limbo – the first circle of Hell, reserved for the virtuous heathen – Virgil introduces Dante to the four great poets of antiquity: Homer, Horace, Ovid and Lucan.[7] In this circle, Dante also meets Aristotle – another of Gladstone's 'doctors' and 'il maestro di color che sanno', 'the master of them that know',[8] but misses King David (another of the figures on Gladstone's memorial tomb) who, Virgil explains, was taken to Paradise by Christ during the Harrowing of Hell.[9]

So, as Virgil was the 'dottore' for Dante – and indeed as Homer, another Gladstonian hero, was for Virgil when he wrote the *Aeneid* in imitation of Homer's *Iliad* and *Odyssey* – so Dante was a 'doctor' for Gladstone.

In memory of Arthur Hallam

Owen Chadwick assumed[10] – and this view was taken up by Richard Shannon[11] – that Gladstone was first introduced to Dante by the posthumous anthology (*The remains*), published in 1834, of the poetry and prose writings of his Eton friend, Arthur Hallam, his 'earliest near friend' who had died suddenly on a trip to Vienna in the previous year at the age of twenty-two.[12]

---

[6] DC, *Inferno*, canto 5, 40. Sinclair translates 'dottore' as 'teacher'. Elsewhere, Dante also repeatedly calls Virgil 'maestro' ('master') and 'duca' ('guide') as well as, famously, 'il mare di tutto il senno' ('the sea of all wisdom').

[7] For a full discussion of the importance of Homer to Gladstone see David Bebbington, *The mind of Gladstone: religion, Homer and politics*, Oxford 2004.

[8] DC, *Inferno*, canto 4, 131.

[9] Ibid. canto 5, passim. Here we already have two of Gladstone's four doctors – Dante and Aristotle – and three of his four memorial figures – Dante, Aristotle and David – mentioned within the same canto.

[10] His opinion of Dante 'came to him with something of the force of a dying message of a friend who was dead': Chadwick, 'Young Gladstone', 248.

[11] Shannon, *Gladstone: Peel's inheritor*, 48.

[12] Morley, *Gladstone*, i. 81.

Paget Toynbee, on the other hand, maintains that Gladstone's interest in Dante dates from his first visit to Italy in 1832 when he too was twenty-two years old: of which more later. Closer inspection of the available evidence, however, suggests that Gladstone's awareness of Dante's importance for Hallam was sparked many years earlier.

Hallam was indisputably the prime instigator of Gladstone's interest in Dante, but this may well have happened when the boys were young pupils at Eton, rather than through the posthumously published work. It could have been triggered by Hallam's youthful but unpolished translation of the sonnets of the *Vita nuova*: these remained unpublished for more than a hundred years because of the censorship exercised by his father, the historian Henry Hallam, who found them crudely executed. They were, however, known at the time to Tennyson and other friends, possibly including Gladstone. Alternatively, the source of Gladstone's first interest in Dante may have been a selection of *Poems* by Arthur Hallam printed privately while he and Gladstone were still at Eton, and which Gladstone notes having read on various occasions in 1830. They include 'Farewell to the south', which on two occasions mentions the importance of Dante. Gladstone's introduction to Dante, through Hallam, thus probably came much earlier than previously thought, at a time when the adolescent Gladstone was emotionally suscep-tible to his young friend's ideas, which he was then predisposed to embrace fully after the friend's death. It is difficult to avoid a comparison between Hallam/Gladstone and Beatrice/Dante in terms of a dear departed friend providing an interface with God. Tennyson faced the same challenge.

Arthur Hallam is perhaps best remembered as the subject of the great epic poem *In memoriam* by his Cambridge friend (and Gladstone's rival for Arthur's affection), Alfred Tennyson, to whose sister Emily he had been engaged at the time of his death. On hearing the news three weeks later, Gladstone wrote:

> This intelligence was deeply oppressive even to my selfish disposition. I mourn in him, for myself, my earliest near friend . . . I walked upon the hills to muse upon this very mournful event, which cuts me to the heart . . . Alas, my poor friend was cut off in the spring of existence.[13]

Shortly afterwards, in the spring of 1834, Arthur's father Henry printed the *Remains* and circulated them privately. It is this book that Chadwick main-tains was Gladstone's first serious introduction to Dante. If so, it was a strange way for Gladstone to embark on the subject of a lifetime's devotion: not because of what the book contains but because of what is consciously excluded, through parental censorship, namely Arthur's translations from the *Vita nuova*.

In his diary entry for 18 June 1834, Gladstone recorded coming home from

---

[13] Ibid.

parliament to dine, and finding a copy of Hallam's book waiting for him. It was

> a sad memorial of death. Tis a sad subject, a very sad subject to me. I have not seen his like. The memory of him reposes gently in my inmost heart, a fountain of tears, which soften and fertilise it in the midst of pursuits whose tendency is to dry up the sources of emotion by the fever of excitement. Read his memoir. His father had done much and undeserved kindness there.[14]

Much and undeserved kindness is recorded – but no indication of any sudden awareness of Dante. The *Remains* comprise much, but not all, of Arthur Hallam's output. The elements in it which relate to Dante include a few lines from the poem 'Farewell to the south':

> Dante, heir
> Of a world's wonder, whom the Almighty gave
> To be an earnest of His power to erect
> Our souls above themselves, so as to leave
> No depth of Love, no height of intellect
> Unknown, unmaster'd[15]

Dante is also mentioned elsewhere. He features in passing, for example, in the sonnet 'Lady, I bid thee' and in Hallam's essay on 'The influence of Italian upon English literature', but by far the most substantial Dante-related item is Hallam's far-ranging critique of Gabriele Rossetti's *Analytical commentary on the Commedia*.[16] Although this critique was apparently received with respect even by Rossetti, it is a strangely unattractive introduction to the subject for any young man, even one as serious as Gladstone. In brief, Rossetti's theory was that the *Vita nuova* was not written when Dante was a young man – and therefore before the *Commedia* – but was a later work designed to serve as a key to the *Commedia*. It maintains that Dante was not only an imperialist, which he undoubtedly was at the time, although he nominally belonged to the pro-pope party, but also a freemason, opposed to Rome's[17] temporal power and spiritual pretensions, and a reformer and heretic who advanced his views on the *Commedia* through elaborate allegories. Whatever the truth of this, the point is that neither Rossetti's anti-papal dispositions nor Hallam's detailed rejection of them represents a sympathetic angle from which anyone approaching Dante for the first time might be fired with enthusiasm. On the other hand, if Gladstone had already become acquainted with the works of Dante through Hallam while at Eton, and had this interest been reinforced

---

14 Ibid. i. 84.
15 Arthur Hallam, 'The farewell to the south', in *Remains in verse and prose*, Boston 1863, ii. 241–6.
16 Gabriele Rossetti, *Disquisizioni sullo spirito anti-papale*, repr. in *The writings of Arthur Hallam*, ed. T. Vail Motter, London 1943.
17 This is quoted in *Writings of Arthur Hallam*, 115.

during his Italian travels two years earlier – on his postgraduate Grand Tour, witnessing the modern significance of the poet in his homeland at a time of longing for freedom and national unity – the debate could simply have provided additional intellectual stimulus which persuaded him that it was time to read Dante.

Other evidence supports the view that Gladstone was well aware of Arthur Hallam's interest in Dante long before the latter's death. In his letter of condolence to Henry Hallam, Gladstone wrote:

> Dante and Shakespeare were certainly the two poets whom he regarded as the highest and noblest of their class . . . I have often heard him complain that Dante was not properly appreciated even by his admirers, who dwell only on his gloomy power and sublimity, without adverting to the peculiar sweetness and tenderness which characterise, as he thought, so much of his poetry . . . Of Milton he always spoke with due reverence; but I do not believe that he recurred to him with so much delight or rated him quite so high as his favourite Dante.[18]

Hallam himself had written, in a letter to his friend W. H. Brookfield on 4 March 1831, and again in August of that year to Tennyson's sister Emily and in the August issue of the *Englishman's Magazine*, that the popularity of 'Homer, Shakespeare and Dante [was] due to the fact that they speak to the hearts of all'.[19]

As regards the *Remains*, Vail Motter points out that Rossetti's essay enabled the young Hallam

> to go beyond refutation and to say some permanent things about poetry, love and allegory. The *Remains* brings us close to that edition of the *Vita nuova* with full translation, notes and commentary, upon which Hallam was working in 1832, and which his death left unfinished.[20]

This is an important point. Arthur Hallam's translation of the *Vita nuova* is nowhere to be found in the *Remains*. In the preface to the work, Henry Hallam acknowledges their existence but says that he excluded them because he found them 'rather too literal and consequently harsh'.[21] The publication of the sonnets a century later – in *The writings of Arthur Hallam*, compiled by the Modern Language Association of America – was possible only because they had been preserved in the commonplace book of Hallam's Cambridge contemporary, J. M. Heath.[22] Had the translations from the *Vita nuova* been published with the *Remains*, they would have made Arthur Hallam the first in the field. As Vail Motter observes:

---

18 Toynbee, *Dante in English literature*, ii. 417.
19 Idem, *Britain's tribute to Dante in art and literature*, Oxford 1921, 78.
20 *Writings of Arthur Hallam*, 116.
21 Ibid. 115.
22 J. M. Heath, commonplace book, fos 189–13, quoted ibid.

That the refusal of an over-scrupulous parent to print the sonnets in 1834 robbed his son of such credit as goes to a pioneer for originality and scholarly initiative, is apparent when it is realised that Charles Lyell's translation of the sonnets and canzonieri of the *Vita nuova*, which appeared in 1835, was the first in English; that not until 1846, with the work of Joseph Garrow, was there a translation of the whole, prose as well as poetry; and that not until 1861, with Dante Rossetti's *The early Italian poets*, was Hallam's project for a translation with full apparatus achieved.[23]

The gentle courtly-love sonnets of the *Vita nuova* would have been a much better introduction to Dante for Gladstone – particularly in view of the way his opinions on women and female virtue were to develop – than Hallam's dissertation on Rossetti's view on anti-papalism in the *Commedia*, notwithstanding the vehement anti-Romanism of Gladstone's early years. And indeed, Hallam's translations from the *Vita nuova* may have been known to Gladstone before he read the *Remains*. Arthur Hallam made no secret of the translation project he was engaged upon. The work was apparently well under way when Hallam wrote to Tennyson, some time between 1828 and 1830:

> I expect to glean a good deal of knowledge from you concerning metres which may be serviceable, as well as for my philosophy in the notes for my actual handiwork in the text. I purpose to discuss considerably about poetry in general, and about the ethical character of Dante's poetry.[24]

On 29 January 1832, to his much less intimate friend, W. B. Donne, Hallam wrote:

> Towards the end of the year I may have ready for the Public . . . a translation of Dante's *Vita nuova*, prefaced by some biographical chatter, & wound up by some philosophical balderdash about poetry & metre & everything. If in the interim you have any views on any of these subjects which you can charitably spare, suggestions will be thankfully received.

If Hallam was in contact about the *Vita nuova* with his mere acquaintances Donne and Heath, not to mention his close friend Tennyson, why not with his equally close friend Gladstone? We know that he sent other poems to Gladstone at a time (1828–30) when, according to Tennyson, his translation of the *Vita nuova* would already have been well under way. In the 1830 edition of a collection of his other poems, he quotes in the title page from a letter of his to Gladstone on 17 June 1830:

---

23 Ibid.
24 From a fragment quoted in Hallam Tennyson, *Alfred, Lord Tennyson: a memoir*, London 1897, 45, and cited by Vail Motter, *Hallam*, 115.

With regard to the poems, I am glad you find anything in them to like; for my own part I have very much outgrown my parental partiality, and they are very discordant with my present view of what poetry ought to be. However, I value them as the record of several states of my mind, which may all be comprehended in a cycle out of which I fancy I am passing.[25]

This was written by Arthur Hallam just three years before he died; eighteen months before he wrote to an acquaintance that he expected soon to finish his English edition of the *Vita nuova*. As we also know, Hallam was in regular correspondence with Gladstone while he was in the process of completing his translation. It seems possible, likely even, that Gladstone had knowledge of the work, whose very nature was more likely to persuade him to become a Dante enthusiast than Arthur Hallam's *Remains*.

One final piece of evidence indicates that Gladstone's first encounters with Dante, *via* Hallam, may well have come sooner than most commentators have hitherto suggested, possibly in his early teens. This is that Hallam's fifty-nine-line translation into Greek iambics of the 'Ugolino' episode from *Inferno* 33, reprinted in the *Remains*, was, according to Toynbee, completed as early as 1824, when Hallam and Gladstone were at Eton together. Gladstone was fourteen at the time, Hallam a year younger. We know, moreover, that Gladstone was conscious of Hallam's very early interest in Dante, since he recalls it in an appreciation of his friend that appeared both in *Youth's Companion* and the *Daily Telegraph* in 1892.[26]

That Gladstone was aware of Hallam's interest in Dante well before his friend's death is further corroborated by the existence, in Gladstone's private library at Hawarden Castle, of a privately published copy of Hallam's *Poems*. It is undated, but it includes a dedication 'to my dear friend from the author'.[27] It therefore predates Hallam's death in 1833. It is followed by a quotation from Cicero, written in a different hand and in different ink, and dated 1836, presumably added by Gladstone. The book includes 'From the south', with its allusions to Dante, which was also included in the *Remains*. While the question of when Gladstone became aware of the importance of Dante remains open, the role of Hallam in that awakening is beyond doubt.

Notes and marginalia

Whatever the trigger that fired Gladstone's enthusiasm for Dante, and whenever it came, it was a powerful one. He began reading the *Commedia* on holiday at the family home at Fasque in Scotland in autumn 1834. Working

---

25 This is quoted in *Writings of Arthur Hallam*, p. xii.
26 W. E. Gladstone, 'Arthur Henry Hallam', *Youth's Companion* (Jan.1898), and 'Personal recollections of Arthur H. Hallam', *Daily Telegraph*, 5 June 1898.
27 This is on the blank front page, handwritten in ink.

on his Italian as he went – and he already had some knowledge of the language from his previous Italian visit – he read two cantos a day, finishing *Paradiso* on 4 December. The next year he 'recommenced with great anticipations of delight the Divine Comedy'.[28]

According to the *Diaries*, there followed thereafter a series of programmes of Dante study every year from 1835 to1838. Subsequently Gladstone carried out ten further bouts of intense study of the poet during the next forty years.[29] This is not, however, necessarily a complete record of his Dante reading. His casual reading is not recorded in the *Diaries*. And he certainly had enough editions of the *Commedia*, including tiny pocket editions, to leave in many places for casual reading.

In-depth Dante study, as distinct from casual reading, usually happened during a parliamentary recess, when Gladstone could devote plenty of time to his subject. In later years he avoided tackling Dante or books about him at all during a parliamentary session. As he told Morley 'I never look at Dante unless I can have a great continuous draught of him. He's too big, he seizes and masters you.'[30]

For serious study, Gladstone appears always to have used the same copy of the *Commedia* from the tens of different editions in several languages and formats kept at St Deiniol's and in the 'Temple of Peace' at Hawarden Castle.[31] His own preferred copy was the Minerva Italian version of the *Commedia*,[32] with a commentary by Baldassare Lombardi, to which he added copious annotations.[33] These deal mainly with linguistic and literary points, and occasionally with geographical ones: Dante's physical arrangement of Hell, Purgatory and Paradise is complex. Generally the notes are not conceptual; rather they are points of clarification and comparison. Gladstone would, for example, add quotation marks if necessary to facilitate his reading of the text, or comment 'ma' (yes, but) where he failed to understand completely what Dante meant. Therefore, except in the instances quoted below, the

---

[28] *Gladstone diaries*, ii, entry for 15 Nov. 1836.

[29] Gladstone's daughter, Mary Drew, corroborates the later Dante reading programmes in her diaries: *Mary Gladstone: her diaries and letters, 1870–1886*, ed. Lucy Masterman, New York 1930.

[30] Morley, *Gladstone*, ii. 497.

[31] There are more than twenty Dante-related works in Gladstone's private study at Hawarden Castle, ranging from a 1572 edition of Bartolomeo Sermatelli's *Discorso sopra la prima cantica del divinissimo theologo Dante d'Alighieri, del bello nobilissimo fiorentino, intitolata Commedia*, to a pocket version, Florence 1822, measuring perhaps one inch by three inches.

[32] The *Commedia* comprises vols i-iii of the five-volume *Opere di Dante*, Padua 1822.

[33] Only the Minerva edition contains Gladstone's own marginalia and endnotes, written in pencil. However, I have also discovered at St Deiniol's what appears to be his own copy of G. A. Scartazzini's Dante handbook, *Dante Alighieri: seine Zeit, sein Leben und seine Werke*, Biel 1869. It too contains handwritten marginalia which will be considered in chapter 7 below.

notes are inconclusive in determining any depth or substance to any specific points of Dante's influence on him.

According to H. J. Jackson, this was not untypical of marginalia written during the period from the early nineteenth century to the present day:

> What seems to have happened is that by and large readers retreated themselves and annotation became predominantly a private affair, a matter of self-expression. Annotating readers went underground. Personal systems of marks became more common . . . but without the explanatory key that enabled another reader to follow it . . . manuscripts indexed with the briefest of subject headings take the place of discursive notes: they would be sufficient for the owner, and no other reader was thought of.[34]

Matthew believes that the short notes compiled inside the front or back covers of Gladstone's books served the practical purpose of providing an index for future reference since a printed index was rare in books in those days.[35] Referring specifically to Gladstone and the uncounted numbers of annotated books preserved at St Deiniol's – and there are many more in the library at Hawarden Castle – Jackson adds that 'he does not seem to be a very forthcoming annotator'.[36] But perhaps this is not crucial, as it is possible to attach too much importance to marginalia. When outsiders study marginalia for clues to the person of the writer, for 'access to the inner life', as John Powell has called it,[37] they are, Jackson comments, assuming 'that marginalia express a reader's impulsive and unguarded reactions to a book' and are therefore an exceptionally reliable guide to personality. This, she concludes is 'a somewhat shaky assumption'.[38]

As regards Gladstone's marginal and endnotes to his copy of the *Commedia*, the theory of a private index for future reference seems sensible. The notes and marginalia are sometimes written in Latin or Greek, occasionally French or Italian, the latter especially in *Paradiso*, where one has the sense that his knowledge of Italian had become more confident.[39] They draw heavily on classical works, particularly Virgil's *Aeneid*, although Milton's *Paradise lost* – which, in a lecture, Coleridge famously compared with Dante, and found in the latter's favour – also features on a number of occasions. At the front or back of each book are lists of topics and their locations. These are difficult to interpret, consisting mainly of references to popes, Florence, similes, fame, trust, the nature of knowledge and the like.

From differences in the handwriting and style of referencing, it would

---

[34] H. J. Jackson, *Marginalia: readers writing in books*, New Haven–London 2001, 73.

[35] Matthew, *Gladstone*, 237.

[36] Jackson, *Marginalia*, 87.

[37] See n. 50 below.

[38] Jackson, *Marginalia*, 87.

[39] See appendix A for a transcription of Gladstone's handwritten annotations at the beginning and end of the three parts of the *Commedia*.

seem that the annotations and marginalia have been written at different times, and perhaps few were written at all until after his first reading of the *Commedia* as a whole. A note to canto 4 of *Inferno*, for example, refers to *Paradiso*, canto 2, although no link between the two is mentioned in Lombardi's annotations. One must therefore assume that Gladstone had already read *Paradiso* before annotating *Inferno*. The variation in the use of Roman and Arabic numerals also implies that he revisited the same text over the years. The numeration varies between Roman numerals with bars top and bottom to Roman numerals without, to Arabic numbers for cantos and lines, thence to page numbers. One assumes that this is the progression, as it moves towards simplicity. It makes no material difference to the substance of Gladstone's annotations, except that it indicates a more mature appreciation of the poem in later additions that are marked with conventional page numbers.

Four notes highlight Dante concepts particularly important for Gladstone. *Paradiso*, canto 3, 86, contains the line 'In his will is our peace' which Gladstone told his future wife Catherine Glynne he regarded as the motto for their marriage;[40] here Gladstone has written in the margin: 'English Church-women'.[41] Secondly, against key lines in canto 30, he has written: 'quoted by AHH' – that is, Arthur Hallam – which provides further confirmation that Gladstone linked his interest in Dante to the influence of his 'first near friend'. The lines thus marked relate the moment when Beatrice described for Dante the Empyrean – the highest heaven – to which she has brought him at the end of his pilgrim's journey as a place full of 'light intellectual full of love, love of true good, joy that surpasses every sweetness'.[42]

The third and fourth notes are the most significant. On the inside front cover of *Purgatorio*, Gladstone highlighted the word 'puttana', 'whore' – the word used by Dante to describe the corrupt state of the papacy in his day. Finally, towards the bottom of the inside back cover of *Purgatorio*, Gladstone wrote: 'an imp. not a Ghib. an RC not a pap'. Gladstone understood that it was possible for Dante (though not an imperialist Ghibelline) to support the emperor against the Church on a matter of principle, although nominally he belonged to the political party (the Guelphs) that supported the pope. It also implies that Gladstone realised that being a Roman Catholic did not mean you were *de facto* a papist. This reinforces the argument that Gladstone, though vehemently anti-papist at the time he wrote *The State in its relations with the Church*,[43] was nevertheless influenced by Dante, inevitably a Roman

---

[40] DC, *Paradiso*, canto 26, 64–6, was the other Gladstone 'canon for living'.

[41] Ibid. p. 50.

[42] 'Luce intelletual pieno d'amore/ Amor di vero ben, pieno di letizia,/ Letizia che trascende ogni dolzore': ibid. canto 30, 40–3.

[43] Gladstone wrote *The State in its relations with the Church*, London 1841, in the middle of his most intense Dante study programme.

Catholic, in the formulation of his ideas on the subject of Church and State.[44]

The handwritten marginalia and endnotes to volume iv of Gladstone's own copy of the *Works of Dante* – the concordance to rhymes and the index[45] – are confined to the second half of the book. They are also almost exclusively geographical.[46] Apart from three personal names (Charlemagne, Philip the Fair and Cicero), they refer either to rivers (primarily), towns or cities, and are marked in the margin with a short line, dash, number or 'nb'. At the end of the index, Gladstone has written 'Total 46 non-Italian'. On the opposite, right-hand page, he lists seven of the towns again: Arli (Arles), Doagia (Douay), Bruggia (Bruges), Guanti (Ghent), Lilla (Lille), Parigi (Paris) and Praga (Prague). On the final two blank pages he has again listed the rivers and place names, some with their *Commedia* references. It is likely that these annotations were made in preparation for his article 'Did Dante study at Oxford?', published in June 1892, which drew heavily on geographical evidence to prove its case. We know from his diary entry for 16 April 1892 that he 'worked a little on Dante's rivers'.[47]

Volume v of the *Works of Dante* includes Boccaccio's biography, various essays on the *Commedia*, and a list of some Italian editions published between 1492 and 1821.[48] On the last page of the book, Gladstone has written what appears to be the total of editions published in each century.[49]

The precise meaning of the various elements in Gladstone's annotation system has presented scholars with a challenge over the years. Ruth Clayton located an incomplete key to the more obvious annotation marks in a volume of John Locke's *Works* in St Deiniol's Library. She quotes John Powell, who undertook the first specific and detailed examination of the annotations, as admitting that 'the scholar will frequently be baffled by a variety of cryptic markings, and that these are better left alone as evidence'.[50] For the purposes of the present discussion, it is not of crucial importance what the individual marks signified but rather the topics that they highlight.

---

[44] See chapter 5 below for the long-term effects of the supposed Donation of Constantine and Dante's interpretation of it. Like Dante, Gladstone believed that both spiritual and temporal power should be invested in the same body for the greater good of mankind.

[45] *Opere di Dante*, IV: *Il rimario e indice*.

[46] Gladstone had a strong interest in topography. Geographical features were much marked in his reading for Bulgaria in 1876–7. I am grateful to Mark Nixon for this information.

[47] *Gladstone diaries*, iii

[48] *Opere di Dante*, V: *Vita e visione di Alberico*.

[49] '1472–? (not legible). Edd/ 16th. 41/ 17th. 5/ 18th. 36/ 1804–21'. This is strong evidence for a nineteenth-century Dante revival (although the data refer only to Italian editions of the *Commedia*).

[50] Ruth Clayton: 'W. E. Gladstone: an annotation key', lecture, St Deiniol's Library, June 2001. Clayton is quoting J. Powell, 'Small marks and instinctual responses: a study in the uses of Gladstone's marginalia', *Nineteenth Century Prose*, special issue xix/3 (1992), 4.

As to Gladstone's handwriting style, it is, though small, not generally diffi-cult to read. The nineteenth-century graphologist J. Holt Schooling described its simplicity as 'a most rare trait, but it may be seen in the writing of men who are remarkable for integrity, sincerity and absence of ostenta-tion'.[51] The life-long consistency of style, even during times of stress, he interprets loyally as 'an altogether abnormal instance of vitality and force'.[52]

In conclusion, Gladstone's awareness of Dante's importance may go back as far as his early teens through his friend Arthur Hallam. It blossomed in his twenties, after the death of Hallam, particularly as he came to know and love the poet's homeland. And it lasted his entire life: his apparent final published reference to Dante was an appreciation of Arthur Hallam published only months before his own death in May 1898. However, while his relationship with Dante was unique in that they shared areas of concern – politics, civic duty, theology – that transcended simple delight in Dante's poetic genius, Gladstone was not alone is his appreciation of the medieval Florentine.

[51] J. Holt Schooling, 'The handwriting of Mr Gladstone from March 1822 to March 1894', *Strand Magazine* viii (1894), 74.
[52] Ibid. 81.

2

The Victorian View of Dante

Gladstone was not the only Victorian Dante enthusiast. Marx read verses to his children when they were ill. George Eliot, said by Mary Gladstone to look like Dante,[1] quoted him liberally. She recorded over a hundred quotations from Dante in her notebooks, and many are identifiable as direct influences in her novels.[2] Tennyson lifted whole lines from Dante and made them his own.[3] Gissing is said to have based the arrangement of his fictional boarding houses on the circles of Dante's *Inferno*.[4] Ruskin called him the 'central man of all the world'.[5] In 'Deucalion', he also recommended reading Dante as a cure for depression while travelling:

> [I] took up my Cary's Dante which is always on the carriage seat, or in my pocket – not exactly for reading, but as an antidote to pestilent things, and thoughts in general, and store, as it were, of mental quinine, – a few lines being usually enough to recover me out of any shivering marsh fever fit, brought on among foulness or stupidity.[6]

Paget Toynbee, who credits Ruskin with being the main agent in spreading Dante's popularity amongst the nineteenth-century *literati*, lists amongst other fans Wordsworth, Byron, the Brownings, the Shelleys, Keats, Carlyle and Henry Hallam.[7]

---

1 Marghanita Laski, *George Eliot and her world*, Norwich 1978, 101. Laski quotes Mary Gladstone as commenting on Eliot's 'great strong face – a mixture of Savonarola and Dante'. Eliot is said to have been not displeased at the comparison. According to Kathryn Hughes it was also while reading Dante that Eliot and her husband John Cross fell in love: *George Eliot: the last Victorian*, London 1998, 334–5.
2 Andrew Thompson, *George Eliot and Italy: literary, cultural and political influences from Dante to the Risorgimento*, Basingstoke 1998, 2.
3 An example is 'Locksley Hall': *Alfred Lord Tennyson: selected poems*, London 1991, 99, 75–6. Tennyson wrote: 'This is truth the poet sings/ That a sorrow's crown of sorrows is remembering happier things.' This is a paraphrase of Francesca da Rimini's lament in *Inferno*, canto 5, 121–3: 'There is no greater pain to recall the happier time in misery.'
4 Michael Wheeler, *English fiction of the Victorian period*, London 1994, 187.
5 John Ruskin, 'The stones of Venice', in *Works*, ed. E. T. Cooke and Alexander Wedderburn, London 1912, xi. 187. There are well over 1,000 references to Dante in the index to Ruskin's works. More tangibly, Ruskin created at his Lake District home Brantwood, near Coniston, a garden based on the terraces of Dante's Mount Purgatory. The garden survives.
6 Ruskin, 'Deucalion', *Works*, xxvi. 224.
7 Toynbee, *Britain's tribute to Dante*, passim. It is interesting to note that the first volume of Toynbee's book covers the period 1380–1800, over 400 years. The second volume, which is of equal length, covers the first half of the nineteenth century, or fifty years: indication

A number of factors converged in the nineteenth century to encourage a revival in the study of Dante. First, there was the widespread interest in all things medieval. Nineteenth-century nostalgia for the perceived simplicity of the Middle Ages, at a time of rapid change and uncertainty in Britain, took many forms. They included Pre-Raphaelitism in art, neo-Gothicism in architecture and Anglo-Catholicism in religion. Nor was medievalism confined to serious culture. Gilbert and Sullivan lampooned popular contemporary poets for their 'medieval air',[8] and Queen Victoria and Prince Albert favoured medieval dress for their costume balls.[9] At the same time, there was the identification of the Renaissance by Burckhardt and others as a recognised period of culture, especially in Italy. In this context, Dante could be located as a proto-Renaissance figure straddling the gap between the Middle Ages and the Modern World.

The opening-up of Europe following the Napoleonic Wars, accelerated by the development of the continental railway system, provided new opportunities for tourism. And there were various new Dante-related tourist attractions. In 1840 a new image of Dante as a young man, attributed to Giotto, was discovered under plaster on the walls of the Bargello in Florence. Now a museum, the Bargello was a prison in the Middle Ages. Previously, images of Dante had been based on his death mask. The new find meant that he could be reinvented as a character of vigour and vitality, and as such a suitable symbolic figurehead for the new Italy. The Bargello discovery, being made by the Anglo-Florentine Seymour Kirkup, also helped to increase interest in Dante in the Anglo-Saxon world in particular. Back in London, Dante Gabriel Rossetti even painted a picture of Giotto painting a picture of Dante. Later came the discovery of Dante's tomb at Ravenna during refurbishment work prior to celebrations for the 600th anniversary of his birth in 1865.[10]

But, above all, there was the appeal of the Risorgimento, the resurgence of Italy as more than just a geographical expression, the rebirth of a nation through the expulsion of foreign powers and the reunification of individual city states. For the first time since the fall of Rome, Italy was perceived as being united in exactly the way that Dante had longed to achieve over half a millennium earlier.

---

enough of the resurgence in the English interest in Dante in the run-up to the Risorgimento.

[8] See their comic opera, *Patience*.

[9] See 'Queen Victoria and Prince Albert at the Bal Costumé' by Sir Edward Landseer (oil on canvas, 1842, Royal Collection).

[10] Dante was known to have been buried within the Franciscan monastery at Ravenna, but the exact location of his remains had been kept secret to prevent their being carried off to Florence, and subsequently forgotten. Ravenna's disinclination to let Florence get its hands on Dante was well-founded. On 20 July 1999 the *Guardian* reported, quoting *Reuter*, that a bag of Dante's ashes had been found by chance, lying on a Florence library shelf. Donated by Ravenna in 1865, they had been put on display in Florence in 1929 but then went missing, possibly when the library moved in 1935.

Translations and commentaries

There was also massive translation activity. Whether this was cause or effect of the Dante revival in the nineteenth century, translations of – and commentaries on – the *Commedia* in particular played a significant part in consolidating the trend. The name of Dante occurred for the first time in English literature in the first book of Chaucer's *House of fame*, which was probably written in 1384, some sixty-three years after Dante's death. There are some indications of an earlier interest. The insertion into the *Compleynt to his lady* – written around the time of Chaucer's first visit to Italy in 1373 – of two fragments of Dante-style *terza rima*, is the earliest instance of the use of this metre in the English language. Chaucer is also believed to have brought back the first copy of the *Commedia* to find its way to England, following another visit to Italy in 1378–9. Toynbee identifies six mentions of Dante by name in the works of Chaucer, and a total of thirty *terzine* (tercets, or three lines of verse) translated directly from the *Commedia*.

The first complete translation of Dante for the English market (but into Latin, not English) is recorded as having been carried out by Giovanni of Serravalle, bishop and prince of Fermo, in the early fifteenth century. It was accompanied by a Latin commentary. The manuscript of this translation is in the Vatican Library, with a preface that indicates that the translation was undertaken at the request of three fellow-delegates attending the Council of Constance (1414–18): an Italian cardinal plus the English bishops of Salisbury and Bath. A copy of the Latin commentary, which is the first known source of evidence for Gladstone's essay contending that Dante studied at Oxford,[11] was presented to the University of Oxford by Humphry, duke of Gloucester, together with an Italian text of the *Commedia*, in 1443.

This interest in Dante did not endure in the short term. His name virtually disappeared from English literature in the second half of the fifteenth century, reappearing in a brief mention in Alexander Barclay's *Shyp of folys* in 1509.

During the Reformation, the Protestants claimed Dante as a champion. This was because, in parts of the *Commedia*, Dante denounces the contemporary Catholic Church, which made him attractive to anti-papist English reformers.[12] This was also one of the characteristics of Dante that endeared him to Gladstone. But bearing in mind the particularly parlous state of the incumbents of the papacy in Dante's day, its corruption, divisiveness and

---

11 What Gladstone does not reveal in this essay, although Toynbee does, is that the bishop of Salisbury had previously been chancellor of the University of Oxford, and was therefore not entirely objective about whether Dante had studied there.

12 Toynbee, *Dante in English literature*, i, p. xix. Toynbee quotes Bishop John Jewel (1522–71) and John Foxe (1516–87) as specific examples.

transfer to Avignon, it is perhaps unfair to take the state of the Catholic Church at that time as typical.

Moving on to Shakespeare's time, Paget Toynbee finds little evidence that he knew Dante. And if Shakespeare didn't know Dante, it seems unlikely that anyone else in Britain did at the time:

> Few who have examined the evidence . . . will have any hesitation in endorsing the conclusion of the well-known Shakespearean scholar, who expressed the belief that 'if Shakespeare had known Dante, he would have used him, and so often, as to leave no doubt on the point'.[13]

In the first half of seventeenth century there was a brief flurry of interest in Italian literature, with Petrarch, Ariosto, Tasso, Boccaccio, Castiglione and Machiavelli among the 400 separate titles translated into English. But by and large, no Dante – who, according to John Hale, was virtually unknown in England even as late as the seventeenth century 'owing to the obscurity of his language and imagery'.[14] Milton, however, was intimately acquainted with the *Commedia*. Writing from Florence in 1638, he names Dante as among the Italian authors he read eagerly. References to the *Commedia* are to be found in every book of *Paradise lost*.

The establishment of a more enduring interest in Italian culture generally is traced by John Hale back to the publication in London in 1659 of the first English–Italian grammar by *emigré* language teacher Giovanni Torriano. Previous to that, the only recorded language aid was the Elizabethan work, *Florio, his firste fruites* (1578) written by John Florio. Florio, son of a religious refugee from the Roman inquisition – and perhaps best known for his translations of Montaigne's *Essays* – dedicated this work to the earl of Leicester 'for the benefit of all Englishmen who took pleasure in the Italian language'.[15]

John Hale comments that part of Dante's appeal was that he could be claimed by two camps: the medievalists and the Renaissance scholars, or what Hale calls 'the Ancients and the Moderns'.[16] The medievalists of the nineteenth century – Nazarenes, Pre-Raphaelites, Gothicists – saw in Dante a symbol of a simpler, more Christian time with clearer values. For them, he represented an age populated by crusaders and troubadours, with a tradition of courtly love, with heaven and hell in their proper places, and damsels in distress being rescued by knights in shining armour. For Victorian Renaissance enthusiasts, on the other hand, Dante was the first man of the New Age. They saw him as steeped in the classics, but writing in the vernacular for the benefit of all his countrymen. Most of all, they saw him exploring the fundamental nature of humanity, man's place in the universe, and the

---

[13] Ibid. i, p. xxiv. The scholar he quotes is F. J. Furnivall, *Notes and Queries* 5th ser. x. 396.
[14] John Hale, *England and the Italian Renaissance*, London 1996, 100.
[15] Ibid. 6.
[16] Ibid. 51.

concept of sin as its own hell – and virtue as its own reward – in a manner that implied a very modern understanding of psychology.

It was during the eighteenth century that Dante's position in the world of letters gradually began to gain ground in Britain, and this was also recognised in the world of art. Pope recognised a 'school of Dante' in his scheme for a history of English poetry, Toynbee reports. In 1782 the first substantial English translation from Dante appeared. Translations of other extracts followed, and English commentators began to study Dante to trace his influence on contemporary writers. Nevertheless, he was not universally appreciated. Paget Toynbee quotes Lord Chesterfield, Horace Walpole, Oliver Goldsmith and later William Wordsworth – although he went on to do his own translation – as amongst those who believed that reading Dante was not worth the trouble.[17]

The Dante translation industry has been credited with re-establishing the poet's credentials in Victorian Britain. But it seems unlikely that the translations would have been carried out in the first place had there not already existed a fundamental interest in the ideas Dante expressed. It may be useful nevertheless to outline the main features of Dante translation in the nineteenth century.

According to Gilbert Cunningham, the *Commedia* has been translated more often than any other post-classical work, with the English-speaking peoples the most prolific of all, although they were late starters. When the first major rendering appeared in English in 1782, in a translation by Charles Rogers, civil servant and art collector, Spanish, French and German translators all had several versions to their credit. During the nineteenth century English writers went rapidly ahead especially when American translators began to swell their numbers in the latter decades of the century. In the two hundred years after Rogers, there were in English eighty-two versions of one or more cantiche, approximately half before 1900 and half in the next fifty years.

The translation currently still favoured by many English Dante scholars is the prose version by the Church of Scotland minister John Dickson Sinclair, born in 1865 on the 600th anniversary of the birth of Dante. The best-read of all time, however – possibly because of her popularity as a crime writer, possibly because her publisher was Penguin – is, Gilbert Cunningham believes, that of Dorothy Sayers (1893–1957): 'the wide circulation of her version in the Penguin Classics probably exceeds the sales of all the other versions put together'.[18]

Yet until 1782 not so much as a complete canto of the *Commedia* had been printed in English translation. There had been a few versions of famous episodes – going back as far as Chaucer – but none of any great merit. Two

17 Toynbee, *Dante in English literature*, i, p. xxxv.
18 Gilbert Cunningham, *The Divine Comedy in English: a critical bibliography, 1782–1900*, London 1965, 150.

more extensive renderings (by William Huggins, 1696–1761, and Dr Charles Burnley, 1726–1814) are said to have existed in manuscript form but both are lost. Of the forty or so translations carried out between 1782 and the end of the nineteenth century, Gilbert Cunningham says 'about half we have found hardly worthy of serious consideration, and half of the remainder as definitely of the second class. Cary, indeed, is the only translator prior to 1900 who combined poetic merit with some degree of literal accuracy'.[19]

Henry Cary is the translator normally cited as having given a boost to the nineteenth-century study of Dante by making the entire original of the *Commedia* genuinely accessible to the public at large. A clergyman, as many English Dante scholars have been, Cary was born in Gibraltar in 1772, educated at Rugby and at Christ Church, Oxford – the college later attended by Gladstone – and took holy orders in 1796. His blank verse translation of the *Inferno* was published in 1805, followed by the whole of the *Commedia* in 1814. It is said to have been a lecture given in London in 1818 by Samuel Taylor Coleridge, comparing Dante with Milton – and finding in Dante's favour, that brought Cary's translation to prominence. Until then it had enjoyed an indifferent reception. Coleridge's support for Dante over Milton would have been a major – stunning, even – endorsement for the poet among the staid anglocentric *literati* of his day. Among the 120–strong audience at the lecture was Lord John Russell, who was later to publish a translation of the Paolo and Francesca episode, harshly reviewed by Gladstone.

After the Coleridge lecture – and following favourable reviews by the Venetian *emigré* Ugo Foscolo, a Dante scholar and Whig *protégé* – Cary's translation performed well. It was brought out by the enormously popular publisher Cassell. In less than three months, 1,000 copies were sold and a new edition was published the following year. A third followed in 1831, and a fourth in 1844, the year of Cary's death. The slab above the spot where he is buried in Westminster Abbey bears the simple inscription: 'The Translator of Dante'. Later editions of the Cary translation (*Inferno* from 1861, *Purgatorio* and *Paradiso* from 1868) are illustrated with prints of engravings by Gustav Doré (1832–83), which helped fix the visual image of Dante and his adventures more firmly in the reader's mind through a contemporary style of illustration to which they could relate.

Alison Milbank[20] emphasises the important role played in early nineteenth-century appreciation of Dante by Ugo Foscolo. Fleeing the Austrians, Foscolo found his way to England and was taken in by the Whig Lord Holland who had also been present at the Coleridge lecture in 1818. It was through Holland's influence that Foscolo was invited by the Whig journal, the *Edinburgh Review*, to contribute a series of articles on Italian

19 Ibid. 200.
20 Milbank, *Dante and the Victorians*.

literature, beginning with Dante. The radical Whig Sir James Mackintosh agreed to translate Foscolo's Italian.

The two articles that appeared in February and September 1818 ran to nearly seventy pages. The second article in particular set Dante, for the first time, claims Milbank, in his own volatile political milieu – a period of new wealth following the expansionist policies of Pope Gregory VII, which brought the French into Italy to balance German imperial pretensions. The article represents Dante as a Romantic figure, the representative of a nascent national culture, a public poet who was also the scourge of tyranny, who conceived and executed the project of creating the language and poetry of a nation – of exposing all the political wounds of his country – of teaching the Church and the states of Italy that the imprudence of the popes, the civil wars of the city states and the consequent introduction of foreign arms, must lead to the subjugation of Italians to external powers, to disgrace. He raised himself to a place among the reformers of morals, the avengers of crimes and the asserters of orthodoxy in religion; and he called to his aid Heaven itself.[21]

Other scholars failed to see any evidence of a more widespread nineteenth-century enthusiasm for Italian literature, and even found the interest in Dante strange. Butler, writing in 1872 in the introduction to his translation from the German of Karl Federn's *Dante and his time* remarked:

> The vogue which the study of Dante enjoys at the present time is a phenomenon somewhat difficult to explain. It is not part of any general interest in the Italian language and literature; which, in England at all events, still suffers under the 'deplorable and barbarous neglect' perceived and lamented by Mr Gladstone a quarter of a century ago.[22]

Yet there is no doubt that in many circles in mid nineteenth-century England it was fashionable to show an interest in Dante, especially in the context of Italian unification. It compares with the intense popular interest – romantic interest, even – in democratic developments in Eastern Europe in the late twentieth century, particularly in Poland and Czechoslovakia. For Victorians, Dante's 600th anniversary celebrations and the discovery of his remains at Ravenna provide the same sort of context. These events, coming just five years after a rejuvenated Italy had achieved, under Victor Emmanuel, the new unified status for which Dante had yearned, and at a time when the English community in Italy was at a peak, helped to consolidate the Victorian interest in Dante in general.

This interest continued into the twentieth century. The *Times* Dante supplement, published to coincide with the 600th anniversary of the poet's death on 14 September 1921, claimed that 'today the appeal of the great poem is wider and stronger than in any former age'.[23] The lasting heritage of

---

21 Ibid. 14.
22 Karl Federn, *Dante and his time*, trans. A. J. Butler, London 1872, introduction at p. vii.
23 *The Times*, Dante supplement, 14 Sept. 1921, iii.

Dante up to the modern day is illustrated in Nick Havely's *Dante's modern after-life* (1998). This collection of essays creates a picture of Dante's enduring influence on writing in English by a number of authors – Pound, T. S. Eliot,[24] MacNeice, Beckett and Heaney amongst others. It includes a translation by Heaney of *Inferno*, canto 2, revised for that specific publication, which may be the most eloquent piece of Dante translation produced to date in English.[25]

Scholarly versus popular appeal

Nineteenth-century interest in Dante was not, however, always perceived as genuine. Ralph Pite comments that Thomas Love Peacock 'with his sharp eye for literary fashion' observed in 1819 (the year after the Coleridge lecture) that 'Dante has suddenly become required reading'. He quotes the Honourable Mr Listless in Peacock's satire *Nightmare Abbey* as remarking:

> I don't know how it is, but Dante never came in my way till lately. I never had him in my collection, and if I had him in my collection I should not have read him. But I find he is growing fashionable, and I am afraid I must read him some wet morning.[26]

While much nineteenth-century interest in Dante was, like Gladstone's, both serious and scholarly, much was also relatively frivolous. This distinction is reflected in the diverse nature of the Dante societies established towards the end of the century. The archives of the Manchester and Liverpool societies indicate that their function was as much social as anything. Press cuttings from the society page of the *Liverpool Standard*, reporting the invariable success of their *conversazioni*, or evening gatherings, form a major part of the records of the Liverpool organisation. The Oxford and London societies, on the other hand, appear to have operated at the other end of the spectrum. Although it has not been possible to trace the records of the London Society, the subject matter of two surviving publications relating to lectures given to the society indicate that its approach was a serious literary one.[27] The Oxford Society, which still exists and has maintained immaculate

---

[24] Eliot, for example, addressing the Italian Institute in London in July 1950, acknowledged his literary indebtedness to Dante as follows: 'I still, after 40 years, regard his poetry as the most persistent and deepest influence on my verse': *To criticise the critic*, London 1965, 125, cited in Stuart Y. McDougal, 'T. S. Eliot's metaphysical Dante', in *Dante among the moderns*, Chapel Hill–London 1985, 57.

[25] Nick Haveley (ed.), *Dante's modern afterlife: reception and response from Blake to Heaney*, Basingstoke 1998. The Heaney translation is at pp. 261–4.

[26] Ralph Pite, *The circle of our vision: Dante's presence in English romantic poetry*, Oxford 1994, 78.

[27] The MLA database identifies William Warren Vernon as having given a lecture to the London Dante Society in January 1907 on 'The great Italians of the Divina Commedia'.

records from the start, was at the time of its inception a learned and select group of twelve academics who met every few months to dine and discuss the finer – and often more arcane – points of Dante scholarship. It has been possible to establish that on 14 February 1886 the august fellows of the Oxford Dante Society, dining at Exeter College, voted to appoint two honorary members. One of them was William Gladstone. The society's secretary at the time was Paget Toynbee.

Despite belonging to such an elite body, Gladstone believed that all men would benefit from taking Dante as a practical guide as well as a spiritual one. But other Dante scholars were clearly irritated at the often indiscriminate, populist enthusiasm for the great Italian poet. One of these was the French commentator Jean-Jacques Ampère (1800–64).[28] Gladstone noted in his diary on 17 December 1866 that he had read Ampère.[29] This was probably, though it is not specified, his collection of three essays, *La Grèce, Rome et Dante* (1848), which the author described as an attempt 'to compare art with the reality that inspired it'.[30] In the third essay of the trilogy, 'Voyage Dantesque', Ampère writes:

> It is a real misfortune for genuine admirers of Dante that fashion has taken up this great poet. It is sad for real enthusiasts to see the object of their devotion profaned by an infatuation that is often little more than a pretension . . . It was a good time for friends of Dante and Shakespeare when . . . they were treated as barbarians! And yet you should not renounce religion just because it is professed by a crowd whose belief is not whole-hearted; similarly, you can not abandon your literary affections just because others jump on the band-wagon. It is essential to remain true to genius and truth *despite this* . . . I am determined to persevere in my love for Dante, even though it is the current craze in both France and Italy, in season and out of season, to admire the author of the *Divine Comedy* whom virtually nobody has read for the past sixty years.[31]

---

28 Jean-Jacques was the son of the more famous André-Marie Ampère, who founded the science of electrodynamics.

29 *Gladstone diaries*, vi.

30 Jean-Jacques Ampère, 'Voyage Dantesque', in *La Grèce, Rome et Dante*, Paris 1848, 1.

31 'C'est un vrai malheur pour les admirateurs sincères de Dante que la mode se soit emparée de ce grand poëte. Il est cruel pour les vrais dévots de voir l'object de leur culte profané par un engouement qui n'est souvent qu'une prétention . . . Oh! Le bon temps pour les amis de Dante et de Shakespeare que celui où tous deux étaient traits de barbares! Cependant, on ne doit point renoncer à sa religion, parce qu'elle est professée par une foule qui ne croit pas au fond du cœur; on ne peut pas abandonner ses affections littéraires, parce qu'il est du bon air d'en afficher de pareilles. Il faut être fidèle au génie et à la verité *quand même* . . . Enfin, je suis résolu à persévérer dans mon amour pour la poésie de Dante, bien que soit aujourd'hui une fureur universelle, en France et en Italie, d'admirer à tout propos at hors de propos, l'auteur de *la Divine Comédie*, que presque personne ne lisait il y a soixante ans': ibid. 231–2. The relevance of the 'sixty years' he mentions is presumably that 1821, the 500th anniversary of Dante's death, precipitated a flurry of enthusiasm for the poet, as indeed did the 600th anniversary of his birth in 1865 and the 600th anniversary of his death in 1921.

Ampère's was clearly a book to be seen reading in the 1880s. In George Gissing's *Born in exile*, the well-established Mr Warricombe seeks to discuss the book with the social climber Godwin Peake to whom his offer of a loan of the book 'seemed a distinct advance in Mr Warricombe's friendliness. Godwin felt a thrill of encouragement'.[32] Moreover, his 'Voyage Dantesque', in particular, indicates that international plagiarism was operating in the field of Dante scholarship at the time. Ampère relates that an earlier edition of this essay had been translated and appropriated by a German with the merest nod of acknowledgement. Then an extract was translated by an Italian who omitted any mention at all of Ampère, decided that the German's name was a pseudonym, and claimed that the real author was the king of Saxony.

While it would be easy to accuse Ampère of elitism, there is undoubtedly in the nineteenth-century representation of Dante in art and literature a distinction to be made between two different approaches. This is inherent in the nature of Dante's work. The complex challenge involved in any attempt to interpret Dante in words, on canvas or in marble, is that he was simultaneously the observer and the observed. Broadly speaking, artists and writers had to choose between aligning themselves with the person or the *persona*, the actor or the author, the poet or the pilgrim. To ignore this distinction, by allowing art and life to elide, can lead to an over-simplification, distortion or misappropriation of Dante's image.

It is a difficult distinction to pin-point. But it is important as a crucial element that sets apart Gladstone's appreciation of Dante from that of many of his contemporaries. Margaret Wertheim makes a distinction between the 'real, historical man' – this would be Gladstone's man – and the narrator of 'the Christian epic of Man's soul'.[33] She compares a 'virtual Dante', moving through real space, with a real man wandering through 'virtual space'. According to her perception, a choice has to be made between a real life and an after-life, between a physical man and a spiritual man. Gladstone's choice would have been for the physical man.

In *Grammars of creation*, George Steiner indicates the key to the difficulty in separating the two modes:

> In Western poetics, the relations between object and presentment, between 'reality' and 'fiction' after the Christian message and doctrine of sacramental transmutation become *iconic*. The poem, the statue, the portrait (the self-portrait most searchingly), the nave, tell of providing lodging for the real presence.[34]

Addressing Dante in particular, Steiner speaks of 'the ability of a craftsman to

[32] George Gissing, *Born in exile*, London 1993, 173.
[33] Margaret Wertheim, *The pearly gates of cyberspace*, New York 1999, 51.
[34] George Steiner, *Grammars of creation*, London 2001, 67.

impose order on the recalcitrance of matter and empirical events. Aesthetic success . . . makes this "order" and "ordinance" perceptible to human feelings'.[35] Under the heading of creativity, Steiner compares 'untruth' with 'fiction', commenting that, 'the pilgrim's exchanges [that] Dante elicits, as it were, from the manifold of his choral monologue, dramatise, analyse in exact nuance, every mode of relationship to predecessors and contemporaries as these are gathered into the fact-fiction of the creative self'.[36]

The fact-fiction of the created self: this may be the key to understanding how Gladstone's appreciation of Dante was significantly different from that of most of his fellow Victorians. Steiner continues: 'One says "Dante", forgetting the live intricacy of the triangulation which connects Dante Alighieri – the actual name "Dante" is used only once in the entire epic – with the narrating "I" and with the persona of the Pilgrim, speaking, feeling in his own substance and seen, as it were, as a third person singular from without.'[37]

Perhaps the simplest way of illustrating this dichotomy is to take a graphic illustration. One of Botticelli's drawings of the Commedia provides an example. In Purgatory, Dante dreams that an eagle – the Dantean symbol of the empire – lifts him up to a higher level (as he believed would be achieved by the arrival of the real emperor, Henry of Luxemburg). In the 'reality' that is the Commedia, he is carried up by St Lucy, sent by the Virgin Mary. But Botticelli (like Gustav Doré after him) chooses to depict the dream eagle, thereby reflecting the idea that was in Dante's head at the time, rather than the 'reality' of St Lucy as per Dante's narrative. It is this same sense of engaging with what is going on in Dante's head – rather than with what he narrates – that distinguishes Gladstone from the many other Victorian followers of Dante.

It is significant that the focus of Gladstone's interest in Dante was concentrated on the later, and deeply serious, Commedia rather that on the youthful, romantic Vita nuova poems much favoured by the Pre-Raphaelites as a source of inspiration. In doing so, Gladstone was aligning himself with the person of Dante rather than the persona, with the real man who was a politician, theologian and philosopher as well as a poet. Despite which, Gladstone and his family maintained strong links with the Pre-Raphaelites and their successors from the 1850s onwards, a connection that was maintained by Mary Drew well into the twentieth century.

The episodes from the Commedia that Gladstone chose for his own translation exercises are considered in greater detail later. Two of them were firm Victorian favourites. One, the story of Ugolino in Inferno, canto 33, was already well known and had been translated by Chaucer as early as 1386. The Paolo and Francesca episode came a close second over the centuries. Though

---

[35] Ibid. 69.
[36] Ibid. 73.
[37] Ibid. 75.

Gladstone did not translate their story, he did commission a sculpture of the ill-fated couple from Alexander Munro in 1851 (*see* plate 4).

It is in Dante's famous tale of Paolo and Francesca da Rimini that the poet's compassion for 'carnal sinners who subject reason to desire' is demonstrated.[38] Dante relates that hearing the story from Francesca (Paolo remains silent) so moved him that he 'swooned for pity'.[39] The story goes that Francesca da Polenta of Ravenna was married to Gianciotto Malatesta, the crippled son of the lord of Rimini. She fell in love with his younger brother Paolo. Her husband took them by surprise as they were about to share their first kiss and killed them both. Contrary to popular belief, which has interpreted Francesca only as the unwilling betrothed of Gianciotto, she had in fact been married to him for several years and had a nine-year-old daughter. The young Dante would have been familiar with the handsome and dashing figure of Paolo, who was Captain of the People in Florence a few years before the tragedy. The horror of the double murder would have hit all Florence. He may have had information which predisposed him to a compassionate description of the lovers. In later years he was on very friendly terms with Francesca's family and spent his final years under the protection of her nephew, then lord of Ravenna. It is difficult to avoid finding parallels between Dante's attempt to present in a sympathetic light the adultery of his sponsor's niece and Gladstone's attempt to present in a sympathetic light, as a woman more sinned against than sinning, the errant wife of Lord Lincoln, his Oxford friend and son of his first political sponsor, the duke of Newcastle.

Gladstone became aware of the story, which fascinated Victorian Britain, in July 1834, when he first read the verse tragedy, *Francesca da Rimini*, by Silvio Pellico. This later became a very successful stage production which owed its success partly to the fact that the liberal Pellico was at the time a political prisoner of the Austrian rulers of Northern Italy. In 1851, when he commissioned the Munro sculpture, Gladstone had just returned from Naples, where he had championed the cause of liberal political activists imprisoned by the Bourbon regime.

Inspired by Rossetti's drawings of scenes from the *Inferno*, Munro had created a plaster model of Paolo and Francesca that was displayed at the Great Exhibition in 1851. Gladstone saw the work, found it very moving and wrote to Munro to ask whether it was available in any other material. Munro replied that it was not, and apologised for the sculpture's 'rough and unfinished detail, caused in the hurry of casting'. These shortcomings, he suggested, could be 'infinitely remedied by its transfer to marble, which would occupy six months and might cost about 250 guineas'.[40] Terms were agreed a week later, and the two men discussed what changes might be made

---

38 DC, *Inferno*, canto 5, 39.
39 Ibid. canto 5, 141–2.
40 Alexander Munro to W. E. Gladstone, 12 July 1851, MS GG 1475.

to 'add to . . . and immensely improve the representation of passion and feeling and tenderness' of the original in the marble version.[41]

Generously, Gladstone made two suggestions. First, that if someone else offered Munro a higher price while the work was being executed, he should feel free to take it; secondly, that he should also feel free to publicise the fact that he had received the commission from Gladstone. Munro, who was still just twenty-seven at the time, was a *protégé* of Gladstone's great friend and confidante, the duchess of Sutherland,[42] and there is a sense that Gladstone was helping further the young man's career as well as commissioning a work whose subject had moved him deeply.

Munro declined the first offer – to sell elsewhere. But he accepted the second – to advertise Gladstone's commission. Almost immediately he attached a card to that effect to the plaster cast at the exhibition. And almost immediately it was removed, since only royal patronage could be publicised. But not before members of the press, and Victoria and Albert themselves, had seen it. The duchess of Sutherland, who was the queen's Mistress of the Robes, conveyed to Munro the royal couple's 'favourable opinion' of his design.[43]

In mid-October the Great Exhibition closed and Munro was able to bring the plaster model back to his studio and begin to transfer the image to marble. Gladstone sent an advance of fifty pounds. Perhaps on the strength of Gladstone's patronage, the young sculptor moved to new premises in Upper Belgrave Place. This had the benefit of workshops; it was also more convenient for Gladstone to call and monitor the work as it progressed, 'should you be so disposed'. The block of marble had arrived and Munro reported it as 'all but spotless and beautifully transparent – such happy fortune that I cannot resist telling you of it'.[44] A few weeks later, Gladstone called in at Munro's studio to see 'my Francesca in his hands'.[45] Meanwhile, the original plaster figure went on display again, this time at the Royal Academy's annual exhibition where Gladstone found it 'very vilely placed'.[46]

About this time, Gladstone sent Munro some 'Dante criticism'. Although

41 Munro to Gladstone, 19 July 1851, ibid.
42 In 1844, when he was nineteen, the duchess arranged for Munro to work on the new Houses of Parliament. She also commissioned a chimney-piece from him in 1849. From that year onward, Munro had work exhibited at the Royal Academy exhibition almost every year. Over the years, he produced likenesses of various members of the extended Gladstone family in the form of busts, medallions and reliefs. In the summer of 1854 he was commissioned by Gladstone's eldest brother Thomas to execute a bas-relief in marble of their parents, John and Anne, for the wall of the family chapel at Fasque. It cost twenty-six guineas and was installed in December 1855: Thomas Gladstone to Munro, June 1854–Dec. 1855, GG MS 450.
43 Munro to Gladstone, 16 Aug. 1851, GG MS 1475.
44 Munro to Gladstone, 1 Jan. 1852, ibid.
45 *Gladstone diaries*, entry for 12 Feb. 1852.
46 Ibid. entry for 1 May 1852.

this has not been traced, it is clear from Munro's reply that it was in Italian and included some notes by Gladstone and his British Museum friend, Anthony Panizzi. Munro wrote 'in energetic protest against [Dante's] unjust comparison to Virgil – unjust to Dante I ever thought it, and I rejoice much, that now I have the authority of your opinion to confirm my own . . . Virgil's lines may catch the ear but they seldom touch the heart – pierce it they never do'. In his letter Munro enclosed a copy of Dante's death masque:

> It is interesting to trace those features of Dante in death, and those of his youth in Giotto's fresco. I shall be glad if you care for it enough to keep it. There are but other two in existence – one in Italy belonging to a nobleman there who gave the duplicate to Professor Rossetti from which the present is taken.[47]

By early November the sculpture was available for collection. Gladstone visited Munro 'and his beautiful work'.[48] The following week it was delivered to Gladstone's house at Carlton Gardens, where it was 'placed on its pedestal in my room – to my delight'.[49] The inscription on the base of the figure reads: 'Quel giorno più non vi leggemmo avante' ('That day we read no more'). The whereabouts of the marble sculpture, after Gladstone lent it to the Manchester Art Treasures Exhibition in 1857, was unknown until it was discovered at an antique shop in Hertford in 1960 and acquired for the Birmingham City Museum and Art Gallery where it remains today, the centre-piece of its Pre-Raphaelite collection. The original plaster version is now at Wallington Hall, Munro's home in Northumberland.

In the field of visual art, the theme of Paolo and Francesca may, Cunningham believes, have been the most frequently represented Dante image. Toynbee also lists more than fifty artistic representations of this subject in one or other of its phases, of which nine are by sculptors. Fuseli (1777), Reynolds (1777), Flaxman (1793), Blake (1824–7), Gallagher (1835) and Westmacott (1838) are among those who painted, sculpted or produced engravings for scenes depicting the couple.

The significance of the inclusion of their tragic story in the *Inferno*, and Dante's sympathetic portrayal of it, has been the subject of continuing debate, particularly since Dante is the only contemporary source of information. From him all future representations are derived. Sinclair maintains that, as with the consignment of Dante's beloved teacher Brunetti to the hellish circle of sodomites, it simply emphasises that it is a fundamental sin to subordinate reason to desire, under any circumstances and whoever you are.[50]

However, in the context of the Victorian perception of women, one interpretation deserves closer attention. Paolo and Francesca fell in love while

47 Munro to Gladstone, 4 May 1852, GG MS 1475.
48 *Gladstone diaries*, entry for 6 Nov. 1852.
49 Ibid. entry for 12 Nov. 1852.
50 DC, *Inferno*, 81.

reading together the story of Lancelot and Guinevere. Francesca admits that 'a Galeotto was the book and he that wrote it'.[51] The implication that reading romantic literature is a dangerous activity for women chimes with, for example, Ruskin's views on female education. In his essay 'Of queens' gardens', Ruskin, writing about the kind of education appropriate for women, specifically excluded romantic literature, commenting that for them, 'the best romance becomes dangerous, if, by its excitement, it renders the ordinary course of life uninteresting, and increases the morbid thirst for useless acquaintance with scenes in which we shall never be called upon to act'.[52] This is the other side of the Victorian view of woman as the angel of the hearth; that, though intrinsically good, she is also intrinsically weak and easily led, and must therefore be protected from herself. It is an issue also taken up by Alison Milbank who provides a feminist reading of the episode.[53]

Of all the Victorian Dante artists, the most prolific was Dante Gabriel Rossetti. Like Foscolo, the Rossetti family is powerful evidence that large numbers of people were moving from Italy to England, as well as *vice versa*. Gabriele Rossetti senior[54] was a librettist to the Naples opera house who escaped to London in 1824, having been sentenced to death for his revolutionary involvement. He became professor of Italian at King's College, London, and produced several works on Dante.

Between them, Gabriele Rossetti and his four children – Maria, William and Christina as well as Gabriel junior – constituted a veritable Dante industry. Between 1849 and 1882 Dante Gabriel alone executed nearly a hundred paintings or drawings of subjects from the *Vita nuova* and the *Commedia*, as well as his translations. Perhaps his most important work is the oil painting – one of several variations on the same theme executed in various sizes to fit the dimensions of his clients' rooms – entitled *Dante's dream*, the original of which now hangs in the Walker Art Gallery in Gladstone's native Liverpool. The negotiations prior to the purchase were tortuous and protracted: the Walker was one of the few places at the time prepared even to consider taking on such an enormous work which was the gallery's first Pre-Raphaelite acquisition.[55] The model for the dead Beatrice – Dante's chaste ideal of feminine virtue and for him the interface between human and divine love – was in fact William Morris's wife Jane. As she was

---

51 Ibid. canto 5, 37. Galeotto was the intermediary between Lancelot and Guinevere; his name became the synonym for a pander.
52 John Ruskin, 'Of queens' gardens', in his *Sesame and lilies*, Orpington 1894, 98.
53 Alison Milbank, 'Moral luck in the second circle: Dante and the Victorian fate of tragedy', in Havely, *Dante's modern afterlife*, 73
54 Although the first name of Rossetti's eldest son was also Gabriel, he changed the sequence of his three Christian names to put 'Dante' first – in itself an indication of the Florentine's popularity.
55 It has not been possible to establish whether the acquisition was in any way influenced by Gladstone's proximity to his native Liverpool, by his Pre-Raphaelite connections or by his brother's status as mayor of the city.

Rossetti's lover at the time, this presents a source of some irritation to Dante scholars, diminishing as it does the fundamental integrity of what Beatrice meant for Dante, and emphasising the danger of confusing person with *persona*. On the other hand, some commentators observe that Beatrice was so idealised after death that in effect she becomes a fiction, or *persona*.

In the same room as the Rossetti at the Walker is Henry Holiday's painting of Dante and Beatrice meeting on a bridge in Florence. Its postcard reproduction is said to be the most popular ever in Florence. The picture depicts a scene from a poem in the *Vita nuova* where Beatrice snubs Dante, who had allegedly been flirting with another woman. Dressed in white, Beatrice is accompanied by friends dressed in green and red. Red, white and green are the colours Dante uses to describe Beatrice's appearance in the earthly paradise in *Purgatorio*. These colours were later chosen for the flag of unified Italy. In Holiday's painting, Dante's cap – usually just red – is coloured with the red, white and blue of the United Kingdom flag, thus underlining British support for the Italian cause.

There is no evidence from the *Diaries* that Gladstone met Dante Gabriel Rossetti,[56] but there were close family links with many other artists from the extended Pre-Raphaelite circle and their successors, as with representatives of the Arts and Crafts movement. Gladstone was painted – or had busts sculpted of himself – by several of them including Millais, Watts and Leighton as well as Munro. He was also responsible for baronetcies being given to Leighton and Millais, whose portraits of him remain the best known, as well as one being offered to George Watts, who declined it.

Finally, mention should be made of visual representations of the Gladstone–Dante connection that span both the serious and the popular, namely the way he fired the imagination of Victorian cartoonists, including Max Beerbohm and the illustrators at *Punch*. Beerbohm, for example, included in *The poet's corner* a drawing depicting Dante at Oxford being interrogated by university proctors demanding to know his name and college (*see* plate 5).[57] R. G. Riewald comments that

> The drawing may have been inspired by a meeting of the members of the Dante Society, held at the City of London College on 9 February 1893, at which the Revd H. P. Gurney read a lecture by William Ewart Gladstone, the English statesman and author, entitled 'Did Dante study in Oxford' [sic]. According to the lecturer, external and corroborative evidence pointed to the conclusion that he did. Beerbohm was then an Oxford undergraduate and he must have heard about the meeting and its proceedings.[58]

---

[56] Gladstone did, however, write to his brother William, the art critic and family biographer, on 16 March 1857, as noted in *Gladstone diaries*, v. This may, however, have been on official business as William worked in the Excise Office at the time.

[57] Max Beerbohm, 'Dante in Oxford', in *The poet's corner*, London 1904.

[58] J. G. Riewald, *Beerbohm's literary caricatures*, London 1977, 34.

Gladstone's reported analysis of whether the poet studied at Oxford was one of his major contributions to Dante scholarship. Completed in his final retirement, it is considered in detail in chapter 6.

It was in 1881 that *Punch* magazine published a cartoon in which Gladstone, dressed as Dante, is accompanied by a Virgil representing the Irish nationalist Daniel O'Connell. They are surveying a scene of rioting Irishmen in the run-up to the Irish Land Act above a quotation from Dante's *Inferno*, canto 11, retitled 'The Irish "Inferno"' (*see* figure 1).

The contemporary Italian experience

For those Victorian enthusiasts, like Gladstone, who were interested in following in the footsteps of the great Dante, the early nineteenth century presented better travel opportunities than they had enjoyed for decades. From 1793 to 1815 England had been almost constantly at war with France, and as a result Italy was virtually inaccessible to English travellers. It is unsurprising, therefore, that when Europe opened up again after the end of the Napoleonic Wars, there was a flurry of interest in visiting Italy, with artists and writers in the vanguard. Time spent in a studio in Rome or Florence was almost mandatory for an aspiring painter, and many writers followed the example of the eloping Barrett-Brownings and took up long-term or permanent residence in Italy, often constructing completely self-contained expatriate communities. As well as being an exciting place to live while the concept of the Renaissance as a significant cultural period was in the process of construction, Italy was also a focus of political and romantic excitement as the country gradually moved towards unity and independence. It was a country whose political struggle attracted the interest and sympathy of liberal mid-Victorian England. It was a place where one could live well at a fraction of the cost of life in England.

However, interest in Italian political developments was not confined to British expatriates in their Tuscan or Roman colonies. Back in Britain, many people – working- and middle-class liberals in particular – watched the Italian struggle with intense sympathy. They regarded the Italian leaders Cavour, Victor Emmanuel, Mazzini and Garibaldi, all of whom had visited, or spent years of exile in England, as national heroes. Of the four men, Mazzini, the idealistic republican, and Cavour, the liberal diplomat who became the country's first prime minister, played the major roles in achieving political unity. But it was Victor Emmanuel, the constitutional monarch, and Garibaldi, the flamboyant guerrilla leader and epitome of the nineteenth-century hero, who had the greatest popular following in Britain.

Gladstone had visited Cavour in early 1859 when he passed through Northern Italy – then virtually in a state of war – on his way home from a brief period as commissioner extraordinary in the Ionian Islands. It was in Milan that he met Cavour and other Risorgimento leaders who took him into

THE IRISH "INFERNO."

"DEATH, VIOLENT DEATH, AND PAINFUL WOUNDS
UPON HIS NEIGHBOUR HE INFLICTS; AND WASTES,
BY DEVASTATION, PILLAGE, AND THE FLAMES,
HIS SUBSTANCE."—DANTE, Canto XI.

Figure 1. 'The Irish "Inferno"' depicting Gladstone as Dante with the Irish
nationalist Daniel O'Connell as Virgil: *Punch* c. 1881.

their confidence about their plans, as a result of which Gladstone arrived back in England sympathetic to change in Italy. This sympathy was reflected in an article by Gladstone which appeared in the *Quarterly Review*. This focused primarily on moves against Austria, which was in occupation of Piedmont, and against the temporal power of the pope – both sentiments Dante heartily endorsed. But despite his support for the Italian cause and his sympathy with Cavour, Gladstone clearly had difficulty in warming to Garibaldi; he may have found him too vulgar, too volatile, a loose cannon in the Italian struggle. As a result, he did little to celebrate this symbol of the new Italy when Garibaldi took up an invitation to visit England in 1864. Nevertheless, a million people turned out to welcome Garibaldi at his first appearance in London, described by *The Times* as 'a working man's reception from first to last'.[59] 'Despite his opportunities, Gladstone did not much encourage the Italianate sympathies of the English radicals, with their republican overtones, and his behaviour during Garibaldi's visit to England can only be described as vacillating. Despite his later claims, Gladstone played an important part in persuading Garibaldi to abandon his planned provincial tour.'[60]

But for his part Garibaldi was well-inclined towards Gladstone, writing to him as he left a note quoted by Tilney Bassett: 'As I leave you, please accept my gratitude to you for your goodness towards me and for the generous interest that you have always shown towards the cause of my country.'[61] Tilney Bassett also quotes another commentator, J. Temple Reader, who wrote to Gladstone: 'My belief is that most Italians look upon you in company with Victor Emmanuel, Cavour and Garibaldi, as one of the founders of Italian independence and unity.'[62]

Despite Gladstone's reservations, Garibaldi was the fashion of the season. Biscuits were named after him, women wore copies of his followers' red shirts and there was an unprecedented demand for Staffordshire figurines and Wedgwood plates bearing his image. But despite Garibaldi's popular appeal, Gladstone was not alone in failing to be amused by the British response to his extravagant appearances. Karl Marx described the whole affair as 'a miserable spectacle of imbecility' and Queen Victoria expressed herself 'half ashamed at being the head of a nation capable of such foibles'.[63]

Whatever else it achieved, Garibaldi's visit reinforced growing popular

---

[59] This quotation appears in *The Victorian vision of Italy* (exhibition catalogue), Leicester Museums and Art Gallery, Leicester 1969, 20.

[60] Matthew, *Gladstone*, 108.

[61] 'En me séparant de vous, veuillez accepter un mot de reconnaissance pour toutes les bontés dont vous m'avez comblés – et pour l'interêt bien généreux que vous m'avez manifesté en tout le temps pour le cause de mon pays': *Gladstone papers*, 110. See also Derek Beales, 'Garibaldi in England: the politics of English enthusiasm', in John Davis and Paul Ginsborg (eds), *Society and politics in the age of the Risorgimento*, Cambridge 1991.

[62] *Gladstone papers*, 83.

[63] *The Victorian vision of Italy*, 21.

interest in Italy as a focus of social, political and cultural inspiration. There were more practical attractions, too, in spending time in Italy. It was a place where one could reinvent oneself; living was inexpensive, the weather was kind and, for artists in particular, the light was ideal. And with improvements in road and rail communications, Italy was becoming easily accessible.

At the beginning of the century, the journey to Italy had been an arduous one. In 1820 Keats took four and a half weeks to sail from Gravesend to Naples, and on arrival there had to remain on board in 'quarantine', though in reality for only lasted ten days. Gladstone, too, reports having to spend days anchored in the Bay of Naples for the same reason. Even travelling over-land took the best part of a fortnight. These conditions prevailed until the advent of the railway which, by the early 1860s, had transformed the journey. In 1863 the ninth edition of Murray's *Handbook for travellers in northern Italy*,[64] first published in 1842 and followed by versions for central Italy in 1843 and southern Italy in 1853, describes the quickest and most direct route from London to Milan as taking only 51¾ hours.[65] Even this time could be shortened by some ten hours if one travelled first to Turin over the Mont Cenis pass. 'Numerous railroads have been opened of late years in Northern Italy', the handbook commented. 'Indeed, this country is little behind others in the continent as regards railway communication.' In 1864 Thomas Cook organised his first excursion to Italy.[66]

This greater ease and speed of access to Italy was good news for anyone travelling to Italy in 1865 for the 600th anniversary celebrations of Dante's birth. Gladstone was not among them. The death of Palmerston that year and the unsuccessful struggle to pass the Liberal Reform Bill gave him little leeway for foreign travel. However, all that changed the following year when Russell's Liberal administration gave way to a Conservative government under Derby following the failure of the Reform Bill. Gladstone was to be in the political wilderness for the next two and a half years, and the first thing he did was to make for Italy. The break provided him, as had previous periods of voluntary exile in Italy, with the opportunity for a concentrated period of Dante study.

---

[64] There are copies of the 1889 edition of the two volumes of Murray's *Handbook to central Italy* (i, Florence; ii, Tuscany) in Gladstone's study at Hawarden Castle.
[65] Gladstone had close links with the publisher John Murray. His diary entry for 22 September 1838 mentions 'corrections of my proofsheets and of the Handbook for S. Germany, for Murray': *Gladstone diaries*, ii. See also introduction, n. 20 above.
[66] Lynne Withey, *Grand tours and Cook's tours: a history of leisure travel, 1750–1915*, London 1998, 153 –5.

3

Gladstone and Italy

In 1893 Gladstone, then aged eighty-three, wrote to his Italian friend, Gianbattista Giuliani, that 'he who labours for Dante labours to serve Italy, Christianity, the whole world'.[1] These three sentiments illustrate why Dante was so important for Gladstone personally. During Gladstone's lifetime, the Italian peninsula was to become one state, a free and united Christian nation, and a force for stability in Europe – as Dante had so fervently desired – for the first time since the fall of the Roman Empire.

Gladstone developed a life-long love of the country. Of fourteen foreign trips he made during his life, nine were to Italy.[2] Some were several months long, often undertaken as part of extended continental tours, and one involved a dramatic personal rescue mission. Italy was the foreign country in which he spent most time, a land he associated with escape, with voluntary exile during periods out of political life, and which provided the opportunity for reflection and respite. It was a place that captured his mind as well as his heart, and Dante was a fundamental part of that attraction, both as a personal moral inspiration and as a political symbol for the new Europe. Unsurprisingly, it was often in Italy that Gladstone followed his most concentrated programmes of Dante study.

Gladstone was twenty-two years old when he embarked on his first trip to continental Europe in 1832 with his brother John Neilson, who took leave from the navy to accompany him. Gladstone had recently graduated from Oxford and, later that year, was to enter political life as the Tory MP for the duke of Newcastle's pocket borough of Newark. At the start of his second Grand Tour in 1838, during which he met his future wife Catherine Glynne, he was twenty-eight. He returned to Italy for a third time in 1849, as a married man of thirty-nine, on a dramatic but unsuccessful mission to bring Lady Lincoln back home. This ill-fated episode resembled nothing so much as a medieval knight's attempt to save the virtue of a distressed damsel.[3] The following year Gladstone spent the winter months (1850–1) in Naples where

---

1   The Standard, 9 Jan. 1893.
2   France and Germany also had something valuable to offer Gladstone, 'but each country appealed to a different element in him: Italy to his heart, Germany to his soul, and France to his mind': Christiane d'Haussy, 'Gladstone, France and his French contemporaries', in Peter Francis (ed.), The Gladstone umbrella, Hawarden 2001, 117.
3   The facts of Lady Lincoln's life indicate there was not much honour left to lose: Colin C. Eldridge, 'The Lincoln divorce case: a study in Victorian morality ', typescript, St Deiniol's Library, Hawarden, GX/X/13.

he celebrated his forty-first birthday. It was on this visit that he witnessed at first hand the mistreatment of political prisoners, made some life-long Italian friends, and conceived such a horror of state repression that commentators have said it was the making of the Liberal in him.[4]

In 1858 Gladstone and his family passed through Italy on their way home from Corfu at the end of his period as commissioner to the Ionian Islands. The islands had become a British protectorate in 1815, and Gladstone's mandate was to make recommendations as to their political future. Later, escaping the cold of England became an added incentive and the family wintered in Italy again eight years on, in 1866–7, spending Gladstone's fifty-seventh birthday at the Benedictine monastery of Monte Cassino. More than twelve years then passed before Gladstone, nearly seventy years old, returned to Italy in 1879, to spend a few weeks there and in Bavaria. In his late seventies he spent two more winter holidays in Italy: a month in 1887–8, two months in 1888–9. These were to be his last visits. From then until his death ten years later, the family wintered mainly in the south of France.

While Gladstone's first visit to Italy formed part of the classic Grand Tour between university and his first parliamentary post, all his subsequent trips to Italy were made while he was a member of parliament for a party in opposition. His second trip took place while he was out of office during the Whig administration of Lord Melbourne, 1835–41, having been under-secretary for war and the colonies in the previous Conservative government. He undertook the third when Russell formed a Whig government, which lasted from 1846 to 1852, and he lost his job as President of the Board of Trade. During the last six Conservative administrations of his political life – two each presided over by Derby, Disraeli and Salisbury – by which time he was no longer a Conservative but a Peelite or Liberal, he made five trips to Italy. The only period in opposition during which he did not travel was the short-lived second administration of Lord Salisbury. Broadly, he exploited the quieter times in his political life to expand his European horizons and in particular his understanding of Italy.

During the half-century or so that Gladstone was visiting Italy the country became more than just the geographical expression it was when he first went there. It progressed from the political divisions carved out of Napoleon's short-lived kingdom by the Congress of Vienna, through various localised wars of independence, to a united country under King Victor Emmanuel II. The nineteenth-century dream of Italian unification, for which Dante was already an icon in his capacity as an advocate of its fourteenth-century equivalent, was one that Gladstone heartily endorsed.

---

4   Gladstone served for the last time as a Conservative in the short-lived administration of Lord Derby in 1852, not long after returning from Naples. He was again Chancellor of the Exchequer, but in the Peelite/Whig coalition, from 1852 to 1855. He held the same office, as a fully-fledged Liberal, in the Palmerston government of 1859–66.

The first Grand Tour, 1832

Gladstone did not begin reading Dante seriously until September 1834, nearly two years after his first visit to Italy. At the time he was on a family holiday at Fasque and devoting much time to a wide range of Italian authors. But his fascination with Italy, along with his frequent frustration with its casual ways, were apparent from the start of his first visit. So, too, was his sense of sympathy for Italy's past history and future aspirations. But the first challenge was to learn the language.

A month into his first six-month tour of Europe Gladstone first noted in his diary that at Turin he had begun learning Italian for which, however, 'I make but little time', he wrote on 3 March 1832.[5] Two weeks later the brothers arrived in Florence where, on 17 March, he recorded: 'Went to see the Cathedral with its portraits of Dante and Hawkwood and last work of Michelangelo. Remained some time, to catch the effect and general character – so important in a building of this kind.' While there, he also witnessed two baptisms and experienced his first revulsion against Roman Catholic ritual: 'Saw two baptisms administered: dissatisfied with the matter, disgusted (I cannot use a weaker term) with the manner of service.' On 19 March he visited the church of Santa Croce: 'Monuments of Galileo, Michael Angelo (who is buried here) – Dante, only erected in 1829 – Alfieri, by Canova – and Machiavelli. A rare assemblage.'

On 29 March John and William arrived in Rome. Two days later they attended St Peter's in Rome. Morley records that it was here that Gladstone 'experienced his first conception of unity in the Church and first longed for its visible attainment'. Here he felt the 'pain and shame of schism which separates us from Rome'.[6] This was a first step to his realisation, much later, that national religions needed above all to be appropriate for the nation concerned and that, in any case, the concept of the universality of mankind transcends such things.

Gladstone started learning Italian seriously on 2 April: 'First lesson in Italian from Armellini. Thought him a good master and agreeable man.' The lessons continued every morning at a relaxed pace: 'I like Armellini much. He gives nothing to prepare in his absence: for, he says, if he does the pupils don't prepare it.' The lessons carried on until the end of the month when the brothers left Rome for Naples, where, on 5 May, Gladstone's antipathy towards Roman Catholic rituals was reiterated in his expressions of disgust at

---

5   To avoid heavy footnoting all references to diary entries in this chapter will be incorporated into the main text as dates. For reference purposes, Gladstone's first visit to Italy is covered in vol. i of the *Gladstone diaries*, his second in vol. ii, his third and fourth in vol. iv, his fifth in vol. v, his sixth in vol. vi, his seventh in vol. ix and his eighth and ninth in vol. xii.

6   Morley, *Gladstone*, i. 64.

the re-enacting of the miracle of the liquefaction of the blood of Saint Gennaro, the city's patron saint. Shortly before leaving Naples, Gladstone expressed his less than complimentary impression of the moral condition of the city in a diary entry that foreshadowed his future confrontation with the city's administration in respect of its treatment of political prisoners. In future, he would famously be describing the government of Naples' behaviour in this respect as diabolical.[7] In doing so, he echoed Dante's condemnation of medieval Florence, its political corruption and moral bankruptcy.

For the present, Gladstone, on a trip to Castellamare from Sorrento on 8 May, wrote of looking across the Bay of Naples to the city in the distance: 'How truly is this a fairy land, full to excess with all the elements of beauty, full to enchantment: what more could one desire in Paradise that its natural character, what more lamentable on this sorrowful earth than its moral condition?' Compare this with the opinion Gladstone expressed of Rome as he left the Eternal City a month later to tour northern Italy on the way back to England. His classical background may have predisposed him to the attractions of Rome rather than those of Naples. But there is also the hint in the diaries of his fascination with the interplay of temporal and spiritual power, epitomised in Rome, that found expression six years later in his first major work, *The Church in its relations with the State*. The publication of this book in December 1838 coincided with Gladstone's next trip to Rome. The Church–State debate was a topic that found a resonance for him later in the works of Dante. For the meantime, though, he noted as he departed the city on 5 June:

> Left Rome at 8am. My acquaintance with it has been short, but long enough to enable me to feel some of its fascination. The scene of two of the most extraordinary and most durable empires the world ever saw – now, even in her decay, the metropolis of a church whose branches extend to the end of the earth – the depository of the noblest collections of the trophies of art in its golden periods, and the resort of its chief votaries in this not wholly degenerate period – crowded with the speaking monuments of the dead . . . clothed in Italy's softest lines, canopied with its most liquid sky, or reflecting back its deepest burning gold – who can visit such a place of 'beauty and decay' without feeling that it opens his mind to what he never knew before and cannot hope to recall elsewhere?

During June the brothers remained in Ravenna, where Dante spent his last years of exile under the protection of Guido Novello da Polenta, and was buried in the monastery of the Franciscan friars. Gladstone wrote on 11 June of visiting the monastery church of Santa Maria del Porto 'where there is . . . the interesting tomb of Dante. Over it is a *basso-rilievo* of the post whose deeply marked countenance is riveted on his work before him. There is an inscription'. Gladstone quoted the inscription:

[7]   Ibid. i. 80.

I sang the laws of monarchy, the beings above, the lines and pit of hell, wandering wherever the fates turned me. But because my part withdrew to better regions, and sought its Actor more happily among the stars, here I, Dante, am shut in, an exile from my native shores; borne by Florence, a mother of scant love.[8]

Gladstone was impressed with the tomb but not with the sentiment: 'I know not that much can be said for this epitaph: it seems to me didactic, spiritless and obscure. I fancy the rhymes warrant one sufficiently in abusing it. But the tomb should by all means be visited – although in a public street, yet it is appropriately environed with the silence and stillness of Ravenna.' Owen Chadwick has interpreted Gladstone's expression of interest in Dante's tomb as evidence of the contrary: 'damned with the adjective "interesting" ',[9] but there seems little reason to doubt that Gladstone used the word interesting to mean precisely that; he was forthright enough in his criticism of the epitaph.

From Ravenna the brothers travelled to Milan. It is illuminating to compare Gladstone's reaction to the well-organised northern city with his earlier responses to Naples and Rome. Milan's orderliness and industriousness clearly appealed to a man for whom order and industry, as for Dante, were something of a personal obsession. On 9 July he commented: 'With what we have seen of Milan as a town, we are much pleased. It has an appearance of wealth, abundance and activity: education is far more general than in other parts of Italy: the streets are very handsome and clean, and the paths in good order: the number of soldiers immense.' By 29 July William and John were back in London.

An eventful second visit, 1838–9

Gladstone's second Grand Tour took place between August 1838 and January 1839. The diary entries compared with six years before show a much more urbane young man. In his Dante studies, he had progressed considerably. He had begun reading the original on 16 September 1834 when he noted quite simply in his diary 'Began Dante's Commedia'. Thereafter he read the work at the rate of two or sometimes three cantos a day, excluding Sundays, when his reading was more specifically devotional. On 4 October 1834, only eighteen days later, he recorded finishing all thirty-four cantos of the *Inferno*. By the time he next visited Italy, his command of Dante seemed confident.

On this second visit to Italy, Gladstone travelled alone. Approaching *via* the Alps in the autumn of 1838, he left the carriage and climbed through the

---

8 'Iura monarchiae superos phlegethonta lacusque/ Lustrando cecini, volverunt fata quousque/Sed quia pars cessit melioribus hospita castris/ Actoremque suum petiit felicior astris/ Hic claudor Dantes, patriis extorris ab oris,/ Quem genuit parvi Florentia mater amoris.'
9 Chadwick, 'Young Gladstone', 245.

Wurmser Loch ravine, where he was reminded of a scene from the *Commedia*. On 19 September he wrote:

> The depth, the range, the barrenness, the sternness, the impregnable adaman-
> tine strength of the almost immeasurable walls of rock whose masses scale the
> very heaven, present a scene that would repay almost any labour, and would
> have aided Dante with his materials for the construction of his Inferno! . . .
> read Dante, on the mountain, while waiting for the carriage 8000 feet up.
> (In Par III. IV)[10]

Gladstone apparently had a copy of Dante readily to hand, even 8,000 feet up a mountain. By way of Milan, he then travelled to Florence where he spent the last week of September but made no mention in his diaries of its most famous son. At the beginning of October he arrived in Rome. On 9 October 1838 he 'translated a little Dante'. The following day, on a visit to S. Andrea della Valle, he admired the decoration by the painter Giovanni Lanfranco of the cupola 'which wonderfully represents the circles of heaven rising in series, the idea of "di soglia in soglia" ['from threshold to threshold]', of Dante's Paradise'.[11] Apart from a trip to Sicily *via* Naples, Rome remained Gladstone's base over the Christmas and New Year period. As always, he was reading assiduously and on 28 November, commenting on Véricours's book *Milton et la poésie épique*, he expressed annoyance that the French author's 'comments on the Paradiso are most unsatisfactory: he compares it with Milton's Paradise and then naturally gives the latter the preference'. Compar-isons between Milton's *Paradise lost* and Dante's *Commedia* were a favourite nineteenth-century exercise. Gladstone was becoming partisan.

On 15 January Gladstone visited the Strada Quattro Fontane in Rome where the works of the painter Joseph Anton Koch (1768–1839) were on display. 'A portfolio of drawings from Dante are very splendid', he wrote, 'I rejoice to find that an artist of genius has so given himself to the King of Poets: it is a noble servitude. Here is the scene of Aristotle and Homer.' Aristotle and Homer were two of Gladstone's heroes, and appear in *Inferno* with other virtuous heathen in Limbo. Like Dante, Aristotle was one of the four 'doctors' – echoing Dante's description of Virgil – from whom Gladstone said he had learned most in life.

A few days later, on 19 January, Gladstone left Italy by boat from Civitavecchia for Marseilles, arriving back in London on the last day of the month – but not before he had taken a major step towards securing his domestic future. The most important element of this Italian trip for Glad-stone had undoubtedly been his growing intimacy with the Glynne family of Hawarden. He had been at Eton and Oxford with Stephen Glynne and had

---

[10] The cantos in *Paradiso* to which Gladstone refers concern the fate of Piccarda, whose maxim 'In la sua volontade è nostra pace' ('In His will is our peace') becomes the 'canon for our living' that Gladstone proposes to Catherine Glynne when she agrees to marry him.
[11] 'From threshold to threshold': *DC, Paradiso*, canto 3, 82.

met his sister Catherine two days before leaving for Italy, shortly before the Glynnes' own departure for the continent. Gladstone had already proposed unsuccessfully to two other women and was keen to take a wife. He almost brought himself to propose to Catherine in the moonlight in the Coliseum, but Catherine chose not to understand what he was saying.[12] He asked her to be his wife by letter in Rome on 17 January, two days before setting off for home.

Catherine eventually accepted him on 8 June of that year, which happened to be the anniversary of the death in 1290 of Dante's Beatrice. The following day Gladstone wrote in his diary: 'I have given her (led by her questions) these passages for canons of our living.' Of the three passages, one was from St Paul: 'Hereafter know I no man after the flesh.'[13] Two were from Dante. The first, from *Paradiso*, canto 26,[14] expresses Dante's preoccupation with the importance of divine order: 'Le frondi onde s'infronda tutto l'orto/ Del Ortolano Eterno, am'io cotanto/ Quanto de Lui in lor di bene è porto', translated in Matthew's footnote as 'The leaves leaf over all the Eternal Gardner's garden, I love in measure of the good that he has lavished on them.' The second, more important, Dante passage is from Piccarda's speech in *Paradiso*, canto 3, an episode which Gladstone later published in translation: 'In la sua volontade è nostra pace/ Ella è quel mare al qual tutto si move', translated in Matthew's foonote as 'In his will is our peace; it is the sea towards which all moves.'

William and Catherine were married at Hawarden Church on 25 July. It was a double wedding. Catherine's sister Mary married Lord George Lyttelton with whom, decades later, Gladstone was to publish his translations from the *Commedia*. Gladstone's happy experience of proposing to, and ultimately being accepted by, a woman he fell in love with in Italy enhanced the special place that the country held in his affections.

In pursuit of Lady Lincoln, 1849

Gladstone's third visit to Italy was a dramatic and short-lived affair. He left England for France in mid-July 1849 and was back less than four weeks later. His mission, unsuccessful as it turned out, was to bring home Lady Susan Lincoln, the wife of his friend Henry who had run off with her lover, Lord Walpole. If unsuccessful in bringing her ladyship home, Gladstone was to obtain evidence of her adultery so that Lincoln could proceed to a divorce.

As with most of the many women at risk that he tried to save during his life, Gladstone failed to redeem Lady Lincoln. She determinedly eluded him

---

12 Matthew, *Gladstone*, 51.
13 2 Corinthians, v. 16.
14 Matthew's footnotes to the relevant diary entry give the location as canto 36, 65. In fact it is canto 26, 64–6.

the length and breadth of Italy. His diary notes that he travelled in the space of ten days from Genoa to Leghorn, to Civitavecchia, to Rome and thence to Naples where he discovered she had again moved on. He then did the trip in reverse, finally travelling from Genoa to Milan, only to discover she had escaped yet again.

At last he tracked her down to a villa near Como where, as Jenkins has described it, 'the pursuit turned into an encounter of a sort, with an obtruding mixture of farce and tragedy'[15] with Gladstone in a state of feverish excitement on discovering that Lady Lincoln was pregnant. Gladstone had entered the villa grounds disguised as a guitarist to obtain the evidence needed for Lincoln to divorce her by private bill:[16] 'It was a day of great excitement, constant movement, overpowering sadness. I saw the Govr. of the Province – the head of the Police – the landlord . . . the levatrice [midwife]. . . . I wrote fully to Lincoln in the evening except the horror reported to me.'

Four days letter, on 3 August, he had composed another 'long and painful letter to Lincoln', commenting in his journal that

> All the delights of travelling are suppressed by the deadly weight of the subject which I carried out with me and now in a far more aggravated form I carry home. I have but one comfort: a hope flows in me, nay a belief, founded perhaps on the worthlessness and brutality of the seducer in this case, that the day of penitence will come, & that then this journey though for no worthiness God knows of mine may have its fruits.

Two days later he reached Lausanne on his journey home. His diary entry for 5 August, after going to church, reflects the depth of his dismay at the fallen woman's predicament:

> Oh that poor miserable Lady Lincoln – once the dream of dreams, the image that to my young eye combined everything that earth could offer of beauty and of joy. What is she now! But may that spotless sacrifice whereof I partook, unworthy as I am, today avail for her, to the washing away of sin, & to the renewal of the image of God.

Gladstone's image of himself as the saviour of fallen women was a recurring theme in his life. His ideal view of woman, as man's ultimate salvation, to be redeemed by him for that purpose if called on, has much in common with the medieval notion of courtly love – the foundation on which Dante's love of Beatrice is based. Gladstone's enthusiasm for attempting to rescue prostitutes was part of a medieval chivalric streak, as will be discussed in chapter 4.

---

15 Jenkins, *Gladstone*, 94.
16 Matthew, *Gladstone*, 80.

Plate 1. Dante on Gladstone's memorial in Hawarden Church.

Plate 3. Dante on the front elevation of St Deiniol's Library, Hawarden.

Plate 2. A relief of Paolo and Francesca da Rimini on Gladstone's memorial.

Plate 4. Sculpture of Paolo and Francesca da Rimini, commissioned by
Gladstone from Alexander Munro.

Dante in Oxford.   Proctor : " Your name and college ? "

Plate 5. 'Dante in Oxford', by Max Beerbohm: an illustration for *The poet's corner*, Oxford 1904.

Plate 6. *Beatrice*, a portrait of Marian Summerhayes, commissioned by Gladstone from William Dyce.

The making of a liberal

Gladstone's next visit to Italy, his fourth, lasted nearly four months. It began as a simple holiday in late 1850, and ended with important political repercussions. It was a source of embarrassment for the British government and marked a significant milestone in Gladstone's development as a liberal. The trip was ostensibly undertaken for the benefit of his daughter Mary, whose eyesight would, it was hoped (correctly, as it turned out) be improved by a change of climate. Mary was two years old at the time. The recent past had not been kind to Gladstone. His daughter Jessy had died earlier in the year, as had his sister-in-law Mary, wife of Lord Lyttelton. Gladstone had been out of office for a lengthy period: the Whig administration of Lord John Russell lasted from 1846 to 1852.

There were, then, many good reasons to travel south. The family left England in late October, arriving on 1 November, All Saints' Day, in Turin, where Gladstone records hearing a sermon on the subject of Purgatory in the church of San Lorenzo, before setting off on a nine-day journey south to Naples. On the way through Italy the party met Henry Hallam and heard of the recent death in Siena of his second son, Arthur's older brother.

Until the last few days of their stay, the Gladstones' visit was unremarkable. The family holiday had been pleasant enough: an innocuous round of theatre trips, cultural sight-seeing, social calls, shopping and the sort of domestic trivia – like protracted negotiations with the local milkman – upon which Gladstone thrived whenever he was at leisure. His main intellectual project at the time was his translation of Farini's *Lo stato romano*, published two years later in 1853. Richard Shannon describes how the Italian excursion, intended as an escape, changed into an entirely different matter:

> Gladstone badly needed to regain his equilibrium, and his instincts were all for the tonic soothings of tourism, art-purchasing, book-hunting, sermonology, theatre, light society. The last thing he anticipated was getting involved in Neapolitan politics . . . If anyone was to be dubbed as the embodiment of Lord Aberdeen's policy of non-interference and forbearance to foreign states it would be Gladstone. When . . . (at a tea party) . . . he came across one Giacomo Lacaita . . . he valued his company not for his dissident politics but for his indefatigable assistance as a cicerone for art-purchasing and sight seeing expeditions.[17]

The politically liberal Lacaita was legal adviser to the British legation at Naples. Shortly before Gladstone was due to return home in January 1851, he heard that Lacaita had been imprisoned, accused of revolutionary activities. Part of the indictment was that he had provided Gladstone with information

---

17 Shannon, *Gladstone: Peel's inheritor*, 229.

to use against the Bourbon regime. Lacaita was released after nine days and, with Gladstone's help, left for England the following year. He became professor of Italian at London University during the mid-1850s.[18] Later, he acted as Gladstone's secretary during the mission to the Ionian Islands. His friendship with Gladstone helped establish the respectability of the Risorgimento amongst Peelites.

Meanwhile, the government of Naples became for Gladstone the focus of a long-smouldering rage. In February 1851 the authorities – with uncharacteristic liberality – permitted him to visit the gaol where political prisoners were held, often in intolerable conditions. He visited other prisons, interviewing inmates and making copious notes, coming to the conclusion that the 'illegal government' of the Kingdom of the Two Sicilies was 'struggling to protect its utter illegality by a tyranny unparalleled at this moment, and almost without a rival amidst the annals of older atrocities'.[19]

Gladstone's invective against Naples is reminiscent of Dante's railings against his contemporary Florence. Dante called Florence the 'city which is a plant of his who first turned his back on his Maker',[20] so corrupt that 'throughout Hell thy name is spread abroad'.[21] Gladstone called the Naples government 'one of the most purely Satanic agencies upon earth'.[22] For Dante, Florence was 'a place which strips itself of good day by day'[23] while Gladstone called Bourbon rule in Italy 'a total inversion of all . . . moral and social ideas'.[24]

Back in England, Gladstone wrote a private letter to Lord Aberdeen about the situation in Naples, if a 12,000-word diatribe can be called a letter. It conveyed information that he feared Aberdeen would find 'painful, nay revolting, to the last degree'. Aberdeen had been Foreign Secretary in the last Conservative government, in which Gladstone had also served, and was regarded as the leader of the Peelites after the former prime minister's death. When Aberdeen failed to take any action, Gladstone released his letter to the press. This letter is an important indicator of Gladstone's development not only as a natural European liberal, but also as a supporter of justice for Italy in particular. He wrote:

> After a residence of between three and four months at Naples, I have come
> home with a deep sense of the duty incumbent upon me to make some attempt

---

[18] Lacaita worked on several important Dante-related works, including the first publication of the Latin lectures on Dante by Benvenuto da Imola (1375). After the reunification of Italy, Lacaita re-entered political life in Italy, but he continued to spend much of each year in England. His son Charles became Liberal MP for Dundee.

[19] Shannon, *Gladstone: Peel's inheritor*, 229.

[20] DC, *Paradiso*, canto 9, 27–8.

[21] DC, *Inferno*, canto 24, 1–3.

[22] Matthew, *Gladstone*, 80.

[23] DC, *Purgatorio*, canto 23, 79–81.

[24] Matthew, *Gladstone*, 80.

towards mitigating the horrors, I can use no stronger word, amidst which the government of that country is now carried on . . . Without entering at length into the reasons which have led me thus to trouble you, I shall state these three only. First, that the present practices of the government of Naples, in reference to real or supposed political offenders, are an outrage upon religion, upon civilisation, upon humanity, and upon decency. Secondly, that these practices are certainly, and even rapidly, doing the work of republicanism in that country . . . Thirdly, the Neapolitan case is not mere imperfection, not corruption in low quarters, not occasional severity . . . it is incessant, systematic, deliberate violation of the law by the power appointed to watch over and maintain it . . . it is the wholesale persecution of virtue when united with intelligence, operating on such a scale that entire classes may with truth be said to be its object, so that the government is in bitter and cruel, as well as utterly illegal, hostility to whatever in the nation . . . forms the mainspring of practical progress and improvement. . . . It is the perfect prostitution of the judicial office, which has made it, under veils only too threadbare and transparent, the degraded recipient of the vilest and clumsiest forgeries got up wilfully and deliberately . . . for the purpose of destroying the peace, the freedom . . . and even . . . the life, of men amongst the most virtuous, upright, intelligent, distinguished and refined of the whole community; it is the savage and cowardly system of moral, as well as in a lower degree of physical torture. . . . Law, instead of being respected, is odious. Force, and not affection, is the foundation of government. There is no association, but a violent antagonism, between the idea of freedom and that of order. . . . I have seen and heard the strong and too true expression used, 'This is the negation of God erected into a system of government'.

Gladstone estimated that there were, at the time, about 20,000 political prisoners in Naples, most of them modest middle-class people without the independent means to support their families during their incarceration. Hundreds were under the death penalty, mainly in the city's notorious Vicaria prison, known for its 'extreme of filth and horror'. Many had gone missing completely, including most members of the former opposition party. Men were being arrested 'not because they . . . are believed to have committed any offence; but because they are persons whom it is thought convenient to confine and to get rid of, and against whom therefore some charge must be formed or fabricated'.

Gladstone's outrage 'reflected at a European level the position which Gladstone had already reached in British politics. Whatever his motives, he found himself unavoidably associated with the Liberals: Conservatives in Britain and throughout Europe, with hardly an exception, deplored his initiative . . . Conservative he might still feel himself, Liberal his language was certainly becoming'.[25]

The period up to the early 1850s was a crucial period in Gladstone's political development. On the topics which had become central to his interests –

---

[25] Ibid. 81.

and European liberalism on the Italian question was one of them – he found himself allied with groups which were not predominantly Tory. He had 'developed a number of interests which made it increasingly difficult for him to co-operate with the Tory rump'.[26] The Neapolitan interlude also brought one important new Anglo-Italian friendship and consolidated another: the first with James (as he became) Lacaita, and the second with Anthony Panizzi. Panizzi, also professor of Italian at London for a while, lived in England from 1823 until his death in 1879. In later life he became head of the British Museum and its principal librarian.[27] Panizzi visited Naples the year after Gladstone. On seeing for himself the appalling conditions under which liberal political prisoners were kept, he berated the Bourbon king, Ferdinand, and demanded changes. When these failed to materialise, Panizzi bought a ship to rescue some prisoners from San Stefano Island. The ship sank off the Norfolk coast shortly after leaving England. It is interesting to note that these two liberal Italians who supported Gladstone in his campaign on behalf of the political prisoners in Naples were both Dante scholars; and both, like Dante, became exiles.

Daily doses of Dante, 1866–7

Gladstone's fifth sojourn in Italy was while on his way home from the Ionian Islands. In late February 1859 he arrived by boat in Venice and travelled by way of Vicenza and Milan to Turin where he caught a train to London *via* Paris on 8 March. The most interesting interlude was his brief meeting with Camillo di Cavour and other Risorgimento leaders.

Gladstone's sixth visit to Italy, during the winter of 1866–7, was much more extended. His government had resigned as a result of the failure of the Liberal Reform Bill. Consequently, the family was free to enjoy a more leisurely time than usual, effectively a four-month sojourn with three months spent in Rome, ten days in Florence and the rest of the time touring or 'posting' between locations. For his study of Dante, it is the most significant of his nine Italian trips. As a temporary political exile, he was particularly well-placed to appreciate the messages of the permanent political exile, Dante.

Four days after arriving in Rome, on 15 October 1866, Gladstone 'began Dante with Agnes and Mary'. His daughter Agnes was twenty-four years old at the time; Mary nearly nineteen. Mary also recorded these reading sessions

---

[26] Ibid.

[27] When Panizzi became keeper of printed books at the British Museum in 1837, the man he beat to the post was yet another eminent Dante scholar, Henry Cary, whose translation of the *Commedia* helped consolidate Victorian interest in the poet. All his life Panizzi remained close to Gladstone, who continued to visit him regularly up to four days before his death at the age of eighty-two.

in her diary; they seem to have taken place after breakfast and to have lasted about an hour.[28] From then on, Gladstone studied one canto or more of the *Commedia* every day, sometimes with his daughters, sometimes with other members of the family party, sometimes alone. But he hardly missed a day. Dante is by far the most frequently mentioned author for the duration of this four-month stay in Italy. He even he read his allocated canto of the *Inferno* on 22 October – a day on which he had an appointment of over-riding importance – with the pope.

Despite negative feelings towards the papacy, which Gladstone shared with Dante,[29] the audience with Pius IX, conducted in Italian, was cordial enough. In his diary Gladstone wrote that, after discussing the queen's health, they moved on to general matters concerning England:

> The exceedingly genial and simple and kindly manner of his Holiness had at once placed me at my ease and I entered freely into the conversation . . . On the affairs of Italy he spoke rather largely and very freely and I not less freely in return . . . With regard to the unity of Italy he made no objection in principle but even seemed to admit it theoretically and to allow that there were practical advantages in it. But he spoke of the present state of things as deplorable. He distinctly complained of the conduct of the Italian Government as inimical to religion . . . I said I trusted . . . that respect for religion would be maintained by the State if it lived in the people. . . . The interview lasted about ¾ of an hour.

Six days later Gladstone returned to the Vatican for a second audience, this time with the family. His own diary entry simply records: 'We went at 3 (reluctantly) to the Pope.' Mary's youthful record of the event is more forthcoming. The pope, she wrote, 'trolled on very good-naturedly, laughing a good deal, for about 20 minutes, asking but few questions, and carrying on the conversation almost alone . . . Altogether we were very much pleased with his kindness and simplicity, but there was something excessively ludicrous in the whole thing'.[30]

Back at the Gladstone lodgings, Agnes and Mary appear to have been reasonably willing Dante students for most of the family's stay in Rome, except for a period before Christmas. On 21 December Gladstone noted: 'Resumed Purgatorio with the girls: but their career in Dante has had a sore interruption.' This was the arrival in Rome the previous week of three of their brothers – Willy, Stephen and Harry. On Christmas Day 1866 Gladstone was feeling unwell and did not go with the rest of the family to a morning service at St Peter's: 'Prudence forbade my running risks by going to

28 Mary Gladstone, *Diaries*, 31.
29 See chapter 5 below. It was the idea of the papacy that Gladstone abhorred, although he could be on good terms with the current incumbent; Dante, on the other hand, respected the office but abhorred its incumbents.
30 Mary Gladstone, *Diaries*, 33.

St Peter's. Instead I lay and read Paradiso III and IV, a much higher exercise than any function merely sensible.'

Gladstone continued to read Dante daily, with or without his daughters, Harry or 'with my party'. One member of this party who spent Christmas 1866 and the New Year period with the Gladstones in Rome was the painter William Blake Richmond, then a widower of twenty-four, who forty years later would be asked to design Gladstone's memorial tomb. The British consul and painter Joseph Severn had introduced him to Gladstone earlier in the year at his home at the Palazzo Poli in Rome. In December Gladstone invited the young man to join a group travelling to the Benedictine monastery of Monte Cassino. The monastery's abbot, Luigi Tosti, hoped Gladstone might help persuade the Italian government to permit the Benedictine rule to continue. The Gladstone party arrived shortly before dusk on 27 December: 'We were most hospitably received', Gladstone noted, 'and much struck by the Abbot. Read Dante.' The following day was the eve of Gladstone's fifty-seventh birthday. Richmond[31] recalled in his diary being woken up early by Gladstone in order to admire the sunrise:

> 'Get up, Willie', he exclaimed, 'and come down with me to see a sight you may never see again!' They hurried together down a dim corridor to an east-facing window which overlooked a vast panorama. A most astonishing dawn was breaking. Gladstone and Richmond watched in rapt silence for over half an hour till the sun had fully risen and the morning chill forced them back from their trance. 'I would have given up five years of my life rather than have missed that!' Gladstone said. 'How near the great creator is, and what a world of beauty he has made for those who can see! Should we not rejoice at such a revelation of this goodness and this might?' He went on to quote from Dante's *Paradiso* in faultless Italian.[32]

The passage that Gladstone recited is not specified by Richmond. But since they were at Monte Cassino at the time, it may well have been from canto 32, where Dante meets St Benedict, founder of the monastery at Monte Cassino monastery and of the first monastic order in western Europe. Benedict tells Dante how he brought Christianity to the pagans in the neighbourhood of Monte Cassino, establishing the religious house early in the sixth century in what had been a temple to Apollo:

> That mountain on whose slope Cassino lies was once frequented on its summit by the deluded and perverse people, and it was I who first carried up there His name who brought to earth the truth that so exalts us; and such grace shone down on me that I drew away the neighbouring towns from the impious worship that led the world astray.[33]

---

[31] Richmond, erroneously, remembered the journey as having taken place in March 1867: Reynolds, *Richmond*, 55.

[32] Ibid.

[33] DC, *Paradiso*, canto 22, 37–45.

Benedict pronounces a bitter censure of monastic life in Dante's time, calling the religious houses dens of thieves. He particularly denounces usury in the Church and the misappropriation of funds that should be spent for the relief of the poor. Gladstone's original interest in Monte Cassino had been triggered by Abbot Tosti's desire to save the monastery from the threat of secularisation. He would raise the matter later with officials in Florence, then the Italian capital, on his way home to England from Rome; but the details of his part in the compromise that was ultimately reached are not known.

From Monte Cassino the party returned to Rome. During the rest of their stay, young Richmond also became a favourite of Catherine Gladstone, who nursed him when he was ill with tuberculosis and introduced him to his future second wife, Clara. Catherine also commissioned from him a portrait of her husband, the first of many such of family members over the years. Gladstone sponsored his *protegé* in a number of artistic and social contexts throughout his life, from proposing him for membership of the Athenaeum, to securing funding for his work on the refurbishment of St Paul's Cathedral.[34]

As well as his comprehensive reading of Dante in the original on this visit, Gladstone also devoted considerable time to reading around the poet while in Rome. He is noted in the *Diaries* as having read *Cantù on Dante* and *Omaggio a Dante Alighieri*, a work edited by Duke Caracciolo di Brienza and published in 1865. He also spent a week reading Ampère's 'Voyage Dantesque'.

While they were in Florence, Mary Gladstone records that, on 14 January, a family party 'went to the Bargello where we saw the old fresco of Dante by Giotto, lately discovered but ruined by restoration'.[35] She does not relate whether her father was present. Possibly not, since his own diary entry for that day includes the comment: 'A hurried day: no Dante'.

On 20 January, by now in San Remo, Gladstone entered in his diary: 'Finished the *Divina Commedia* again. Each time it is an event in life, and suggests very much.' He had been in Italy for almost exactly a hundred days. The three books of the *Commedia* contain one hundred cantos: thirty-three for each of three cantiche, plus one introductory canto. The Dante project was neatly dealt with. The next day the family party left for England.

---

[34] Richmond, in turn, cherished Gladstone's friendship greatly. After visiting Hawarden in the autumn of 1888, when Gladstone was seventy-eight, he wrote that 'Our walk today reminded me of the younger life, and a great store of gratitude is laid up in my heart for you. If older men are always aware of what they impress on their young friends to whom they are good enough to talk, freely, kindly and openly, it would I believe become a habit for the wise to open out in perfect fellowship to the ignorant. You, in those days of my childhood, set me afire, and that fire has never seen its end; your kindness took me out of many wanderings, and however little you may know it, so was it. Anyhow, this is the lesson I learned mainly of you, "to always be careful of each word, than it should express the meaning in hand. This surely is education" ': Reynolds, *Richmond*, 227

[35] Mary Gladstone, *Diaries*, 41.

Trip number seven

It was to be twelve years before Gladstone next visited Italy, during which time he completed his first six-year period as prime minister of the Liberal government and was within months of embarking on his second. He had, in the meantime, visited continental Europe, but not Italy. After resigning his ministry in 1874, he spent two weeks in Germany with two of his children – Willy and Helen – visiting his sister Helen and his friend, the eminent German Catholic theologian and Dante scholar, Ignaz von Döllinger.

The 1879 holiday was a short trip by Gladstone's standards: just five weeks touring in Bavaria and Italy, with a ten-day central stop at the Grand Hotel in Venice. But from the time he left England on 15 September until two days after he returned home on 21 October, he read Dante every day except the occasional Sunday which he kept clear for more devotional reading.

As ever, the entries – usually the first of each day – are sparse, mainly just 'Read Dante' with occasional additions such as 'Read four cantoes', 'good progress', 'Read Dante – passing into the third great division'. In Munich on 11 October he met up with Döllinger again: 'Went to Dr Dö[llinger] in the forenoon; and had a long walk with him in the afternoon. Conversation on Dante and on various matters of Theology.' The next day he was back again: 'Again with Dr Döllinger at 2: at 4 he entertained us most genially to dinner, and we sat till 8 . . . Read Dante: got more learning from Dr D. about the old commentaries.' The next day he was back on tour, and even his relative neglect of Dante rated a mention: '(on train). Read hardly any Dante: all was busy'.

Back in England on 23 October, Gladstone entered in his diary 'Finished my Dante'. It was to be the last diary entry that refers specifically to the original work. All future entries refer to books of commentary on Dante, his life and work. Bearing in mind Richmond's comment at Monte Cassino in 1866 on the readiness with which Gladstone could quote from memory a substantial passage from the *Paradiso*, it may well have been that Gladstone now knew the *Commedia* virtually by heart.

Wintering in Italy, 1887–8, 1888–9

In 1886 Gladstone's third ministry ended. His first Home Rule Bill for Ireland had failed and the Liberal party was defeated at the polls. He was to be out of office for six years, until August 1892. Italy beckoned. The family spent two consecutive winters in Italy during this time, a five-week trip based in Florence in 1887–8 and a slightly longer trip the following winter to Naples, where they spent Christmas and New Year.

During the first of these trips, Gladstone's reading around the subject of Dante was extensive. During the second there are no diary entries referring to

Dante-related reading. This may have been because, at the time, Gladstone was writing about, rather than reading about, Dante. Only weeks before he formed his fourth and last government in August 1892, Gladstone had an article published in *Nineteenth Century* on the possibility that Dante had visited Oxford. Whether or not he was correct in asserting that he did, Gladstone's 5,000–word argument is a masterpiece of Dante scholarship. It must have taken some considerable time to compose and may already have been in preparation during his last visit to Italy.

This possibility is reinforced by the fact that Gladstone's reading during the first of these two winters in Italy – 1887–8 – was primarily of a new book by the Swiss Dante scholar G. A. Scartazzini[36] that revived the question of Dante at Oxford. Add to this the fact that, when back in England in March 1888, Gladstone began to read Boccaccio's biography of Dante, the first to provide evidence to suggest that Dante was indeed at Oxford.

Gladstone, now nearly seventy-eight years old, was also keen to escape the rigours of a British winter. After spending Christmas at home, the family left London for Paris on 28 December 1887 for a five-week stay in Florence. According to Morley, Gladstone had a throat complaint, and his doctor had advised a warmer climate – and a Trappist regime of silence. For a man once described by his arch-rival Benjamin Disraeli as inebriated with the exuberance of his own verbosity, that must have been quite a challenge.

Two weeks before their departure, on 15 December, Gladstone began a daily reading around Dante. This was of commentaries, in particular Scartazzini's companion to Dante, a commentary on his work by Cornoldi[37] and another Dante book by G. A. G. Carducci. The reading of Scartazzini continued daily, except for one Sunday. On 12 January there was an excursion to Santa Maria Novella, the Baptistery[38] and the front of Dante's house, then back to read Scartazzini. On 22 January Gladstone was nearing the end of the Dante companion and clearly reluctant to stop reading, despite the fact that it was a Sunday, and Sundays were normally given over to devotional reading. He noted in his diary by way of an excuse: 'The study of Dante is very sabbatical'. The following day he wrote: 'Finished Scartazzini's real great work'. Six days later, on 29 January, he embarked on the next opus: Carducci's *L'opera di Dante: un discorso*. Matthew gives the publication date of this work as 1888 – publisher unknown – which means that Gladstone must have seen it very soon after it was published. A week later he was back with

---

36 Although the English version of G. A. Scartazzini, *A handbook to Dante*, trans. A. J. Butler, was not available until 1893, various versions and editions were available in Italian and German at the time of Gladstone's visit to Italy in the winter of 1887/8. Scartazzini's *Dante: seine Zeit, sein Leben und seine Werke* had been published in 1869 and read at the time by Gladstone.

37 G. M. Cornoldi, *La Divina Commedia: a commentary*, n.p. 1887.

38 The Florence Baptistery had a special importance for Dante. It is mentioned three times in the *Commedia* – twice in *Paradiso* (canto 15, 134; canto 16, 47), and once in *Inferno*, canto 19, 17.

Scartazzini and his 'Nachtrage' [sic], that is supplements or indices, by which Gladstone probably meant Scartazzini's German-language *Zur Dante-Bibliographie* of 1871.

The next winter sojourn was slightly longer and this time included the Christmas period. The family left London on 19 December 1888, arriving in Naples three days later. There were no diary entries relating to Dante for this period. However, Gladstone may already have been working on 'Did Dante study at Oxford', the major intellectual preoccupation of his last decade. He arrived back in London on 20 February 1889. Gladstone never went back to Italy.

Italian contacts

Since Gladstone visited Italy primarily in a private capacity, his dealings with the leading Italian public figures of the day were mainly conducted back in England, in an official capacity. But he followed Italian affairs with particular interest; three of the leading contemporary Italians whose progress he monitored closely were Garibaldi, Cavour and Mazzini.

George Eliot called Mazzini 'the prophet of the new Italy',[39] as Dante was of the old. Although, in Britain, the revolutionary aroused public sympathy and indignation in equal measure, one might have expected Gladstone to be attracted by Mazzini's vehement anti-papism and his contention that only 'God and the people' could liberate Italy. In fact, there are just two brief mentions of Mazzini in the *Diaries*, and both are negative. On 19 October 1849 Gladstone commented that 'Lord Aberdeen spoke ill of Mazzini.' Nearly half a century later, on 25 February 1893, he reflected on his own 'disapproval of Mazzini's line'. Gladstone did, however, keep himself up to date with Mazzini's thinking by reading most of his writings immediately on, or soon after, publication.

With Gladstone's innate love of order, it may have been the 'loose cannon' element of Mazzini's behaviour that irritated him, as in the case of Garibaldi. If, as was widely believed at the time, Gladstone was responsible for persuading Garibaldi to call off his provincial tour of Britain, it may be he feared that Garibaldi would excite political feeling in the provinces.[40]

Gladstone and Garibaldi met almost every other day during the latter's two-week visit to London in 1864, which began 12 April: 'Met Garibaldi. We were quite satisfied with him. He did me much more than justice.' A diary entry for the following day mentions 'The Young Garibaldis'. On 16 April, Gladstone 'dined at Lord Palmerston's to meet Garibaldi' and the next day was 'at Stafford House . . . on Garibaldi's movements. In a conversation he

[39] Thompson, *George Eliot and Italy*, 4.
[40] Derek Beales, 'Gladstone and Garibaldi', in Peter Jagger (ed.), *Gladstone*, London 1998, 145.

agreed to give up the provincial tour'. Matthew adds that 'Gladstone later claimed "there was nothing political in the conversation . . . not one syllable about the desire of the Government that the General should leave escaped my lips".'[41]

Three days later, on 20 April, the Gladstones hosted a farewell dinner and party for Garibaldi. Gladstone noted: 'In the evening a great entertainment to Garibaldi came off. Before the door, at night, say a thousand people, all in the best humour: the hall and stairs full before dinner . . . Dinner and evening party both seemed to go well. A hostile deputation invaded us at ten: but we ejected them.'

On 24 April Gladstone had another 'conversation with Garibaldi: the utmost I could get from him was that it would be sad if the Italian people should lose its faith'. The following day he 'bade farewell to Garibaldi at 8'. A month later, on 10 May, Gladstone entered in his diary that he met the Garibaldi Committee. He asked the deputation to see him as he wished to clarify his role in Garibaldi's departure.

Gladstone was slow to recognise Garibaldi as a worthy representative of anti-papalism. The two men

> Had in common a passionate and bitter hostility to the pope and his temporal power. Garibaldi's went even further than Gladstone's, of course: he had little sympathy with dogmatic Christianity of any brand, whereas Gladstone professed himself a (non-Roman) Catholic . . . it is doubtful whether sufficient weight has been given to Gladstone's anti-papalism . . . He wrote of the papal states as 'a foul blot upon the face of creation'.[42]

Gladstone remained, as his pamphlet of 1874 on *The Vatican decrees* showed, 'the virulent enemy of the papacy, its temporal power and its claims to infallibility. This was the strongest of the bonds that linked him with Garibaldi'.[43] And yet the two apparently failed to connect, despite Garibaldi's expression of gratitude to Gladstone for the 'generous interest that you have always showed to the cause of my country'.[44]

Cavour, whose acquaintance Gladstone first made when the count visited England in August 1852, shortly after becoming president of the Piedmont Council, he met again in London in December 1855. At Turin in March 1859 – a crucial time in the evolution of the new Italy – Gladstone spent an hour alone with Cavour on his way back to England from southern Italy. They never met again. Within months of becoming Italy's first prime minister, Cavour died. Gladstone continued to read his works, published posthumously. Cavour's *Thoughts on Ireland, its present and its future* he first read in 1868. In April 1893 he reread it around the time that the Liberals'

---

41 *Gladstone diaries*, vi. 269n. Matthew is quoting *The Times*, 11 May 1864.
42 Beales, 'Gladstone and Garibaldi', 149.
43 Ibid. 156.
44 See chapter 2 n. 61.

Second Home Rule Bill was being defeated, and again two years later in retirement. Perhaps the principles of independence, democracy, freedom from foreign intervention and self-determination that Gladstone sought for Ireland stretched back through what Cavour's modern Italy had achieved, to medieval Florence – and Dante's dream of a fair and just society.

Gladstone was not alone at the time in his commitment to the Italian cause: it enjoyed considerable support in Victorian Britain. Nor should the recreational element of his visits to Italy be disregarded: the country was an increasingly popular tourist destination. But Dante was more for Gladstone than mere holiday reading, more than just a source of local colour: he was a source of fundamental ideas concerning civic duty, morality, liberty and the universality of mankind. And, as a politician, Gladstone was in the privileged position of being able to act on those ideas to influence events.

4

Images of Womanhood

Gladstone admired women greatly. He admired them sometimes too much, and he admired them sometimes unwisely. But admire them he did. His instinctive feeling, in the true chivalric tradition, was that the ideal woman represented sinful man's interface with God. 'Friendships with women have constituted no small part of my existence', Gladstone wrote to his friend, the courtesan-turned-evangelist Laura Thistlethwayte in 1869.[1] The types of women in his life ranged from his saintly mother and older sister to prostitutes; they included the greatest society hostesses of the day and problem women like his younger sister Helen, Lady Lincoln and his near-nemesis, Mrs Thistlethwayte. But there is a consistency in his treatment of them all that fits comfortably into the matrix of medieval courtly love, epitomised in Dante's treatment of Beatrice. For Gladstone, women who failed to meet the feminine ideal were to be helped back to it. He believed that fallen women fell through no fault of their own, but for reasons such as poverty and male deceit.

He made it clear how far his own friendships would go. The infatuated Mrs Thistlethwayte came to his room at her home one night, her 'hair let down – the rippled ringlets to the knee', reminding him of Tennyson's *Godiva*.[2] But he was gently insistent when her letters mentioned love that they must 'keep the word within the bounds prescribed by honour and pre-existing duty'.[3] Otherwise, innocent expressions of affection were acceptable; as Dante said: 'Amore/acceso di virtù, sempre altro accese,/ pur che la fiamma sua paresse fore' ('Love kindled by virtue always kindles another, if only its flame appear without').[4]

With respect to women, Gladstone was the modern version of the Pre-Raphaelite knight.[5] 'Anything he tried to see nobly, particularly in women, he saw through the categories of medieval chivalry.'[6] This was primarily an allusion to Gladstone's rescue work with fallen women, as he walked the streets of London on a mission to save damsels in distress from the dragon of prostitution. Gladstone's contemporary at Oxford, the journalist

---

1 *Gladstone diaries*, viii, appendix at pp. 557–7.
2 Ibid. viii, entry for 12 Dec. 1869.
3 Ibid. viii, entry for 6 Jan. 1870. Gladstone refers to the 'weighty word' that Thistlethwayte uses to describe her feelings.
4 *DC, Purgatorio*, 10–13.
5 Matthew, *Gladstone*, 160.
6 Ibid. 324.

Martin Tupper, commented that, even in their university days together, Gladstone

> in his religious outlook [was] moved more by a broad humanity than by dogma. He is insistent on the need for more compassion for the sinner, and he could not, he said, bring himself to regard even the most consistently erring women as other than one of God's creatures, for whom salvation was not only possible but an absolute necessity for which every Christian should fight. The Magdalen is in some ways a figure for whom he has the greatest reverence.[7]

The chivalric comparison, the blend of duty and romance, applies to most aspects of Gladstone's relationships with women, be they saints or sinners or something in-between like his reformed courtesan friend. On the one hand, he sought out prostitutes – many of whom hid in doorways to avoid being 'saved' – and aspired to raise them to a better life, with an almost reckless disregard for the threat to his own reputation. At the same time he treated the virtuous women of his intimate acquaintance with a reverence that echoed the tradition of courtly love: a tradition that found an expression in Dante that is both ancient, in that it follows conventional ideals, and modern, in that it deals with real people and their psychology. This aspect of the Commedia may have struck a chord with the young Gladstone, coming to Dante as he did at a time of intense turmoil in his emotional life.

The basic elements of courtly love were that it was regarded as an ennobling force, that the beloved woman was seen as superior to her lover and that love itself should ideally remain unsatisfied physically, since adultery was a sin as well as a social disturbance. Foster described it as

> a phenomenon of the decline of feudalism: for it emerged within the feudal structure as an order of feelings and attitudes that in some respects went clean contrary to the external order imposed by custom and law. In this external order, the ruler was normally and emphatically the male; medieval society was by and large patriarchal. But in the order of courtly love we find the ruler, the belted knight, habitually on his knees before a woman.[8]

Foster insists that courtly love had roots that went down deeper than any class differences or particular social structure. 'The cult of the feminine had nothing, I repeat nothing, to do with social status.'[9] Equally, Gladstone's idealisation of women was independent of class.

The most significant relationships in the early lives of both Gladstone and Dante were with virtuous young women who, they believed, provided a means of salvation for their own, morally inadequate selves. For Dante this was his childhood friend, Beatrice Portinari. For Gladstone it was his sister Anne. Beatrice provided the inspiration for the Commedia, the writing of

---

[7] This is quoted in Richard Deacon, The private life of Mr Gladstone, London 1965, 28.
[8] Kenelm Foster, 'Courtly love and Christianity', in his The two Dantes, London 1977, 21.
[9] Ibid.

which could be described as the ultimate act of intellectual chivalry. Trailed in the closing lines of the *Vita nuova*,[10] the poem becomes Dante's atonement to Beatrice for turning after her death away from theology to a study of philosophy (or possibly other women). It was this dereliction that led him to the 'dark wood' of bewilderment where the action of the *Commedia* begins. Gladstone's three volumes on the work of Bishop Joseph Butler, written after his retirement from politics, have been similarly described as 'written as a debt to theology' for having made public life and not the Church his career.[11]

When Gladstone's sister Anne died in 1829, he lost the person to whom he felt closest in the world. In 1833 he also lost his 'earliest near friend'[12] Arthur Hallam. In 1835 his mother died when he was still only twenty-five years old. Gladstone was without a soul mate for a decade after Anne's death, until he married Catherine Glynne in 1839. During this period of repeated romantic disappointments – he proposed marriage twice and was twice rejected – there may have been comfort in discovering an immortal beloved like Dante's Beatrice, described in terms he could relate to his own dead sister.

Later there were other people whom Gladstone loved and lost. There was the death of his infant daughter Jessy, and the death soon after in childbirth of his sister-in-law Mary Lyttelton. There was the suicide of Mary's husband George, Gladstone's old friend and colleague. There was the assassination in Dublin of the Irish Secretary Frederick Cavendish, husband of Lucy, daughter of Mary and George, whom the Gladstones had brought up as their own. But it is the earlier losses in life – like that of Gladstone's sister – that have the most effect. And it is often the earlier books – like the *Commedia* for Gladstone – that have the most enduring influence.

A significant factor in the Dante/Beatrice and Gladstone/Anne parallel is that it was in death as much as in life that the female influence was felt. Immortalised in the *Commedia*, the *persona* of Beatrice was no longer a teenage sweetheart or even a respectable young Florentine matron. She became the older, wiser, saintly woman in an intimate relationship with a mortal, sinful, less mature – if not actually younger – man in need of correction. Both Dante and Gladstone seem comfortable with this balance of power. In his relationship with his wife, too, Gladstone followed the chivalric convention of finding her the more moral creature, he the greater sinner.

Dante's youthful feelings for Beatrice are expressed in his collection of poems and treatises on the art of poetry, *La vita nuova*. It was this anthology of young love as much as the mature *Commedia* that crystallised Dante's *persona*

---

10 'I hope to compose concerning her what has never been written in rhyme of any woman': Dante Alighieri, *La vita nuova (Poems of youth)*, trans. and intro. Barbara Reynolds, London 1969, 99.
11 H. C. G. Matthew, 'Gladstone and the University of Oxford', *Oxford Magazine* clxx (1999), 4.
12 Morley, *Gladstone*, i. 81.

for nineteenth-century artists, particularly the Pre-Raphaelites. But it is the second half of the *Commedia* that establishes the image of Beatrice as saint, saviour and Dante's interface with God. A similar outline of Gladstone's relationship with Anne emerges clearly from his *Diaries*.

From 'dear Anne' to 'departed saint'

Beatrice was twenty-four years old when she died; Dante was twenty-five at the time. Anne Gladstone died aged twenty-six, when her brother was nineteen. By dying prematurely, these two beautiful young women lent themselves to idealisation as symbols of perfect womanhood in the medieval tradition. The tradition of courtly love was second nature to Dante; and it was one for which, temperamentally, Gladstone was ideally suited. But the influence of the courtly love tradition in no way diminishes the fact that these were two real, intensely and intimately loved young women. More than representing just an idea of purity and innocence, they provided the hope of salvation; they were the personal and partisan interlocutors by means of whom the two men hoped ultimately to reach the sight of God.

Gladstone's diary, which he began when he was fifteen, was inspired by his sister who encouraged him to keep an account to God for his use of time. They display an exceptional degree of closeness between the siblings – an intensity almost – indicating that Anne was for William more than the average sister, as Beatrice was for Dante more than the average childhood friend. Even allowing for the Victorian view of the ideal woman as the angel in the house, Gladstone's attachment to Anne was an anxious one, possibly anticipating future loss.

During the first year of Gladstone's diary, there are several brief entries about his sister, who was also his godmother. Most of them refer to her ill health, together with that of their mother. In one of the earliest entries, written when the family was living at Cheltenham Spa, he noted: 'Mother ill – cd not go to Cheltenham. Anne ill with sore-throat'. It was an oft-repeated refrain, as the family moved from one smart watering-hole to another in search of a remedy that would improve the two Annes' health. 'Dear Mother and Dear Anne fatigued'; 'Dear Anne not feeling well'. After Gladstone returned to Eton, he continued to monitor anxiously his sister's health. 'Dear Anne . . . in bed some time.' 'Dear Anne as been in the house some days. May God give her relief.' Anne was so precious to William, and so good and noble as well as ill, that an early association of goodness in women with frailty must have been inevitable.

Back at home for Christmas, Anne's health continued to fluctuate, although on Christmas Eve 1825 – her birthday – she was able to come down for dinner: 'God bless her – She dined with us all (first time all together for two years) though not feeling very well. She gave lots of presents to us all.'

Already, within the first six months of his diary, Gladstone indicated a preoccupation with Anne that far exceeded his interest in any other family member. This included even his mother although she, being equally saintly and equally sickly though more remote, is often referred to in the same breath. On 7 January 1826, Gladstone was again expressing concern: 'Dear Anne bilious.' The following day he noted: 'Struck by the reflection, that inasmuch as the path of the Christian to Heaven is steeper than that of his fellows, inso much as it leads to a *higher place* – as in ascending a hill and a mountain. Very applicable to Mother and A. Dear Anne ill.' The next day 'Dear Anne' was 'still ill with bile'; the day after that: 'Dear Anne ill still – as also Dear Mother with headache.' Things were looking up on Wednesday 11 January: 'Anne a little better – Mother little better', and again on the Thursday: 'Both invalids better' and the day after that: 'Invalids again better'.

Entries for his Easter holiday back at Cheltenham follow the pattern of the Christmas break, this time with his brother Tom joining the invalids. In mid-April Gladstone was back at Eton and busy reading works by writers as diverse as Milton and Molière, Homer and Darwin. At half term he stayed at Eton where he spent much time with Arthur Hallam. For a while, family concerns faded into the background as Gladstone enjoys a more independent life. His correspondence with Anne dwindled until 18 July when he writes,

> received a letter from Dear Anne, with one from Mr G. to my great surprise desiring my immediate return home, and enclosing letter for Keate (his head-master); on account of Dear Anne's late severe illness, and Dear John's con-templated departure in a week. Went to Keate: he kind; gave leave; Tutor very kind; Dame too. Sorry for this summons itself; sending up, any other things, done away with by it: but far, far more anxious as to the cause.

Clearly, the family feared that Anne was dying. Gladstone travelled through night and arrived back home at Seaforth near Liverpool at breakfast time: 'Found nothing so immediately evil as I had feared. Dear Anne however thin and weak, and Mother especially very anxious.' The summons home seems to have been a false alarm and Gladstone coped with the anxiety by being busy and organised: reading, writing imaginary speeches, letters, accounts, diary entries. On 24 July a diary entry in Greek indicates that an operation had been carried out on his sister. The next day his brother John set off for two years in South America and William seems agitated but grateful that 'Dear Anne, please dieu restored to health'. The state of Anne's health is mentioned daily in the diary for the next five days, often coupled with comments on the health of her mother. There are also several entries during this period mentioning that Gladstone 'drew Anne in chair'.

By the autumn Anne was ill again. 'Dear Anne ill with sore throat', he wrote on 8 September and with mounting anxiety, on an almost daily basis 'Dear Anne still ill'; 'Dear Anne had a blister on'; 'Dear Anne's throat still very bad'.

Back at school, Gladstone was able again to some extent to compartmen-talise his parents and siblings, as in future he would compartmentalise his wife and his children when they were at Hawarden and he in London, or at the great houses where he often spent his weekends. Dante did much the same while in political exile from Florence while his wife held the family together back home. Reinstalled at Eton, Gladstone's letters to and from home become less frequent, and the influence of friends like Arthur Hallam more marked. Correspondence with Anne becomes patchy – perhaps because she felt too weak for any sustained writing, until on 11 February he received long and most excellent and pious letter 'from my beloved sister – unworthy as I of such an one'.

Easter 1827 found young Gladstone back at Seaforth where he 'found Dear Anne fully as well as expected'. And again begin the anxious entries: 'Drew Anne in chair' with almost obsessive daily regularity. Drawing his sister in a chair seems to have become a therapeutic activity for both of them.[13] In August William was back at Seaforth for the summer holidays and resuming his mildly compulsive activity: 'Drew Anne in chair' was entered in his diary on nineteen days in one month alone.

In September 1827, shortly before leaving for his final term at Eton, Gladstone learned that he was to go up to Oxford. Once again, when away from home, Gladstone's preoccupation with his ailing relatives subsides as his interest in other areas of life increases and his life expands. In December he is back and again noting: 'Drew Anne in chair'.

Christmas Eve 1827 was Anne's twenty-fifth birthday: 'Thank God for her passing it in better health than the last . . . Above all, let us thank Him for the good gift which he has bestowed upon her of a true and fervent Christian spirit and heart.' From Seaforth Gladstone travelled in the New Year to Wilmslow to be crammed for Oxford in Homer, Cicero, Euclid, Greek Testament and other subjects by one Revd Turner. It was 5 February before he wrote to Anne. With many social distractions in Wilmslow, Gladstone rather neglected his correspondence, though Anne wrote to him frequently enough. Back home for Easter, they read and discussed what he had been learning in the course of long evening conversations 'in which may God render useful to me a miserable sinner'. Every day they sat together and read the Bible or other devotional works and sermons. Anne's health fluctuated. She began to deteriorate again; she became 'not very well', then 'less well than usual'. But they persevered in their reading programme and soon his sister recovered enough to join the family for meals again, and to sit outside. Then came another 'bad week . . . May God bless my dear sister, and make her to grow in every grace'.

In autumn 1828 Gladstone went up to Oxford. Thereafter, his diary entries were much taken up with sermons by Pusey, a co-founder of the

---

[13] It is uncertain whether in 'drawing Anne', Gladstone was sketching his sister – in which case, there is no evidence of any drawings surviving; or whether he was pushing her around in a wheelchair, his usual phrase for which elsewhere in the diary is 'drawing out . . . in chair'.

Oxford Movement, readings of the classics and books on theology. It was November before he found time to write to Anne. His diaries are mainly filled with details of whom he had breakfast with, who was at chapel and his increasingly wide reading of classical, religious and mathematical works. Anne wrote to him regularly during the term but it was December before he responded. And then it was the Christmas vacation and time to return home to Seaforth where he found 'Mother . . . much improved – but Dear Anne, I much fear, weakened'. Two days later, he began reading St John's Gospel with Anne and his brother Herbert, 'to which an hour a day is to be allotted, and from which I hope to receive benefit'. Reading with Anne was an almost daily feature in Gladstone's diary during the Christmas break, until his return to Oxford in mid-January. Immediately he is immersed again in the round of studying and socialising. A letter arrived from Anne on 28 January; but before he could reply to it, Gladstone received, on 9 February 'a most affectionate letter from H.J.G [his sister Helen] but sad accounts of Anne. "Sad!" '. He wrote to his sister three days later but received no reply, unsurprising given the state of her decline. 'Dearest Anne alarmingly ill at night' is his diary entry for 18 February.[14]

Anne Mackenzie Gladstone, William's sister, godmother and spiritual mentor, died in the early hours of 19 February 1829. Gladstone was suddenly without the one woman in the world (except the remote figure of his mother) upon whom he could rely as a benchmark for contemporary female virtue. His entry in his diary, outlined in black, reads: 'At 20m to 3 A.M., our dearest sister Anne breathed her last without a struggle or a groan.'

Over the next two weeks Gladstone documented his grief for his dead sister in terms reminiscent of Dante's lament for his dead Beatrice. At this stage, Gladstone had not read Dante. When, five years later, he first began the *Commedia*, a work created primarily to celebrate a virtuous young woman, it must have struck a chord. The image of the female beloved, whose moral integrity confers such authority in the after-world that it creates an interface between man and God, is what Gladstone was looking for. For Sunday 22 February he recorded,

> found all in great grief, especially my dear Mother, but looking to the High and Mighty One for support. Saw the pale remains of Dearest Anne, but felt in weeping over them, that my tears were entirely selfish. Blessed and praised be God's Holy Name for thus calling to Himself first from among us one who was so well prepared, so thoroughly refined, so weaned from earth, so ripe for Heaven . . . Listened to the accounts of Dear Anne's deathbed scenes, with an interest which must be felt under such circumstances even by those whose feelings are as little tender and as much abstracted as my own.

---

14 This entry and those up to 2 March were added after the event.

The next day, three days before Anne's funeral, Gladstone noted that a strange apathy had overcome him:

> Dear Anne's remains were still open. I felt a wonderful apathy, considering how many opportunities I had enjoyed of conversation and intercourse with my dear deceased sister: of knowing her character: of estimating her powers of mind and her tenderness of heart and her numberless Christian graces; how unworthy I had been of the love, and the attention, with which the departed saint had honoured me, as well as others more worthy.

He questions his grief as selfish and indulgent, when she was in a better place, and hopes, like Dante with Beatrice, to honour her memory by following in her footsteps:

> If this comparative apathy was the result of a *just* view of the case, it was well: if it arose from that estimate which Christianity teaches us to form of time and eternity, life and death, earth & heaven; and from – not a careless belief – but a deep-rooted conviction that *she* was happy, and that *our* first and highest duty, after suffering the duty of tears to be paid, was to seek what she had sought, and to honour her memory in following (by God's grace) her footsteps. But it was not so. It was from a torpor of mind and habitual selfishness who she (who is gone) was freed from, and from which 'good Lord deliver us'.

The following night, Gladstone observed his brother John's 'melancholy pleasure of weeping over Anne's cold remains'. On the next day, 25 February, he added: 'This day the remains of dearest Anne were inclosed in their last earthly house. The lead was soldered over the shell and all placed in the outer coffin – which then remained on the bed where she breathed her last. Read burial service . . . to Mother.'

The funeral took place the following morning and Gladstone described it in his diary in detail, down to the precise order of the coaches and who was in them. His tendency to make lists, to categorise and clarify, was a frequent response to stress. Although trivial, the preoccupation with order and the detailed structure of the *Commedia* may have been another of its characteristics with which Gladstone was later to identify. The day after the funeral he set about making an inventory of Anne's books with his brother Herbert, and there is 'much copying' over the next few days, including parts of his brother Tom's recollections of their sister. Back in Oxford, on Thursday 5 March, he began 'arranging all my letters from Dear Anne and other papers . . . Labelled the letters and read a good many: it is delightful to dwell on what Tom beautifully calls "the sweetening recollections of that spirit which was but too pure for an impure world" '.

From then on Gladstone marked each anniversary of his sister's birthday, remembering it, as Matthew has commented, 'as a special day of religious observance, rather in the manner that Newman remembered his experience of conversion'.[15] The memory of his sister's 'ascendancy to Heaven served almost as a vicarious conversion', and Gladstone was still commemorating it in his diary in 1878.

The correspondence between William and Anne Gladstone (as distinct from his diary references to it) from the period between his departure for Eton in 1820 and her death in 1829 reveals a tenderness that is palpable. There are 144 surviving letters from her during that period, and twenty-nine from him, beginning in 1822: he frequently teases her that she places too great a debt of letter-writing on him and begs her to write fewer but longer ones. The content of the letters is mundane enough. The very young Gladstone frets about lost stockings and sickly servants, reports on a visit to the circus and calls her his 'little witch'. The young teenager discusses with her the appointment of Canning as Foreign Secretary and calls her the Gladstone family's own 'Secretary of State for Foreign Affairs, Home and Colonial Affairs' all in one.[16] His later letters deal more with the affairs of the wider world – political issues and social events at Wilmslow and then at Oxford. He worried over the deaths of parents of his friends, talked about lectures he attended, books he read, sermons he heard and the difficulty of getting decent rooms in college. It is clear that Anne fulfilled the role of surrogate mother while the real one was indisposed. This is reflected in the fact that he hardly ever wrote to his mother nor she to him – and it was Anne to whom he looked to 'execute his commissions' on an everyday basis.

Most of their letters, while unfailingly affectionate and supportive, deal with day-to-day domestic matters rather than affairs of the soul. But one letter hints at a literary interest of young Gladstone's that would find an echo in Dante. Anne's birthday was on Christmas Eve. One Christmas Eve, probably in 1825, William wrote her a poem.[17] This appears to be original in that it contains many amendments and revisions, indicating that it was not a copy of someone else's work. Well over a hundred lines in length, it begins as a conventional Christmas composition. But after the seasonal section, it changes to describe a heaven/hell or salvation/damnation scenario. There is no comparison between this and the *Commedia* in terms of depth of thought, understanding of life or linguistic sophistication. Gladstone was a child with little life experience at the time of writing, while Dante was a middle-aged former statesman, respected theologian and renowned philosopher. Yet in this formulaic young poem, there is a vision of eternity that may have found resonance in the *Commedia* when Gladstone came to read it some years later.

The relevant section of the composition – some twenty or so lines – is

---

15 Matthew, *Gladstone*, 7.
16 Gladstone to Anne Mackenzie Gladstone, 26 Sept. 1822, GG MS 745.
17 It may have been 1824. There are two different dates on the manuscript: the dedication at the bottom of the poem reads 'WEG to AMG, December 24, 1825', but the date on the cover is 1824. It is not possible to ascertain the correct date from documents on either side, since they are dated June 1824 and March 1827 respectively.

quoted here as it appears not to have been published elsewhere. After the Christmas seasonal part, Gladstone wrote:

> And where fell Satan's varied wile
> Decoyed the victims of his guile,
> He feels the lack of fire;
> Down, down the dark abyss of hell,
> His deeply muttered curses tell
> His unavailing ire.
> See gnawing Envy War and Strife
> & Every passion, cease;
> And see each new Regenerate Life
> Bring forth the fruits of Peace;
> And man with man, and child with child
> Hold commerce faithful, constant, mild.
> From every rock, from every plain breaks out
> The loud, unconquerable shout,
> Hail! All Hail!
> And Natures chorus, hill & dale & tree
> Re-echo full the symphony
> While the wide Heavens vaulted arches sing,
> Thousands of thousands on celestial wing,
> And all the sound of God in triumph sing
> Hail! All Hail!
> Adown the gulf of death and Hell
> The shuddering demons hear their funeral knell
> Trembling and pale!
> And through the regions of th'abyss they fly
> The wrath of Heaven's majesty.
> The rays of Thy salvation gleam
> With endless, universal beam,
> The stream of Thy salvation pour
> From sea to sea, from shore to shore,
> And every tribe from every distant land
> Fill the wide Heavens with exulting band
> And unalloyed with plaints of woe
> The tuneful measures of the Heaven's flow.[18]

The death of Gladstone's sister Anne was followed a few years later by that of his mother Anne. Of her Gladstone wrote, in true Victorian mode,

She departed in seraphic peace, like the gentleness of her own disposition . . . She was eminent in the discharge of every duty: she sorrowed for sin: she trusted in the atonement of Christ. But this was not all; these elementary sentiments of religion were matured in her by the power of God, and she was made partaker of the nature and very life of the Redeemer, and her will con-

---

[18] Gladstone to A. M. Gladstone, 24 Dec. 1824, GG MS 745.

formed to his. Therefore, being like him, perfected through suffering, she had no new thing to learn, no fresh character to assume, upon translation to the world of spirits . . . Two only have been taken from our family: and both are angels in heaven.[19]

Gladstone had now lost both the important women in his life. His relationship with his mother had been quite distant – Matthew has suggested that one reason that Gladstone was comfortable associating with prostitutes was because he had relied on servants for company in his early life, and was at ease in the company of the so-called lower classes – but nevertheless she had still represented, like his sister, the angel of the house.

Of Beatrice, Dante wrote, 'Often people said, when she had passed: "This is no woman; this is one of the fairest angels of Heaven". And other said: "She is a miracle".'[20] Dante's response to the death of Beatrice[21] seems much more emotional than Gladstone's to the loss of either his mother or his sister, his dear 'departed saint'.[22] The more reserved Gladstone, on reading Dante a couple of years later, found a voice that articulated his own grief. Simon Reynolds has commented that it was not his language, his structure or his vocabulary alone that made Dante so innovative, 'It was in the gradually increasing admittance of reality into the enclosed garden of poetic convention that Dante made his most original and creative discoveries.'[23] This combination of reality and idealism struck a chord with Gladstone. That he had not read Dante before Anne died reinforces rather than weakens the argument that his sensibilities had developed independently along parallel lines. When he came to read the *Commedia*, it will have offered a potential channel for emotional release.

Other women

There were many other women in Gladstone's later life. After marriage, his extended family became enormous, as was his London circle of friends, many of whom were women. Particularly important were his 'difficult' women: his sister Helen whose life was a series of rebellions including an unsuccessful engagement, drug addiction and conversion to Roman Catholicism; Lady Lincoln; and Mrs Thistlethwayte. But there are few points of identification with other female characters – good or bad – in the *Commedia*.

There are few women in the *Commedia* at all, reflecting their lower public

19 W. E. Gladstone, *Autobiographica, 1871–2*, ed. John Brooke and Mary Sorensen, London 1981, ii. 6.
20 Dante, *Vita nuova*, 75.
21 Ibid. 82–3.
22 Matthew, *Gladstone*, 6.
23 Dante, *Vita nuova*, 17.

profile in the Middle Ages. Those that do appear are often stock figures from classical literature and mythology, often borrowed from Virgil: for example, Cleopatra, Dido, Helen and Medusa. Or they are local or contemporary characters introduced as a means of enabling Dante to declaim against the vices of the Italian cities whence they originated. For example, there is Manto, supposed founder of Mantua, or Sapia from a famous Guelph family in Siena, who act as narrative devices enabling Dante to attack the current Mantuan and Sienese administrations. In Purgatory, there are Rachel and Leah, the symbols respectively of the active and the contemplative life, and Beatrice's friend Mathilda. Examples from Paradise include the Holy Roman Empress Constance in the company of lesser spirits, placed there to demonstrate that all are equal in heaven, plus other established figures such as Mary, Rahel, Sarah, Rebecca, Judith, Ruth and many more Old Testament women who believed in the coming of Christ, together with St Anne and St Lucy.

But there are no female figures, other than Beatrice, whose lives or characters may be seen to provide parallels with Gladstone's own experience of women, except perhaps for Francesca da Rimini, the *Commedia*'s 'fallen woman' par excellence.

Many of Gladstone's significant friendships were with women who were both older and of a higher social provenance, possibly compensating for his remote relationship with his mother, women like the duchess of Sutherland and Lady Waldegrave. In the Thistlethwayte letter quoted earlier, Gladstone continued: 'Valued and precious friendships with women . . . formed no small part of my life. To be prized by women in general is in my opinion a great glory, because of their gift of judging character: but it is a glory I cannot claim and do not deserve.' Gladstone was temperamentally inclined to revere older, wiser women, which is essentially what Dante turns the young Beatrice into in *Paradiso*.

Paradiso was Gladstone's preferred cantica of the *Commedia*. Today it is the least popular, partly because of its intense preoccupation with medieval cosmology and theology, partly because relentless bliss is generally less compelling than the blood-and-guts drama of the *Inferno* or the pilgrims' progress through *Purgatorio*. Yet, as Morley wrote, this was not the case with Gladstone:

> He once asked of an accomplished woman possessing a scholar's breadth of reading, what poetry she most lived with. She named Dante for one. 'But what of Dante?' 'The Paradiso,' she replied. 'Ah, that is right,' he exclaimed. 'That's my test'. In the Paradiso it was, that he saw in beams of crystal radiance the ideal of the unity of the religious mind, the love and admiration for the high-unseen things of which the Christian church was to him the sovereign embodiment. The medieval spirit, it is true, wears something of a ghostly air in the light of our new day. This attempt, which has been made many a time before, "to unify two ages" did not carry men far in the second half of the nineteenth century. Nevertheless, it were an idle dream to think that the dead

76

hand of Dante's century, and all that it represented, is no longer to be taken into account by those who would be governors of men.[24]

John Sinclair wrote of *Paradiso* that it was,

above all, the Cantica of Beatrice. That one of the blessed should watch with particular care over the well-being of individuals living the hard and perilous earthly life was a prevalent idea of the time, but the poet's choice of Beatrice for that office is an invention that gives to this third Cantica a beautiful note of humanity and affection.[25]

An additional attraction of *Paradiso* for Gladstone was that here Beatrice comes into her own as a woman. Virgil, as the voice of human reason and the symbol of state and empire, guides Dante, as Dante guides Gladstone, through Hell and Purgatory. But it is Beatrice, as the embodiment of the perfect woman, the manifestation of divine love and the symbol of the Church triumphant, who ultimately leads him to God. One of Beatrice's most endearing characteristics, as she and Dante approach the highest heaven, is that she becomes increasingly more beautiful. It is in terms of physical attractiveness that Dante tries to convey the beauty of her soul. The overall impression of Dante's personal tenderness for a beautiful and holy woman may have been intensely attractive for Gladstone at an emotionally fraught period of his life.

Sins of the flesh

And what of women of compromised virtue? Inappropriate sexuality was the main factor behind the fall from grace of Gladstone's 'problem' women. But probably no discussion of Gladstone and women could avoid making some mention of the sexual trials in his own life, specifically in the context of his relationship with the prostitutes he sought to rescue. Briefly, current opinion favours the view that Gladstone's rescue missions were well intentioned, though foolhardy, potentially damaging to his career and ultimately unhelpful to the vast majority of women he approached. Naivety seems to be the worst he can be accused of, though the after-effect of his visits to beautiful young prostitutes is a more complex matter. It is also a fact that Gladstone did not choose this mission at random. He was directed to it through his membership of The Engagement, a group of friends who came together in 1844 under the protection of John Keble, founder of the Oxford Movement. The Engagement has been described by Matthew as 'a layman's substitute for clericalism'[26] and by Richard Shannon as a 'characteristic expression of the

---

24 Morley, *Gladstone*, i. 151.
25 DC, *Paradiso*, 29
26 Matthew, *Gladstone*, 22.

Tractarian impulse of the time'.[27] The first of the twelve rules imposed on members of The Engagement was that they undertake regular good works, and donate one-tenth of their income to charity. Initially Gladstone fulfilled this by working with destitutes of both sexes before 'specialising' in women. He is believed to have spent some £80,000 attempting to rehabilitate them.[28]

Magnus goes so far as to call Gladstone's rescue work a 'sublimation':

> He had experienced a call to enter the Church, and he had not responded to it. He had nursed the idea of a sacred union between Church and State, and he had watched it dissolve into air. In his rescue work he found a priestly office which he could fulfil as a layman, and in which his duty to God and man could be discharged together. No consideration on earth could have induced him to abandon it until old age enfeebled him.[29]

More significant for the purposes of Dante comparisons is his personal response to the prostitute activity. The publication of his diaries revealed for the first time that after these encounters Gladstone sometimes had recourse to the scourge – marked in the diaries by a small whip symbol. This was a means of sexual self-control expressly approved by the Tractarians. It was also the way Dante punishes seducers in *Inferno*,[30] and warns the faithful in *Purgatorio*. To this extent Gladstone can claim a historical precedent for his self-inflicted correction. Dante is purified of lust by passing through the flames of Purgatory. Lust is one of three sins to which Dante admits in the *Commedia*; the others are pride and anger. Gladstone admitted to the same three.

Gladstone's prostitute rescue work was at its most intense from the mid-1840s to the late 1850s. At times he took an uncomfortably close interest in his cases and had actively to curb his enthusiasm for seeking them out. One such was Marian Summerhayes, whom he met in 1859. Summerhayes was a courtesan and artists' model, much more refined than most of the girls he had been trying to save. She was also very beautiful, and soon Gladstone was seeking her out virtually every day. He had known her for less than a week before he commissioned his friend, William Dyce, to paint her portrait. Like his fellow Pre-Raphaelite Alexander Munro, who had executed the marble sculpture of Paolo and Francesca for Gladstone a few years earlier, Dyce was a *protégé* of Gladstone's confidante, the duchess of Sutherland.[31]

---

[27] Shannon, *Gladstone*, 171.
[28] This would equate to £4m. at present-day values, according to figures provided by the Treasury. In summer 1999 the Treasury quoted an inflation rate of 50:1 for the mid-nineteenth century compared with the present day.
[29] Magnus, *Gladstone*, 107.
[30] DC, *Inferno*, canto 18, 36–7.
[31] Dyce had already painted his own version of *Francesca da Rimini*, which was exhibited at the Royal Scottish Academy in 1837.

The portrait of Summerhayes, originally entitled *Lady with a coronet of jasmine*, is now known as *Beatrice*, and hangs in the Aberdeen Art Gallery (*see* plate 6). The identity of the sitter was unknown until the publication of volume v of the *Diaries* in 1978 but from the start she was widely held to represent Dante's ideal woman of the *Commedia*. Five years after its completion, a Dante scholar in Florence wrote to Dyce that the model was 'a perfect Florentine type'. Dyce had, she maintained, used the same hair decoration as that used by Botticelli, 'a touch that adds beauty to the picture. I like this one better than any of the many Beatrices I have seen'.[32]

Dyce's correspondent was mistaken about the hair decoration in one important respect: the Beatrice of the *Commedia* was wearing a crown of olive branches (symbolising wisdom), not of jasmine (which traditionally represent purity), when Dante met her in the Earthly Paradise at the top of Mount Purgatory. But visually the Dyce and Botticelli images – and their messages – are very similar.

Within a few weeks of their acquaintance, Gladstone realised that his emotions were not under control and 'my thoughts of Summerhayes require to be limited and purged'.[33] The relationship ended shortly afterwards. It is not known what Gladstone had paid for the Summerhayes portrait. But in June 1875 he sold it at auction for £420.

As regards sins of the flesh in other people, Dante and Gladstone both tended to compassion, perhaps because they were no strangers to temptation themselves. *Inferno* is often interpreted as a place where Dante delighted in taking particular revenge on his enemies. Yet he also included in the seventh circle, with the sodomites, his old friend the distinguished Florentine academic Brunetto Latini.[34] Featuring Latini was a useful narrative device to enable the two Florentines to discuss the state of their native city. But it also indicates Dante's willingness, in sexual matters, to show unconditional compassion for the sinner while conceding to God absolutely the power to condemn him. John Sinclair explains it thus: 'This was a strange and terrible instance . . . of a noble nature inwardly disfigured, and he (Dante) dared not refuse to speak of it just because the man had been his friend, as if he should measure men by their relation to himself.'[35]

This same compassion Gladstone showed in various ways with all sorts of women. The women were as different as Lady Lincoln, Laura Thistlethwayte, Helen Gladstone and Katherine O'Shea, Charles Parnell's married mistress and useful go-between in the Irish Home Rule affair. Gladstone was accused of having turned a blind eye to the Parnell–O'Shea affair on grounds of expediency. Morley reports Gladstone as responding: 'Because a man is called

---

[32] Clara Detmold to William Dyce, *Dyce papers*, quoted in Marcia Pointon, 'Gladstone as art patron and collector', *Victorian Studies* xix (1974), 92.

[33] *Gladstone diaries*, entry for 1 Sept. 1859.

[34] DC, *Inferno*, 15.

[35] Ibid. 202.

leader of a party, does that constitute him a censor and a judge of faith and morals? I will not accept it. It would make life intolerable.'[36] Of this response Roy Jenkins comments:

> Gladstone could often be self-righteous and sometimes priggish, but he was not a hypocrite, and he had seen too much of life and enjoyed the company of too many women whose virtue was not perfect for a straightforward even if long-standing case of adultery to cause him moral revulsion. Furthermore, he must have been uneasily aware of how often he had heard rumour of Parnell's relationship with Mrs O'Shea without it causing him either to decline dealings with the Irish leader or to avoid Mrs O'Shea herself as an occasional go-between. As soon as the outcome of the divorce case was known, Gladstone took his stand on the likely political consequences and not on morals. And to this position he stuck.[37]

Nor did Gladstone totally abandon 'poor Lady Lincoln', 'once the dream of dreams', in her later years. Gladstone had supported her husband in his divorce case against her in 1849. Despite this, in 1881 – not having seen her for over thirty years – he undertook to help Lady Susan Opdebeck, as she was known, by virtue of her second marriage to her Belgian courier, to manage her finances and help relieve her poverty. He even enlisted the services of Mrs Thistlethwayte.

Everyday women

And what about the wives of Dante and Gladstone, real women who defy easy categorisation. Little is known about Dante's wife Gemma Donati and much about Gladstone's wife Catherine Glynne. What they had in common is that they were socially superior to their husbands on marriage and that they spent a great deal of time apart from them. Dante was in political exile for much of his married life while his wife remained in Florence, which she was entitled to do in her own right. Gladstone was away from Hawarden Castle, his wife's family home, for up to six months at a time while Catherine held the fort. Madonna Alighieri seems to have been relaxed about Dante's devotion to Beatrice – which being in the courtly tradition, represented no infidelity – and even agreed to their daughter Antonia taking the name Beatrice when she became a nun. Mrs Gladstone, too, was aware of her husband's nocturnal 'rescue' missions and on occasions took in the prostitutes he had 'saved' and found work for them. Circumstances required that these wives of remarkable men lead capable, practical lives in the shadow of their famous husbands and the evidence is that they did it well. Of Catherine Gladstone, Matthew wrote:

[36] Morley, *Gladstone*, ii. 435.
[37] Jenkins, *Gladstone*, 570.

In an age when the public position of women was fast changing, she was an important icon, her own commemorative plate next to her husband's on many a sideboard. She was the first woman regularly to sit on the platform at political speeches. She energetically organised various homes and hostels, especially for children, and was an unembarrassed fundraiser. She was the first President of the Women's Liberal Foundation . . . Gladstone's comments in his diary usually present her as distanced from the political world in accordance with his view of the proper sphere of femininity . . . In fact, she was an integral part of his political world.[38]

Eugenio Biagini observes that 'Dante's idealisation of his lost love Beatrice . . . contributed to the young Gladstone's construction of gender roles'.[39] Before he read Dante, Gladstone already intensely idealised one dead female relative; he was still a young man when he married Catherine Glynne, who added an extra and different dimension to his perception of women. Dante reinforced essential aspects of Gladstone's chivalric approach to the female – particularly his belief in their fundamental goodness. But in Catherine he came to realise that fun, warmth, rude health and a robust nature were perfectly compatible with goodness and piety; and indeed probably enhanced those virtues.

However much he revered women, Gladstone's attitude to the growing movement towards equal rights was a complex one. He supported the invidious Contagious Diseases Acts, despite his prostitute rescue work. He opposed divorce and loathed the idea of contraception. About the benefits of further education for women, he remained uncertain, despite his daughter Helen's success as Vice-Principal of Newnham College, Cambridge. And he resisted to the end taking responsibility for promoting the female franchise. Catherine Gladstone was obliged to stand down from the chairmanship of the Women's Liberal Federation in 1892 (in a letter of resignation drafted by her husband) because its increasingly pro-suffrage stance was at odds with Gladstone's contention that such a move was premature. And in April that year he wrote to Liberal MP Samuel Smith, who had sought his endorsement of the Woman's Suffrage Bill he was about to present to the House of Commons, saying he appreciated that Smith meant well, but he hoped that the house would reject the bill. He expressed his reservations in terms redolent of medieval chivalry:

I have no fear lest the woman should encroach upon the power of men . . . The fear I have is lest we should invite her unwittingly to trespass upon the delicacy, the purity, the refinement of her own nature, which are the present sources of its power.[40]

---

38 Matthew, *Gladstone*, 615–16.
39 Biagini, *Gladstone*,12.
40 Samuel Smith, *My life-work*, London 1902, quoted in *Gladstone diaries*, xiii. 19.

5

Religion and Faith

As young men both Gladstone and Dante had considered taking holy orders, Dante as a Franciscan – in the *Commedia* he still wears girdle that signifies his allegiance[1] – Gladstone in the Church of England, as he explained to Catherine Glynne on their engagement.[2] Dante's whole life was closely bound up with the Franciscans. After the early death of both his parents, he was educated by the Franciscan brothers at Santa Croce in Florence; if he studied or taught at Oxford, he is likely to have done so under Franciscan protection. His body remains in the Franciscan monastery at Ravenna despite repeated attempts by Florence to reclaim it. While Dante dedicated his major work to Beatrice, who brought him back to theology after a long flirtation with philosophy in the 'dark wood', Gladstone's retirement work on Bishop Butler has been described as recompense for a lifetime spent in politics instead of the Church.[3]

Both men also had a powerful belief in Hell. For Dante this was part of the conventional theology of his time; for Gladstone it was a more radical view in nineteenth-century Britain when the concept was waning, rather to his annoyance, despite the popularity of Dante. In *Studies subsidiary to the works of Bishop Butler*, he complained that

> Among believers in the future state there are no denials of the abstract proposition that punishment awaits the wicked after death. But the proposition seems to be relegated at present to the far-off corners of the Christian mind, and there to sleep in dark shadow, as a thing needless in our enlightened and progressive age.[4]

As Nick Havely has observed

> It is, on the face of it, odd that Dante should be so revered by the Victorians when his work is based on a doctrine they found intolerable: the idea of eternal punishment for the damned. If you experience your spiritual state as an event, not a choice, then there is no reason why you should be punished for it. You are innocent of your own state of belief . . . For some, belief is impossible.[5]

---

1 DC, *Inferno*, canto 17, 6–9.
2 *Gladstone diaries*, entry for 9 June 1838.
3 Matthew, 'Gladstone and the University of Oxford', 4.
4 W. E. Gladstone, *Studies subsidiary to the works of Bishop Butler*, Oxford 1896, 212.
5 Havely, *Dante's modern after-life*, 97.

Gladstone and Dante also both saw the world as a place of exile after the Fall, and life as a journey back to God. Dante lived his exile in a very practical, as well as a symbolic way. That he saw life as a pilgrimage to his eternal home – if not to Florence – is clear from the structure of the *Commedia*, and Dante's progress from the moral confusion of the dark wood, through the three-day descent into the horrors of Hell, then the trials of Purgatory, to Paradise and the beatific vision of God. Of *Purgatorio*, in particular, John Sinclair wrote that its whole subject 'is the perfecting, by penitence and fellowship and prayer, of the life of man among men'.[6] Gladstone's view of life as pilgrimage is exemplified in his retrospective reviews, or annual 'breast-beating', as Jenkins calls them.[7] In these the penitent evaluates and reflects on the progress he has made – social, cultural and political but above all spiritual – in the previous twelve months.

But it is primarily on the vexed question of the importance of keeping separate the power of Church and State that the thoughts of Gladstone and Dante converge. They understood that Church and State were the dual and mutually independent guardians of the welfare of mankind, with both the spiritual and the secular deriving their separate but equal authority directly from God. The two men are particularly in agreement as regards the dangers – equally real and present in the fourteenth century as the nineteenth – of a politically ambitious papacy. Both of them, in different ways, abhorred the papacy in their own times, although they could respect certain incumbents, where deserved. And both of them, in different ways, believed passionately that temporal and religious influences – the power of the State or Empire versus the Church or papacy, should be kept separate.

For Gladstone, as he expressed it in *The State in its relations with the Church*, the state existed to implement the principles of the established Anglican Church, and work towards bringing about the kingdom of heaven on earth:

> If, therefore, we believe that the connection of Church and State, rescued on the one hand from Papal, and on the other from Erastian tyranny of either power over its ally, be comfortable to the will of God, essential to the well-being of a community, implied and necessitated by every right idea and civil government, and calculated to extend and establish the vital influences of Christianity, and therewith to increase and purify the mass of individual happiness, then, as holders of that belief, are we all the most imperatively to its defence in this the most critical period of its history.[8]

Gladstone gave a copy of this book to Catherine during their courtship in Italy. She accepted him anyway. But it was not universally well received. Jenkins comments that it was mostly considered, even by Tories, as

---

6 DC, *Purgatorio*, 445.
7 Jenkins, *Gladstone*, 293.
8 Gladstone, *State and Church*, 3.

a foolish book, making up in portentousness . . . what it lacked in sense and judgement . . . [Its] only self-protective aspect was that it was extremely diffi-cult to read. Few can have penetrated its opaqueness to the full monstrous intolerance of the doctrine, which broadly amounted to a policy of no public service throughout the British Isles for anyone who was not a communicating member of the Church of England.[9]

The views expressed in the book are not views that Gladstone sustained. Morley comments that in 1843 Gladstone's theocratic ideal had been destroyed by practical experience. His opinion by then was that 'of public life, I certainly must say, every year shows me more and more that the idea of Christian politics cannot be realised in the state, according to its present condition'.[10] His increasing knowledge of the world and its infinite variety persuaded him that what was right and fitting for one country – such as an Anglican theocracy for England – could not be so for a country like Italy, where the national religion could not be other than Roman Catholic. That the Church had a duty to act as the State's conscience, the fountain of its morality, remained valid. But young Gladstone had also claimed that the state had the responsibility to maintain the Christian truth professed by the Church of England, without which one could allegedly not be regarded as a true citizen; the Church in exchange deserved the unqualified support of parliament. With time, Gladstone came to realise that the ideal of limiting state support to confessed Anglicans was unworkable in a religiously plural-istic society such as Britain. It could not accommodate Dissenters or Roman Catholics, let alone Jews, all of whom would be excluded from public office, regardless of how competent they were, or however upstanding as private citizens. This clearly was neither fair nor liberal.

Over the years, Gladstone's attitude mellowed into a liberal Broad Church approach that embraced equality of treatment for all religious communities – and even an accommodation with Catholicism in countries where that was the tradition. Gladstone would become comfortable, for example, with the Old Catholicism of his friend Döllinger, who took an historical rather than a doctrinal, Rome-centred approach to Catholicism, and was later excommu-nicated by the pope for declining to accept the new doctrine of papal infallibility.

But while Gladstone's catholicity continued to mellow, his antagonism to the Roman Catholic Church, and the continuing inability of the contempo-rary papacy to refrain from meddling in temporal affairs, remained a constant.[11] As David Bebbington has observed:

---

9   Ibid. 54.
10   Morley, *Gladstone*, i. 183.
11   Ironically, the prominent Victorian journalist W. T. Stead called Gladstone himself a 'kind of secular pope': Travis Crosby, *The two Mr Gladstones: a study in psychology and history*, New Haven–London 1997, 1.

Anti-erastianism was to remain a driving force in his later career. Perhaps most deeply felt of all, however, was the need to defend freedom against Roman Catholic domineering. Gladstone hated the despotic international authority of the Vatican that prevented national Catholic bodies from expressing their own genius in the manner of the orthodox Churches of the east. He detested the oppressive and incompetent administration of the Papal States together with its theoretical justification of the pope to temporal power . . . The whole Roman Catholic system that ensnared his closest friends, seemed intent on repressing personal liberty. Rome was the sworn foe of liberty.[12]

Gladstone never overcame his dismay at the defection to Rome of those who were close to him. When his sister Helen converted in 1842 he told her that her 'soul was staked for all eternity'.[13] On hearing of the conversion of Henry Manning, he said he felt as if Manning had 'murdered my mother by mistake.'[14] On her conversion to Rome, he sacked his cousin Anne Ramsden Bennett, co-translator of Lo stato romano. As late as 1854 he wrote to Samuel Wilberforce on the occasion of his brother Robert's conversion to Rome: 'Could I, with reference to my own precious children, think that one of them might possibly live to strike . . . such a blow, how far rather would I that he had never been born.'[15] But the personal was also political.

Five centuries earlier, Dante had warned time and again of what could happen – and did happen in his native Italy – when the pope usurped civil power. It is a theme that recurs throughout the Commedia. Particularly powerful are his outbursts against the desperate political conditions that prevailed in his own time in the Italian peninsula in general, and in his native Florence in particular. After meeting the poet and fellow-Florentine Sordello in Purgatorio, Dante launches into a bitter analysis of the city's current political woes. This found a strong echo with nineteenth-century Italians desperate for liberty from foreign rulers and politicised popes. Dante's argument is that the evils of his own time resulted primarily from the material ambition of the Church and the papacy's success in usurping the civil power of the Holy Roman Empire, while the Hapsburg emperors failed to assert their due authority, particularly in the Italian city states, which, like Dante's beloved Florence, were descending into anarchy and strife.

The idea that the empire had an active obligation to guard the frontiers of its jurisdiction against ecclesiastical encroachment was fundamental to Dante's thinking. It found its fullest expression in his Latin work, De monarchia. The dates for this book are not known, but it clearly post-dated

12 Bebbington, Mind of Gladstone, 140.
13 Gladstone to Helen Gladstone, 10 May 1842, GG MS 751.
14 This is quoted in Bebbington, Mind of Gladstone, 144.
15 Matthew, Gladstone, 246. It is almost inconceivable that Gladstone could write this, just four years after the death of his infant daughter, Jessy.

the *Commedia*, since Dante wrote in Latin that he was repeating what he had already said in *Paradiso*: 'Sicut in Paradiso Comediae dixi.'

Gladstone first read *De monarchia* in 1861, and he read it again in 1887. But since, by Dante's own admission, there is a total consistency of views on the issue of Church and State in this work and the *Commedia*, reading *De monarchia* will only have confirmed those ideas that they already shared.

James Bryce, a contemporary of Gladstone's, called Dante's book 'an epitaph' rather than 'a prophecy' for the prospects of empire in Italy at the time:

> Weary of the endless strife of princes and cities, of the factions which within every city strove against each other, seeing municipal freedom, the only mitigation of turbulence, vanish with the rise of domestic tyrants, Dante raised a passionate cry for some power to still the tempest, not to quench liberty or to supersede local self-government, but to connect and moderate them, to restore unity and peace to hapless Italy.[16]

Dante – who was influenced by the Franciscan concept of the virtue of poverty – believed that, ideally, the Church should operate not only without jurisdiction, but without money as well. So he felt particularly aggrieved by the individual popes under whom he suffered. It was partly on grounds of his hostility to the papacy that he was exiled from Florence at all in 1302, although this was primarily a political, rather than a religiously-motivated, move.

Papal abuse was represented at its worst in Dante's lifetime by three popes in particular: Nicholas III (in Dante's childhood), Boniface VIII (during his active political life) and Clement V (when, in exile, he was writing the *Commedia*).[17]

John Sinclair called Dante's predicament *vis-à-vis* popes 'a crescendo of iniquity'. It was

> a kind of apostolic succession from Nicholas, reputed the first of the papal simonists – and a great one – through Boniface, the protagonist in his age of the most inordinate pretensions of the Church to political predominance, a worldly, unscrupulous and powerful ecclesiastic – and incidentally the corrupter of the public life of Florence and the cause of Dante's exile – to Clement, treacherous, lecherous and servile to France, the leader of the Church into its seventy years of shame at Avignon.[18]

Bryce described the significance to nineteenth-century Italians of Dante's view on papal power as crucial:

[16] James Bryce, *The Holy Roman Empire* (1864), London 1925, 312.
[17] For a full discussion of the subject see George Holmes, 'Dante and the popes', in Cecil Grayson (ed.), *The world of Dante*, Oxford 1980, 18–43.
[18] *DC, Inferno*, 244.

Dante prayed for a monarchy of the world, a reign of peace and Christian brotherhood: those who, five centuries later, invoked his name as the earliest prophet of their creed strove after an idea that never crossed his mind – the gathering of all Italians into a national state. Yet this he and they had in common – to exclude the papacy from the sphere of secular government.[19]

The most striking element of the Church–State debate is how much both Dante and Gladstone hated popes. Dante respected the office while abhorring the corruption of its recent occupants, Celestine V and Boniface VIII in particular. In *Paradiso*, St Peter complains: 'Quello ch'usurpa in terra il luogo mio/ . . . che vaca nella presenza del Figliuol di Dio,/ fatt'ha del cimiterio mio cloaca/ del sangue e della puzza; onde 'l perverso/ che cadde di qua su, là giù si place' ('He who usurps my place . . . which in the sight of the Son of God is empty, has made of my tomb a sewer of blood and filth, so that the apostate who fell from here above takes comfort there below'). A little later, he adds: 'Non fu nostra intenzion . . . / . . . che le chiavi che mi fuor concesse/ divenisser signaculo in vessillo/ che contra battezzati combattesse' ('It was not our meaning . . . that the keys which were committed to me should become the device on a standard for warfare on the baptised').[20]

Gladstone abhorred the notion of papal infallibility as a complicating factor in nineteenth-century Italian politics in particular, and an inherent threat to national allegiance in any country. In his work *The Vatican decrees and their bearing on civil allegiance: a political expostulation* (1874), he outlines the potential conflict of personal loyalties for a Roman Catholic who felt committed both to the pope and to his own country. On the other hand, Gladstone's personal encounters with Pope Pius IX in October 1860 were cordial enough. Moreover, when his sister Helen wrote to him from Rome in 1855 to say she had met the pope who promised to remember Gladstone in his prayers, he replies that he found him 'a very decent man'.[21] Yet one of the few words that Gladstone copied into the back of his own copy of the *Inferno* was 'puttana' ('the whore') – the word used by Dante to describe his perception of the papacy in his time, its corrupt alliance with the French crown and its desertion of Rome for Avignon. One of the strongest statements on the evil of the papacy assuming temporal power is expressed in *Purgatorio*, canto 16.

Rome, which made the good world, used to have two suns which made plain the one way and the other, that of the world and that of God. The one has quenched the other and the sword is joined to the crook, and the one together with the other must perforce go ill, since, joined, the one does not fear the other.[22]

[19] Bryce, *Holy Roman Empire*, 314–15.
[20] DC, *Purgatorio*, canto 27, 22–7; canto 46, 49–51.
[21] Gladstone to Helen Gladstone, 19 Feb. 1855, GG, MS 752, fo. 3.
[22] 'Soleva Roma, che 'l buon mondo feo,/ due soli aver, che l'una e l'altra strada/ facean

Throughout the *Commedia*, Dante blames the ills of contemporary Italy on the papacy and its misuse of temporal power. Through its interference in politics, it set Christian states against each other when it should be confronting infidels. Dante also condemns the Church for corruption, greed and extortion. The first pope in *Inferno* is Celestine V 'who made the great refusal'[23] by stepping down to clear the way for Boniface, whose intrigues were a direct factor in Dante's own exile. Celestine preferred to return to the obscurity of non-commitment rather than address the Church's current problems. He is placed with other Neutrals – the souls of those who lived for themselves alone – in the first level of Hell. This categorisation is an original creation of Dante's, outside all the traditional systems of Hell. It emphasises the degree to which duty and integrity were paramount for Dante, as for Gladstone, in any form of public life. That the uncommitted are the object of a particular contempt on Dante's part has a clear autobiographical significance. These innumerable seekers of safety first, who take no risk either of suffering in a good cause or of scandal in a bad one, are described as Dante believed them to be in life – the rubbish of the universe, unfit for Heaven but barely admitted to Hell. They follow a meaningless shifting banner that never stands for anything. Dante's principles, as manifested in this scene, chime with Gladstone's in acting in politics according to one's conscience.

Boniface, in Dante's view the shameful antithesis of everything the papacy should represent, has no place in Hell, at least not yet, since the *Commedia* is nominally set in 1300, when Boniface was still alive. In other parts of Hell damned priests abound. Virgil identifies many of the 'tonsured ones' amongst the Avaricious and the Prodigals of the Fourth Circle as popes and cardinals.[24] In the Circle of the Infidels, Pope Anastasius is condemned for all eternity to lie in a stinking tomb.[25] In medieval tradition this fifth-century pope was persuaded to deny the divine birth of Christ.

Canto 19 begins with a bitter denunciation of simony, again emphasising Dante's preoccupation with the corruption of the Church. These sinners – who abused sacred things for sordid ends – are punished by a reversal of contemporary baptism practice. Plunged head down in narrow pits like communal fonts, they are tortured with fire on the soles of their feet, rather than being immersed in holy water. Dante compares the scene with the Baptistery in Florence and takes the opportunity to refute publicly an earlier charge made against him – probably of sacrilege – when he broke a Baptistery font to save someone from drowning.[26] The practice of simony angers Dante

---

vedere, e del mondo e di Deo./ L'un l'altro ha spento; ed è giunta la spada/ col pasturale, e l'un con l'altro inseme/ per viva forza mal convien che vada,/ però che, giunti, l'un l'altro non temer: DC, *Purgatorio*, canto 16, 106–12.

23 DC, *Inferno*, canto 3, 60.

24 Ibid. canto 7, 37–48.

25 Ibid. canto 11, 8–9.

26 Gladstone witnessed two baptisms there during his first visit to Florence and felt profoundly uneasy at the ritual: *Gladstone diaries*, entry for 17 Mar. 1832.

profoundly, as did any corrupt practice of the Church, and he sternly rebukes one of the damned – Pope Nicholas – even as he reiterates his reverence for the papal office. Other popes and high-ranking clerics mentioned in *Inferno* and *Purgatorio* include Adrian V, Archbishop Boniface of Ravenna, Clement IV, Gregory I, Martin IV. *Paradiso*, of course, is full of appropriately saintly ones.

Among those in paradise is Constantine, the first Christian emperor, who removed the imperial government to Byzantium in the fourth century. He was believed to have endowed the Church, in the person of Pope Sylvester, with imperial dominion in the west; this belief was based on the Donation of Constantine, an ancient document, now acknowledged to be a forgery. Though the emperor himself finds eternal bliss in heaven,[27] it is back to this document, which Dante believed to be genuine, that he traces the ills of contemporary Italy, in that through it the realms of Church and State, and the offices of pope and emperor, first supposedly became confused. Dante's argument was that the Donation of Constantine was fundamentally flawed, indeed illegal. The emperor had no power to abrogate imperial authority, nor had the Church the power to receive it. No single emperor or pope could disturb the dual nature of their respective spheres: the one had no right to bestow, nor the other to receive such a gift. The Donation is mentioned in Gladstone's *The State in its relations with the Church*.

In Dante's Italy, in political terms, the Guelphs broadly supported the pope and the Ghibellines the emperor. But the margins were often blurred. Dante, like Gladstone, changed allegiance when conscience required it, preferring to be led by the requirements of the common good than narrow political traditions. Though a (White) Guelph, it was to the Emperor Henry VII of Luxemburg that Dante looked to bring peace to Italy. Henry followed two emperors – Rudolph of Hapsburg and Albert I – who had failed to come to Italy at all, let alone to be crowned, and showed no interest in Italian affairs. Henry was crowned first in Milan, then in Rome, and Dante had great hopes of him – not just to save Italy from internecine strife, but to put an end to his own political exile. Dante had been one of the priors of Florence sent to San Gimignano on a diplomatic mission during which the (Black) Guelphs – at that time supporting the pope – took control of the city. Dante was exiled from Florence in 1301, never to return.

The terms of exile were harsh. He was charged with intrigue against the peace of the city and hostility to the pope. A heavy fine was imposed and he was banned from holding public office in Florence for the rest of his life. His property was confiscated and he was sentenced to be burned alive if caught. His sons, when they came of age, were compelled to join him in exile, although his wife, a member of an old Florentine family, was entitled to remain in the city in her own right. So began Dante's wanderings. Exactly

27 DC, *Paradiso*, canto 20.

where he went and when is not known in detail, although Can Grande della Scala at Verona and Guido Novello da Polenta, Francesca da Rimini's nephew, at Ravenna were among his sponsors.

Under Henry of Luxemburg, Dante's hopes for peace in Italy, and his own return to Florence, were revived. Dante wrote to his fellow citizens urging them to welcome Henry as emperor. When Henry met with strong opposition, Dante sent a bitter letter to him, urging him to put down the rebellion quickly; he also addressed a letter in similar vein to Florence using abusive terms which could not be forgiven. When Henry's expedition failed, and the hope of empire died with him, Dante was not included, understandably, in the amnesty granted to certain exiles. Later, amnesty was offered on the condition that he acknowledge his guilt and ask forgiveness publicly. With a stubbornness reminiscent of Gladstone, he refused and his death sentence was renewed. Despite his failure to help achieve either peace for the Italian region or his own rehabilitation, Dante's stance was to make him the hero of the Risorgimento.[28]

There are three major quotation referring to passages from the *Commedia* in *The State in its relations with the Church*. The first refers to *Paradiso* 2, line 123; the third to *Paradiso* 30, line 40. The second, and most significant, refers to *Paradiso* 3, line 30, and fits in with Morley's 'faint echo' of Constantine. Gladstone writes: 'When Dante wrote the "Ahi Costantin" it was of the supposed donation of temporal sovereignty to the bishop of Rome that he meant to record his disapprobation. But the union of the Church and the State must have been found a powerful instrument of extending influences of religion.'[29] Morley explains that:

> In the early pages of this very book, Mr Gladstone says that the union of Church and State is to the Church of secondary though great importance; *her* foundations are only the holy hills and her condition would be no pitiable one, should she once more occupy the position she once held . . . Faint echo of the unforgotten lines which Dante cries out to Constantine what woes his fatal dower to the papacy had brought down on religion and mankind.[30]

Taking into account the level of anti-Catholicism in Victorian Britain, Dante's antagonism towards many medieval popes may have helped endear him to Gladstone. But the reality is more complex, as Gladstone understood. In writing on the inside back cover of his own copy of *Paradiso*, the words 'an imp. Not a Ghib'., and, beneath that: 'a RC not a pap', Gladstone recognised in Dante a political conscience similar to his own, a recognition which also

[28] For the significance of Dante as a Risorgimento icon for the Victorians see p. 31 above.
[29] Gladstone, *State and Church*, 70.
[30] Morley, *Gladstone*, 134.

helps to explain his affinity with Roman Catholic statesman, despite his personal anti-papalism. 'An imp. Not a Ghib'. implies that Gladstone understood that Dante was a pan-European imperialist though not a Ghibelline, not a member of the party that traditionally supported the emperor for purely power-political reasons. On the contrary, Dante was a Guelph, traditionally therefore a supporter of the pope. Yet he would ally himself with the Ghibellines if he felt the greater good of Italy required it, and support Henry of Luxemburg as the only chance for peace and unity in the region.

The annotation 'a RC not a pap' reinforces the point. Gladstone sees Dante as embracing the national religion personally, while disowning contemporary popes for their abuse of power. With this Gladstone could identify. His own thinking on the Church–State issue was also motivated by the ambition to achieve what was best for his country. For him, the soul of nineteenth-century Britain was threatened by corruption, dissent and disunity as was medieval Italy for Dante. And both, in their different ways, laid some blame on the separation of temporal and spiritual power and the divided loyalties it created. This same reservation lay behind Gladstone's rejection of the doctrine of papal infallibility and the degree to which the doctrine compromised British national loyalty.

Life's journey back to God

When he began the Commedia, Dante was already acquainted with life as exile – from public position, from family and friends, from home and property: from everything, not just from God. Exile was his condition as well as his theme. 'The subject', Dante wrote in his famous letter in Latin to his friend and sponsor Can Grande della Scala at Verona, explaining the structure of the Commedia, 'is man either gaining or losing merit through his freedom of will'.[31] In the letter Dante makes various points of comparison between parts of his Commedia and the Bible. Gladstone, on the other hand, compares it with a more recent account of a journey through the vicissitudes of life. In his diary entry of his reading for Easter Day, 6 April 1890, he notes reading 'Bunyan's Pilgrim's Progress: a clear cut objectivity reminding one of Dante'. Roger Sharrock makes the same comparison, while commenting that The pilgrim's progress 'is not intellectual or highly organised as in the sophisticated religious allegory of Dante'.[32] The parallels between Dante and Bunyan (a Dante for the working classes?) extend beyond their work to their personal lives. Bunyan's dream began in a 'den' in the 'wilderness of life';[33] Dante's in a

31 Dante Alighieri, 'Letter to Can Grande della Scala', trans. John Marchand, University of Illinois, http:ccat.sas.upenn.edu/jod/cangrande.English.html, 6.
32 John Bunyan, The pilgrim's progress, London 1987, ed. Roger Sharrock, introduction at p. xv.
33 Ibid. 11.

'dark wood where the straight way was lost'.[34] Both allegories lead through the spiritual exile of confusion, misery and gradual enlightenment to Bunyan's Celestial City and Dante's Beatific Vision respectively.

Bunyan, who supported Parliament in the civil war, was imprisoned after the restoration of the monarchy for his refusal to cease preaching. He could have been released at any time if he had agreed to stop preaching and conform to the Church of England. Roger Sharrock describes it as a measure of Bunyan's personal integrity that he refused to do so.[35] In this he resembles Dante, who would not admit publicly a guilt he did not feel, even to secure his return home. Sharrock comments that, in *The pilgrim's progress*, Bunyan rendered the spiritual autobiography he wrote earlier while in prison, *Grace abounding to the chief of sinners*, 'into the objective form of a universal myth. All Christians searching for the truth and prepared to reject a hostile society are comprehended under the figure of the wayfaring man earnestly pursuing his pilgrimage'.[36]

There are several parallels with Dante and his *Commedia*. Dante called his work his 'universal volume' as Bunyan called his a 'universal myth': both were intended to appeal to all mankind. Initially, Dante was exiled from Florence as a purely political move – he was banned in his absence when the administration changed. He too had opportunities to return to his home and family – as Bunyan had to leave prison – had he been prepared to declare himself guilty of crimes of which he felt innocent. Gladstone, too, endured periods in the political wilderness. He, too, was prepared to resign over a matter such as the Maynooth affair.[37] In this instance, he voted with the government for an increase in the grant to a Roman Catholic seminary in Ireland on the pro-Irish grounds that to do so was good governance, but then resigned since he opposed the move as a matter of personal anti-Roman Catholic conscience.

If Gladstone, like Dante and Bunyan, saw the world as a place of exile and life as a journey back to God, this was not necessarily how an outside observer saw his life, Dean Plumptre of Wells for one. Plumptre formally dedicated the section on Purgatory in his *Commedia and canzionere* to Gladstone, as follows:

> Not thine the exile's weary lot to tread
> The stairs of others as with weary feet,
> Nor yet in lonely wanderings still to eat

---

[34] DC, *Inferno*, canto 1, 2.
[35] Bunyan, *Pilgrim's progress*, p. ix.
[36] Ibid.
[37] On the question of exile, Gladstone's periods in the political wilderness were nothing compared with the exile he was partly responsible for inflicting upon his apostate younger sister Helen, 'emotionally as well as morally', according to Matthew, *Gladstone*, 329. Helen, who failed to conform either to the family norm or to Victorian social standards in terms of acceptable female behaviour for the time, was reduced to spending most of her adult life abroad.

The doled-out bitter griefs of others' bread.
Thine is rather to have nobly led
Where others halted, or would fain retreat;
To steer the State, tho' fierce the storm winds beat,
On to the wished-for haven, sails full-spread.[38]

Plumptre's verses make specific reference to *Paradiso*, canto 17, 58–60, where Dante complains that in exile other men's bread is salty and other men's steps are steep.

In Gladstone's case, the concept of life as progress towards the divine is expressed mainly in the diary entries for his birthdays, sometimes those made on New Year's Eve, and occasionally those written on the anniversary of his late sister Anne's birthday, on Christmas Eve. The last week of each year was thus always for Gladstone an emotionally charged period. Reading the entire sequence of his 'retrospects' for that week, over the years, one sees the boy become the adult, the student become the politician and the thrusting young statesman become the weary fourth-time prime minister in his eighties, longing for a period of 'peace between the theatre and the grave'. And yet in his annual critiques Gladstone repeatedly finds himself falling short of 'the true Christian pattern'.[39] Key words such as progress, improvement, change, upwards, onwards ascent, backsliding path, way, guide, appear year after year as he struggles to contain his perceived sins, shared with Dante, of impurity, envy, anger and pride. The diary entries cast a fascinating light on the private man, the husband, brother, father, confidant and colleague as he negotiated his own personal pilgrimage through life, and many contain Dante references, or Dante-related issues that reinforce the life-as-journey metaphor.

When his sister Anne died in 1829, Gladstone had not yet begun to read Dante. But his idealisation of her was to follow a pattern that he would later recognise in the *Commedia* in Dante's treatment of Beatrice. For the present, he simply recorded on New Year's Eve: that 'This year brought us an awful loss in Anne's infinite gain – But He who made her can raise up such another.'

On his thirty-first birthday, 29 December 1830, Gladstone was commenting on his performance in subordinating his will to the divine – one of Dante's key objectives in the *Commedia*: 'as to real progress in religion – the subjugations of the will and affections – I see no progress: though I may have clearer notions perhaps: which if so increase guilt . . . may God keep one during the coming year from day to day may I approach more a practical belief that He is my friend, I mine enemy'.

His next birthday came just prior to his departure on the Grand Tour, when he asked God to guide his path: 'And now let me pause for a moment

---

38 Henry Plumptre, *Commedia and canzionere*, London 1886. His 'Hell' Plumptre dedicated to Dean Church of St Paul's, and his 'Paradise' to the Princess Royal.
39 *Gladstone diaries*, entry for 29 Dec. 1893.

on the even of departure to offer my unworthy prayer, that in whatsoever country we may be, God himself may be our guide, and may direct our path so as shall most effectually conduce to the fulfilment of his purposes in us.'

His birthday entry for 1834 sees Gladstone still preoccupied with 'his worst fault', lust, a sin he shares with Dante. 'Besetting sins' were still troubling him two years later, in 1837, on his twenty-eighth birthday. In his retrospect of the past year he finds 'accumulated cause for gratitude: but no progress I am afraid against my besetting sins – unless it be in respect of envy . . . O for a sense of Divine Will, an earnest and continual design to read accept and follow it'. Gladstone's twenty-ninth birthday, in 1838, was spent in Rome on the trip during which he was to meet his future wife. The birthday entry, taken from his travel diaries, deals almost exclusively with cultural and social events rather than the state of his soul. By his thirtieth birthday he had married Catherine.

In 1839 his end-of year review reads: 'The last twelve months has seen less done and more received from God: a slight progress as respects relative duties. . . . United to my Catherine, I now stand in the eye of God charged with a double responsibility and ought the more to seek grace to meet it.' For the first time, he is writing as a married man. But whereas Dante left his wife in Florence when he went into exile, and Bunyan's Christian leaves his wife behind in the first part of The pilgrim's progress, Catherine is for Gladstone 'a help towards Heaven', as Beatrice was for Dante.

By his thirty-first birthday, in 1840, Gladstone was already anticipating his thirty-fifth. Quoting the opening line of the Commedia, when Dante finds himself 'midway on the path of life', he commented: 'I approach al mezzo del cammin di nostra vita . . . In apparent bulk this year yields better than the last. In the true growth of man it has made at no point more than slow and feeble progress, at some perhaps less.'

Gladstone's next birthday entry has echoes of Dante's climb up Mount Purgatory, or of Christian the Pilgrim and his ascent of the Hill of Difficulty, when he writes: 'how long and steep is the ascent before me before I attain to any level of true Christian virtue'. The following year, 1843, brought with it a more detailed analysis of his progress on the path to God: 'again I have before me the awful question, what is the state of the soul before God, and what movement has there been in that state . . . since there are no bounds to the tender mercy of God in Christ He may yet bear with me until my steps be well and firmly set in the path of holiness'.

In 1844 Gladstone achieved in reality Dante's mid-life point, as he repeats in his diary towards midnight of the day before his birthday, finding as he writes that 'the spiritual is unspeakably sad'. On his birthday itself he added: 'Now commences as it were the downhill of my life. . . . I am older than was the Redeemer in the flesh. Is He in any sense my pattern . . . have I made any true progress in the work of salvation?'

Gladstone was too busy to write a retrospect for his thirty-sixth birthday, but made up for it the following day with a bout of 'breast-beating': 'Against

my greatest foes alas I cannot think it had been a year of real progress.' Again
the next year he notes that he is short of time to write at length but observes
that 'if there be progress yet it is so small as to escape from vision'. 'Still and
always the continuing stream of mercy it is that waters and invigorates my
hopes', he adds, again recalling Dante's Lethe and Christian's River.

In 1847 Gladstone was thirty-eight years old and seemed quite pleased
with himself. Despite a year fraught with financial difficulty, he expresses
gratitude in his birthday diary entry – in images which find their counterpart
both in Dante and in Bunyan – for 'the wonderful mercy of God which is
indeed for me . . . both a shadow from the heat and a shelter from the storm'.

The following year Gladstone completed his fourth decade. His birthday
entry is sombre, as he feels he has lost his way:

> It is not my outward so much as my inward life that grieves me . . . If I could get
> back or rather get the spirit of a child, the way would be plain . . . These
> decade birthdays are greater even than the annual ones. How blessed would it
> be if this should be the point from whence is to spring a lowlier and better life.

By late 1850 Gladstone was in Naples. He had been out of office since his
resignation over the Maynooth affair but still remained an MP for Oxford
University. After his brief visit in 1849 in pursuit of Lady Lincoln, Gladstone
returned to Italy with his family on an extended visit. It was again a fraught
period in his life, with his protest against the Bourbon regime in the city and
its treatment of political prisoners. He was also greatly unnerved by the
recent conversions of his friends Hope and Manning and his sister Helen. Yet
the *leitmotiv* of his birthday note remained personal. It had been a year of
'anxiety and of labour', he wrote. 'Would to God I could add it had been one
of progress in obtaining the mastery over my most besetting sins.'

By 1852 Gladstone was back in England and back in office as Chancellor
of the Exchequer in Aberdeen's Whig-Peelite government. As a result, he has
less time to dwell on his shortcomings in the pilgrim's progress of life, and less
time to write about them, apart from the main recurring one: 'The year which
closes on me closes in one respect darkly: I have made no progress against the
besetting sin often mentioned . . . Yet I trust my ultimate aim has not been
wholly corrupt; and in some other matters my life might seem less unhopeful.'
Two years later his entry was more expansive:

> In looking back over the stained course of my life, I have cause to feel yet more
> keenly my need to escape before long from a sphere of so much temptation so
> sorely oppressing me. I refer particularly to the sins of wrath, impurity, and
> spiritual sloth. The first of them seems to toss me like a tempest. Of the next I
> can only hope it has not been more flagrant. But as to the last I feel its bonds
> to be heavier than ever.

Gladstone admits to wrath, impurity and sloth. He has previously mentioned
envy as one of his weaknesses. Dante's 'besetting sins', as symbolised by the
leopard, lion and wolf that threatened him in the first canto of the *Commedia*,

are lust, pride and envy; he also admits to anger, as is shown in several episodes in the poem. In their own personal pilgrim's progresses through life, Gladstone and Dante had very similar failings to deal with. Two days after his forty-fifth birthday entry, Gladstone is echoing other Dante images, this time from *Purgatorio*, when he recalls the ship of souls in which the pilot angel brings the penitent dead across the ocean to Mount Purgatory and the 'little bark of my wit' ('la navicella del mio ingegno')[40] of his narrative that brings Dante thither: 'At night I heard the bells ring in the New Year . . . O mighty stream we cannot arrest thee but we can load our little vessel as it floats on thy bosom with good fruits of holy living.'

On the last day of 1856 Gladstone bemoans the increasing calls being made on his time and energy 'in that the ties which bind me to this world [are] growing more numerous and stronger'. He lists politics, church struggles, literature 'which has of late acquired a new & powerful hold on me', family finances, a wife and seven children as just some of the demands which divert him from his pilgrim's purpose: 'What a network is here woven out of all that the heart & all that the mind of man can supply. How then am I to have my conversation in heaven in the sense of having my loins girt and my lamp burning and of waiting for the Lord before the morning watch?' The confusion caused by being too much taken up by the things of the world has echoes of the dark wood of earthly confusion in which Dante found himself at the start of the *Commedia*.

The following year Gladstone was forty-eight: 'How long a time to cumber the earth: and still not know *where* to work out the purpose of my life. But God I trust will clear my way.' On New Year's Eve he added: 'I dismiss another year with a growing sentiment that my life must come to its crisis while I do not see in myself the inward preparation, which would be the surest sign that God was going to make the way plain.'

His next birthday, in 1858, found Gladstone on Corfu as commissioner extraordinary. 'My birthday brings me no joyful sense of progress in my weakest of points', he wrote, 'only the still warm ashes of hope in the mercy and boundless love of God.' His entry for the last day of the year repeats Dante's classic river/stream image of life's inexorable progress. He writes that 'the stream of time flows on and we launch a new year . . . May the God of justice do justice here, whether through me or through some channel less clogged with sin'.

For his half-century Gladstone was back in England, and writing in his diary: 'Behold me then arrived at the close of half a century in this wayward world. Half a century! What do those little words unfold! Grace and glory, sin and shame, hopes, fears, joys, pains, emotions, labours, efforts; what a marvel is this life, what a miracle the construction of it for our discipline?'

And yet, for all his apparent ease with the devotional concept of life as a

---

[40] *DC, Purgatorio*, canto 1, 2.

finite pilgrim's progress, on this his fiftieth birthday there creeps in a very personal note of resentment at getting old: 'There is in me a resistance to the passage of time as if I could lay hands on it and stop it: as if youth were yet in me and life and youth were one!' This sentiment is repeated the following year, 1860: 'I feel within me the rebellious unspoken words, I will not be old!' The following day he worked on an earlier translation of the Ugolino episode from *Inferno*, prior to its publication the following year in the volume of translations from various languages undertaken with his brother-in-law Lord George Lyttelton.

His fifty-second birthday found Gladstone 'encircled with the richest store of domestic blessings' but still battling with his own particular version of Bunyan's Slough of Despond or Dante's Circle of the Neutral: 'If I contemplate myself my rejection of mercies, my clinging to sin, my cold & wasted heart, all might inspire despair. But on the other hand I do not see the signs of divine abandonment: the same love and patience follow me and strive with me and will yet I trust conquer in the end.'

Five years later Gladstone spent his birthday in Rome where he was wintering with the family, and reading Dante daily. After the failure of the Liberal Reform Bill, the government had resigned and he was out of office. That year he wrote no birthday retrospective assessing his spiritual progress, but commented on New Year's Eve, as he read his Dante, that he wished 'that the old year sped away from me with wings less charged'.

In the annual review for his fifty-ninth birthday in 1868, the pilgrim's pathway image returns: 'This birthday opens my 60th year. I descend the hill of life. It would be a truer figure to say I ascend a steepening path with a burden of ever gathering weight. The Almighty seems to sustain and spare me for some purpose of His own deeply unworthy as I know myself to be.' The lengthy entry for this day concentrates on the burden imposed by his public life which impedes his spiritual progression. The torments he describes himself as suffering echo several of the torments of the *Inferno* and the penances of *Purgatorio*:

I feel like a man under a burden under which he must fall and be crushed if he looks to the right or left, or fails from any cause to concentrate mind and muscle upon his progress step by step. This absorption, this excess . . . is the fault of political life with its insatiable demands which do not leave the smallest stock of moral energy unexhausted and available for other purposes. They certainly however have this merit: they drive home the sense that I am poor, and naked, and blind and miserable: and they make forgetfulness of God not a whit less unintelligible than it is inexcusable, though it is one thing to remember and another to obey. Swimming for his life, a man does not see much of the country through which the river winds, and I probably know little of these years through which I busily work and live, beyond this, how sin and frailty deface them, and how mercy crowns them. But other years as I hope are to come, a few at least in which yet ampler mercy will permit to learn more of my own soul and to live for that kind of work which perhaps (I have never lost the belief) more especially belongs to me . . . even may yet come to be as a doorkeeper in the house of my God!

The end of 1870 found Gladstone in the middle of a difficult government re-shuffle and again unable to focus clearly on his inner life. Again, he expresses the desire to see an end to his public life – his own 'dark wood' – the better to concentrate on the advancement of his spiritual one: 'The sentiment has deepened in my mind that my life can attain neither its just balance nor its true basis till it shall please God to give me a lawful opportunity to escape from the present course of daily excess which is for me inseparable from my place and calling.' The same sentiment was expressed on his birthday the following year. By now he was sixty-two and felt that 'my life is but half life while it is oppressed entangled and bent as it now is with the heavy burdens upon me which exhaust in public affairs the moral force of the soul'.

On New Year's Eve 1873 Gladstone wrote: 'The year ends as it were in tumult.' It was a year in which he had been both Chancellor of the Exchequer and prime minister; he had seen the defeat of the Irish Universities Bill and had tried, unsuccessfully, to resign:

> My constant tumult of business makes other tumult more sensible. Upon me still continued blessings rain: but in return I seem to render nothing except a hope that a time may come when my spirit, instead of grovelling may become erect and look at God. For I cannot, as I now am, get sufficiently out of myself to judge myself, and unravel the knots of being and doing, of which my life seems to be full.

'Catherine [grows] more noble and more heroic, as well as stronger, from year to year', he added, echoing Dante's description of Beatrice growing brighter and more beautiful as she comes closer to God: 'la donna mia ch'i'vidi far più bella' ('I saw my lady become more fair').[41]

1874's birthday found Gladstone still seeking, unsuccessfully, a more peaceful life, but 'I find myself in lieu of the mental repose I had hoped engaged in a controversy'. It was the year that the Liberals were defeated and Disraeli came to power at the head of a Conservative government. 'But I do not regret anything except my insufficiency and my unworthiness in this and in all things', he wrote. 'Yet I would wish that the rest of my life were as worthy as my public life, in its nature and intent, to be made an offering to the Lord Most High.'

In 1877 Gladstone celebrated his sixty-eighth birthday without much enthusiasm. 'I have no marked or cheering advance to report to myself', he wrote. 'The gap continues to be wide between my measure of perception and my standard of action. The day of death seems to make its approach felt with

[41] Ibid. canto 8, 15.

a sense of great solemnity.' He was still subdued on New Year's Eve: 'So passes over the year to join its fellows in eternity: laden with marks and with sins. O that I could but live my personal life which however speckled with infirmity is upright in intention and less unfit to be offered up through Christ to the Most High.' The following year there was no birthday entry, but Gladstone made up for it with a New Year's Eve report: 'It has been a year of tumultuous life. And such life will not let my hard heart soften and break up as the soil after a frost, but keeps it stony, so that I am almost driven to ask whether God will finally have to break it by some more crushing stroke.'

Gladstone's annual retrospectives for the early 1880s are sparse and lack a spiritual dimension. Again prime minister, and now in his seventies, he seems overwhelmed by the heavy cares of government and hoping that 'my political work is all but done'. On his seventy-eighth birthday, in 1887, Gladstone was on the train from Paris to Florence and too busy to write in his diary. Once more out of office, under a cloud over the death of Gordon at Khartoum, and smarting over the defeat of the first Home Rule Bill for Ireland, he had again chosen temporary exile in Italy. 'All I can see is that I am kept in my present life of contention because I have not in the sight of God earned my dismissal', he wrote from Rome. On the final day of the year he added:

And so we ring out the year. In scenery and weather almost heavenly. Would that the spectacle I see within me corresponded with them. At any rate I learn more and more from year to year how deep and penetrating are the roots of selfishness: how subtle, sudden, untiring, manifold, the devices and assaults of the Evil One within the soul.

The lengthy entry for Gladstone's eightieth birthday in 1889 focuses on a review of his health and it is clear that matters of state are taking up a lot of his energy. On holiday again in Italy he wrote: 'I feel however that I never can get at the true measure of my sinfulness until I am permitted to pass into the condition of a simply private person.' The following year, he again reviewed the political events of the time and the lack of space they afforded him in life adding: 'All my life I have cherished from day to day the idea of some peace between the theatre and the grave. I can well understand, indeed an inward voice makes reply, that the rest is a privilege and "thou hast not earned it: hast not reached the condition which qualified you to rise to a higher spiritual level".'

1891 saw the death of Parnell and the prospect of a fourth ministry for Gladstone looming the following year. 'It is a singular lot', he reflected on his birthday. 'I am not permitted the rest I long for: Amen. But I am called to walk as Abraham walked, not knowing whither he went. What an honour. Yet I long long to be out of contention: I hope it is not a sin.' A year later Gladstone was back in office as prime minister and writing in his diary: 'May God at the length give me a true self-knowledge. I have it not yet.' He was eighty-two years old. At the end of the year he noted:

And so is drawn the curtain of the year. For me it some ways a tremendous year . . . An increased responsibility undertaken with diminished means. That I of all men should have come to a position which in its way is perhaps without parallel. But the stays are wonderful, almost incredible. The fountain of mercies is inexhaustible . . . Lead me through duty unto rest.

On his birthday the following year he noted that 'I sometimes hope it has been a year of some improvement: certainly of more avid sense of need. But oh how far I am, at all times and in all things from the true Christian pattern.' The entry for 1894 is not long but Gladstone marks the closing year with a commentary on the Thirty-Nine Articles and the nature of sin. The 1896 entry in the *Diaries*, two years after his final retirement, was more concerned with health and family matters that anything else:

My long and tangled life this day concludes its eighty-seventh year . . . I do not enter on interior matters. It is so easy to write, but to write honestly nearly impossible. . . . Would that in looking back I could discern any decided features of improvement. Would that I did not on the other hand see many grievous crimes. Many unlawful fears and detections. Should I most blame myself for these, or bless God for His infinite mercies? May those mercies provided for us relieve me and may a melancholy retrospect of the past bring forth good fruits in prayer and watchfulness for the future . . . O may my day . . . bring to my mind and consideration of my day of death.

This was Gladstone's last birthday 'retrospect'. His personal pilgrimage back to God ended eighteen months later, on Ascension Day 1898.

In whose footsteps?

It could be argued that it was Bunyan's experience and the Puritan tradition that informed the Victorian concept of life as a journey; that in writing his year-end retrospects as progress reports on his path back to God, Gladstone as pilgrim was simply following a contemporary pattern as conventional as the diary-keeping itself. And indeed Gladstone remembers first reading Bunyan as a boy of ten: '*The pilgrim's progress* undoubtedly took a great and fascinating hold on me, so that anything which I wrote was insensibly moulded by its style; but it was by the force of the allegory addressing itself to the fancy and was very like a strong impression received from the Arabian nights.'[42]

Two points argue against the Bunyan model being the definitive one for Gladstone. Some Victorian commentators already sensed that the allegorical journey of Bunyan's pilgrim Christian echoed the earlier one of Dante. A reverse interpretation of the *Commedia* in terms of a Bunyanesque journey

---

[42] Morley, *Gladstone*, i. 10, quoting an undated 'fragment of record in Gladstone's own hand'.

appears in a late Victorian work entitled *Dante's pilgrim's progress* by Emilia Russel Gurney,[43] a book dedicated to the bishop of Ripon in memory of three lectures he gave on the *Commedia* in 1884.[44] It comprises key extracts from Dante accompanied by author's notes 'on the way', including comparable passages from Bunyan and Milton, amongst others. The selection comprises reflective rather than dramatic interludes from Dante's poem and concentrates primarily on the trials and tribulations, questions and fears, of Dante the pilgrim, together with Virgil's responses and explanations.

By objectivising Dante's subjective first-person narrative – simply by substituting 'The Pilgrim' where Dante wrote 'I' – and by concentrating on Dante's personal journey to the almost total exclusion of the many other life stories that cram the *Commedia*, Gurney achieves a remarkable Bunyanesque effect. The capitalisation of virtues and vices – Truth, Cowardice, etc. – together with Gurney's legitimate description of parts of Heaven and Hell[45] in terms such as 'The Valley of Humiliation',[46] make parallels between the two allegories seem quite pronounced.

There is no suggestion that Bunyan was directly influenced by Dante. There were very few, and then only partial, translations of the *Commedia* into English in the seventeenth century, and Bunyan is not known to have read Italian. However, Bunyan was fully conversant with the works of Milton, who did read Italian, and Bunyan may have absorbed elements of the *Commedia* indirectly by this route. Gurney's interpretation indicates that, steeped as the nineteenth century might still have been in aspects of the Puritan tradition, there existed nevertheless a European awareness of Dante acting as an intellectual precedent. In Gladstone's case, his greater affinity with Dante – as a fellow politician and statesman – than with Bunyan, is likely to have meant that he reached back beyond Bunyan to take Dante's more erudite literary, mystical, moral and allegorical journey as the starting-point for his own spiritual one. Sinclair describes Dante in canto 17 of *Paradiso* as

> blood-brother to Bunyan's Mr. Valiant-for-Truth, who said, at the end of his journey: I am going to my Fathers, and tho' with great difficulty I am got hither, yet now I do not repent me of all the trouble I have been at to arrive where I am. My sword I give to him that shall succeed me in my Pilgrimage,

---

43 Emilia Russel Gurney, *Dante's pilgrim's progress; or, the passage of the blessed soul from the slavery of the present corruption to the liberty of eternal glory*, London 1897.
44 The bishop was clearly still giving Dante lectures five years later. Gladstone records that he attended one such lecture at Grosvenor House 'and spoke briefly': *Gladstone diaries*, entry for 6 Apr. 1889. In 1896 the bishop gave Gladstone a copy of Michelangelo Caetani's *La materia della Divina Commedia*, Florence 1894, according to a dedication on the front cover of a copy in the library at Hawarden Castle.
45 Though not of Paradise, where Dante in any case transmutes in Gurney's work from 'the pilgrim' to 'the disciple'.
46 Gurney, *Dante's pilgrim's progress*, 93, commenting on DC, *Purgatorio*, canto 1, 100–14.

and my courage and skill to him that can get it. My Marks and Scars I carry with me, to be a witness for me that I have fought his Battles who will now be my Redeemer.[47]

Gladstone's annual retrospectives have none of the richness of either *The pilgrim's progress* or the *Commedia*. Yet, however anchored these two allegories may be in personal life experiences, they are presented within a fictionalised narrative; their characters are only representative realities. A real life, such as that which emerges from Gladstone's diaries, is less neat and more complex; it resists form and has no controllable plot. In Gladstone's case it seems sometimes to be making little progress towards heaven. But the pilgrimage metaphor, the sense of a journey undertaken towards an identifiable moral destination, is as powerful in Gladstone's as in either of the other two works.

Christian the pilgrim had many companions along the way, both false and true. Dante had two: Virgil (reason/empire) and Beatrice (faith/Church). Gladstone had Dante as his companion on the journey back to God. Is Gladstone likely to have felt constrained in this by the fact that the guide on his soul's journey back to God was Roman Catholic? Almost certainly not, any more than Dante was by Virgil's paganism. A medieval Italian poet was unlikely to be other than, at least notionally, Roman Catholic. As Kenelm Foster observes in connection with Virgil's importance for Dante:

> Because the hero of the *Divine Comedy* is a Christian, the poem is Christian, but through two-thirds of it the hero is guided by a pagan. And even 'guided' is too weak a term. Virgil in the poem is the hero's 'leader', 'master', 'teacher', 'lord'.[48]

The same applies to Dante's guidance of Gladstone. Virgil could not have been a Christian; Dante could not have been an Anglican. Ultimately, it was qualities such as morality, conscience, duty and the submission of personal will to the will of God that fitted Dante for the role of Gladstone's guide.

47 DC, *Paradiso*, 255.
48 Kenelm Foster, 'The two Dantes', in *The two Dantes*, 156–89.

6

The Literary Dimension

Gladstone's literary output on Dante was not extensive. There is nothing to compare with his three volumes of studies on Homer (1858), nor with his four–volume translation of Farini's *Lo stato romano* (1853), an attack on the temporal power of the pope. Yet, although he did not write extensively on Dante, what he did produce – three translations (1835–7, published 1861), a critical review of a Dante translation by Lord John Russell (1844) and a controversial essay on whether Dante studied at Oxford (1892) – reflects a profound study of his subject.

An accomplished classicist who took a double first at Oxford in 1831 in Literae Humaniores, as well as in mathematics, Gladstone was also an enthusiastic modern linguist. According to Matthew, 'Gladstone's scholarship was linked to a wide range of languages . . . in languages he was a genuine European, and he matched his abilities by being well read in the literature, theology and politics of most of the European states.'[1]

Matthew was speaking in 1998 at Gladstone's old college, Christ Church, on the centenary of the statesman's death. He makes no mention of the quality as distinct from the breadth of Gladstone's command of modern foreign languages. Mark Davie, approaching Gladstone's translations of the three Dante passages as a professional linguist, comments that 'even his best efforts are uneven'.[2] Valerio Lucchesi endorses this. Gladstone's approach to foreign languages was pragmatic rather than refined. As Roy Jenkins observed: 'His concepts of a common civilisation and of a united Christendom, which were strong, convinced him that an educated Englishman ought to be able to communicate in all the principal languages of civilised Europe. So he did so.'[3]

This description of Gladstone's vision of a commonality of man echoes Dante's concept of the whole of creation as 'a single volume',[4] an idea that as early as the eighteenth century found resonance in the internationalism of the Whigs.[5] Gladstone corresponded and conversed in German with Ignaz von Döllinger. He corresponded in French with the one-time ambassador to London, and later French Foreign Minister, François Guizot. He did so

---

1 Matthew, 'Gladstone and the University of Oxford', 5.
2 Mark Davie, 'Not an after-dinner relaxation: Gladstone on translating Dante', *Journal of European Studies* xxiv (1994), 400.
3 Jenkins, *Gladstone*, 15.
4 DC, *Paradiso*, 435.
5 Milbank, *Dante and the Victorians*, 11.

despite the fact that Guizot's command of English was such that he had translated into French all thirteen volumes of Edward Gibbon's *History of the
decline and fall of the Roman Empire*. In 1889, when in Paris for the celebrations commemorating the centenary of the French Revolution, Gladstone
gave several speeches in French, some impromptu and one from the top of
the Eiffel Tower. When he was briefly and, as Jenkins put it, 'eccentrically'
commissioner for the Ionian Islands, Gladstone made a major policy speech
on 4 February 1859 to the Greek-speaking Corfu National Assembly in
Italian, the traditional language of the professional classes. Though Morley,
with characteristic loyalty, called it 'an eloquent address',[6] Jenkins wrote: 'It
is possible on this occasion that speaker and audience were united in an equal
imperfection in their grasp of the language which he had decided should be a
bridge between them.'[7] Several of the speeches Gladstone gave while in the
Ionian Islands were delivered in Greek, but classical rather than modern, and
thus 'incomprehensible to the audience, some of whom supposed them to be
in English and Italian'.[8] On the two occasions when Gladstone had audi-
ences with the pope, both were conducted in Italian. During his lifetime
Gladstone also acquired some Spanish and even a little Norwegian. He may
not have been a subtle practitioner but, according to Jenkins, his approach to
modern foreign languages made up with vigour what it lacked in finesse:

> His attitude to modern languages was reminiscent of a tank cutting its way
> through undergrowth. It was not subtle. His letters, even in French, whether
> to station masters or statesmen, lacked much sense of elegance or idiom, or the
> subjunctive (which, had he been French, would have been made for him), but
> he could say what he wanted to.[9]

He could say what he wanted to. And Italian was frequently the language he
chose when he wanted to express his most intimate thoughts. 'There is but
one qualification I have for writing about Italian literature and language – an
intense love of it.'[10] He quoted Dante when proposing marriage to Catherine
Glynne. He also wrote in Italian when recording in his diary events that had
a deep emotional effect on him – particularly after episodes in his 'rescue'
work with prostitutes, or when he was rejected in his earlier proposals of
marriage to Caroline Farquar in 1837 and Lady Frances Douglas in 1838.
Dante did something similar. While breaking new ground by writing in
Italian for the first time with the *Vita nuova* and the *Commedia*, Dante would
nevertheless revert to Latin on occasions when he was emotionally over-

6   Morley, *Gladstone*, i. 450.
7   Jenkins, *Gladstone*, 15.
8   Matthew, *Gladstone*, 116.
9   Jenkins, *Gladstone*, 15.
10   Gladstone to Anthony Panizzi, 4 Dec. 1849, quoted in Agatha Ramm, 'Gladstone as
man of letters', *Nineteenth Century Prose* xvii (Winter 1989–90), 9.

whelmed.[11] And yet Gladstone's tendency to write in Italian implied no great attempts at secrecy, and certainly not at secrecy from his nearest and dearest:

> In the diarist's lifetime, no particular precautions were taken to keep the manuscript, beyond a little elementary coding in its text. . . . The current volume lived in his pocket; in an age when gentlemen's pockets were often picked, this perhaps explains why he frequently put entries on sensitive points into Italian. Most of his immediate family, and a few of his servants, could read Italian easily; the precaution could not have been aimed at them, whom in any case he trusted.[12]

Gladstone began to learn Italian seriously as he read – and in order to read – the *Commedia*. He had a few language lessons on his first visit to Italy, and began reading the *Commedia* in 1834 after the publication of Arthur Hallam's *Remains*, through which the desire to study Dante in depth came to him with the 'force of a dying message from a friend'. But Gladstone's family circumstances at the time also meant that there was a deep emotional void to be filled. In the space of a few years he had lived through the death of his beloved sister Anne and his saintly mother, as well as that of his first close friend. His nervous state had produced at least two dreams of an extreme religious nature bordering on 'visions'. His vulnerability at this time may have predisposed him to embrace the sort of promise of consolation that Dante's own beatific vision offered.

Translations with Lord Lyttelton

The *Translations* were published in 1861, twenty-seven years after Gladstone first started to read Dante; but his contributions were in fact completed between 1835 and 1837. By the publication date, Gladstone already had half a political career accomplished. He had been an MP, first for Newark, then for Oxford University, President of the Board of Trade and Colonial Secretary (in a Conservative government), then Chancellor of the Exchequer (first in a coalition, then in a Whig administration). Nor was his translation of the three passages from the *Commedia* his first published translation from Italian. His English version of Farini's volumes on the Roman state from 1815 to 1850, had already been published in 1853 and illustrates his now well-established linguistic versatility. His at times frantic literary output was symptomatic of an overall almost manic level of activity during those years. During Gladstone's private crisis of the 1840s and 1850s,

11 Dante, *Vita nuova*, 29–32, 43.
12 M. Drew, *Catherine Gladstone*, London 1920, 7. The impression created in Mary Drew's biography of her mother is that the latter's command of Italian was better than that of her future husband when they first met.

perhaps his most remarkable ability was that of living life with equal intensity at many levels, and, in these years, without being fully committed to any. It was this ability to change levels, to design railways for the Hawarden estate, to denounce at length Montalbert's *Des Intérêts Catholiques au XIVe Siècle* in the *Quarterly Review*, to translate Farini's *Lo Stato Romano* and to produce the most famous budget of the century, all within the space of a year, 1853, which gave Gladstone his great public weapon – surprise, and his great private resource – variety.[13]

After William Gladstone and Lord George Lyttelton married the Glynne sisters, their relationship remained a close one. When Gladstone was at the Colonial Office, he made his brother-in-law under-secretary. It was to support him after Mary died in 1857 that Gladstone suggested publishing his Dante translations as part of a joint anthology. Lyttelton was then severely depressed. He became increasingly unwell over the years and, in 1876, committed suicide by falling into the stairwell at his London home. Gladstone visited the scene to persuade himself that the fall was an accident, commenting that the staircase was dangerous and 'confirmed the notion I had previously entertained of the likelihood that he never meant at all to throw himself over, but fell in too rapid a descent, over the banisters'.[14] In denying his brother-in-law's suicide, Gladstone saved him from the seventh circle of Dante's *Inferno* where, in the wood of the suicides, souls who have uprooted themselves from their bodies are imprisoned in great trees. Once a virtue in classical times, suicide became a sin for Christianity. Even men of integrity like Dante's Piero delle Vigne, the most influential statesman of his time in western Europe, and for more than twenty years the emperor's chief adviser in the struggle with the papacy, went to hell for it. As a suicide, Gladstone's brother-in-law, despite a similar life of public service, would be condemned to a fate for which Dante said 'such pity fills my heart'.[15] Having failed to help Lyttelton live, Gladstone adopted an attitude of denial about his death. For Dante, Piero delle Vigne was a 'wounded soul' ('anima lesa')[16] rather than a hideous sinner, but consigned to hell nevertheless.

But Lyttelton's death was a long way off when he and Gladstone produced their *Translations*. The book includes Greek and Latin versions by Lyttelton of originals by Milton, Dryden, Tennyson, Gray and Goldsmith. Gladstone's contribution comprises translations into English from Greek (Aeschylus, Homer), Latin (Horace, Catullus), German (Schiller) and Italian (Dante and Manzoni). The Manzoni poem is his *Ode on the death of Napoleon*. The Dante pieces are the Ugolino episode from *Inferno*, canto 33, 1–78, originally translated by Gladstone in 1837, the Lord's Prayer from *Purgatorio*, canto 11,

---

13 Matthew, *Gladstone*, 95.
14 Ibid. 327, quoting from the diary of Lyttelton's daughter, Lucy Cavendish.
15 'Tanta pietà m'accora': *DC*, *Inferno*, 171.
16 Ibid. 169.

1–21, translated in 1835, and the speech of Piccarda Donati from *Paradiso*, canto 3, 1–85, also translated in 1835. The *Translations* were published by Bernard Quaritch in 1861, with a second edition in 1863. Several copies of the 1863 edition are still in circulation: St Deiniol's Library has one, as has Quaritch itself (now an antiquarian bookseller in Golden Square, London, but then based at Piccadilly), as have a handful of universities worldwide. One copy of the first 1861 edition is held at Keele University. The verso to the title page of the first edition indicates that the original print run was '500 Vellum, 25 copies on large paper'. The Latin inscription opposite translates as: 'At their joint wish, in memory of their double wedding'.[17] The printer was W. M. Watts, Crown Court, Temple Bar. The Keele copy was bound by Burn of Kirkby Street, and carries a sticker indicating that it was sold at some stage by John Smith of St Vincent Street, Glasgow. This may indicate that it belonged originally to some friend of the Gladstones in the vicinity of their estate at Fasque. The 1863 edition is without the dedication; again it was printed by W. M. Watts of Temple Bar, but this time the print run was bigger. The verso of the title page reads: 'The Edition consists of: 750 copies on Fine Paper. 25 copies on large Paper. 3 copies on vellum. April 1863.' Beside the word 'vellum' has been hand-written 'No. 3' and the signature of the publisher. Quaritch has tracked down another first edition. It carries the bookplate of Charles Hagart and is inscribed by Gladstone on the initial blank: 'Mrs Hagart/ with the kindest regards of / WG'. The Hagarts were old friends of the Gladstones. Quaritch believe that the woman in question may have been Charles Haggart's mother, of whom Gladstone had written in his diary thirty-three years earlier: 'Met Mrs Hagart, the beauty; & a very clever and fascinating woman'.[18] Since then Mark Nixon has sourced a third copy of the first edition – that which belonged to Gladstone's principal private secretary, Eddy Hamilton, which is signed by both Gladstone and Lyttelton.

Publishing was never Quaritch's main activity, although its publishing rate was relatively high in the 1860s. Bernard Quaritch, a German *emigré* who at one time acted as the English correspondent of Marx and Engel's *Neue Rheinische Zeitung*, opened his own bookshop in 1847 on what is now Charing Cross Road, and was keen to keep a high profile by association with important people. Gladstone was an early *habitué* of the inner sanctum where Quaritch received his top clientele, which included Disraeli, Ruskin, Burton and a host of other great and influential book-collectors. Quaritch believe the *Translations* may have been, if not a vanity publication, at most a courtesy

---

[17] 'Ex voto communi in memoriam duplicum nuptiarum': W. E. Gladstone and Lord Lyttelton, *Translations*, London 1861, title page.
[18] *Gladstone diaries*, entry for 12 May 1828. Additional information from Theodore Hofmann at Bernard Quaritch, who notes that this copy is 'in the original pink wavy-grained boards with glazed cloth spine'. This description resembles that of the 1863 edition located at Hawarden Castle Library in February 2001.

publication for an esteemed client and a means of promoting the Quaritch name in the best circles.[19]

All Gladstone's Dante translations remain faithful to the rhyme structure (*terza rima*, i.e. aba-bcb-cdc-ded etc) of the original. Although English 'may ill submit to the form of terza rima', wrote Gladstone, 'yet to use any other specific form of verse is complicating the first act of violence – ie translation – by a second'.[20] Dante himself hated translations, writing in the *Convivio* that translators were traitors. The difficulties facing any translator of Dante are dealt with comprehensively in Sayers's notes to her translation of *Inferno*.[21] Gladstone's translations frequently also succeed in matching the internal cadences of the original. But his verse is based on the most common metrical pattern in English prosody, the iambic pentameter. This comprises five feet of two syllables each, unlike the hendecasyllable lines of Dante, which produce thirty-three syllables for each terzina, intentionally the same number as there are cantos each of the three Cantiche of the *Commedia*. The difference in metric pattern is less noticeable than the obvious attempt made by Gladstone to match the rhyme and the rhythmic structure of the original.

Why did Gladstone choose the passages he did: Ugolino, the Lord's Prayer and the story of Piccarda? Do they have anything in common?

The Ugolino episode is the longest in the *Inferno*, and his position one of the lowest. His sin was cold-blooded treachery and therefore a deeper, more inhuman, more paralysing sin than all the forms of violence or of simple fraud. Its penalty is the numbing, hardening and disabling of the soul with cold. Ugolino used his country's misfortunes to further his own ambition and intrigued with whichever party, Guelf or Ghibelline, promised to reinforce his power – the antithesis of the politics of conscience that both Dante and Gladstone stood for. Dante described Ugolino's selfishness and hate as he dies immured with his children:

> The long months reckoned only by the returning brightness of the moon through the window-slit of the prison – the warning dreams and the sudden sound of the nails in the door below – the last days of stony despair and death, and the father, blind, dying, yet with the strength to outlive all his children and bearing with him into Hell all the energy of his hate which is now his life that cannot die, 'his tenderness and paternal piety being turned to ferocity and rage'.[22]

Ugolino's story stands in marked contrast to that of Francesca da Rimini, one of Gladstone's favourites but not one he translated. Hers is the record of a great though illicit love, his of as great a hate. Her love (and his hate) holds

[19] Private information from Richard Linental at Quaritch.

[20] Gladstone, 'Lord John Russell's translation', re. Russell's 'Translation of the "Francesca da Rimini" from the Inferno of Dante', which appeared in the *Literary Souvenir* for 1844.

[21] Dante, *The Divine Comedy: Hell*, 55–65.

[22] DC, *Inferno*, 416.

her to her lover (and him to his enemy archbishop Ruggiero, whose brain he gnaws) forever in an association that makes their earthly memories an eternally present agony. These two episodes, with that of Ulysses in the twenty-sixth canto, are the greatest examples of dramatic imagination in the whole poem. John Sinclair commented: 'Francesca, Ulysses and Ugolino each tell their own tales, of love, of daring, of agony and hate, and in each case, by the power of imaginative sympathy, Dante penetrates to the heart of the sinner so that his sin is forgotten and he is, as it were, restored for his sheer human worth to the human fellowship.'[23]

The story of Piccarda Donati, the subject of Gladstone's third passage for translation, concerns the daughter of a celebrated Florentine family to whom Dante was connected by marriage. Dante places her in the Heaven of the Moon among the virtuous who failed to keep their religious vows. Unlike Ugolino's ambition and his attendant terror – and one reading of the episode has him eating his dead children, so great was his hunger – Piccarda rejoices in self-effacement. 'Our affections rejoice in being conformed to His order . . . the power of charity quiets our will and makes us will only what we have and thirst for nothing else.'[24] As a girl, Piccarda became a nun, but she was abducted from the convent by her brothers and forced into a hated marriage. She died soon afterwards. It is to her that Dante gave one of his best-remembered lines: 'In His will is our peace'. This sublimation of personal will to the will of God links all the stories Gladstone chose to translate. Ugolino's sin was personal wilfulness. Piccarda subjects her own will to the divine and acquires heavenly bliss as a reward. And Dante's expanded version of the Lord's Prayer that Gladstone translated exhorts: 'Not my will but Thine be done'.

Whatever prompted Gladstone personally in his choice of passages to translate, the fact remains that Ugolino was a firm Victorian favourite generally, as were Ulysses and Paolo and Francesca da Rimini. These three tales are among the most dramatic narrative episodes from the *Commedia*, also the most universal, the most articulate and the most self-contained. They fired the imagination of many writers, painters and sculptors – and, indeed, composers of music[25] – throughout the nineteenth century.

'Not an after-dinner relaxation'

Gladstone, like many contemporaries, was captivated by the tragic but moving story of the adulterous couple Paolo and Francesca da Rimini. Killed by the jealous Gianciotto Malatesta – his brother and her husband – and

---

23 Ibid. 415.
24 DC, *Paradiso*, 51–3.
25 Donizetti (1797–1848), Liszt (1811–86), Verdi (1813–1901) and Tchaikovsky (1840–93) were among the most prominent nineteenth-century composers who set passages from Dante to music.

condemned to the circle of the lustful, they have at least the satisfaction of seeing Gianciotto condemned to an even lower level of Hell. He rots in Caina, in the ninth circle, with other traitors to kindred. While in 1851 Gladstone had commissioned from Alexander Munro the sculpture of Paolo and Francesca, his family had one side of his memorial tomb at Hawarden decorated with an illustration of the lovers. It is perhaps surprising therefore, that Gladstone chose the grim tale of Ugolino, rather than that of the devoted couple, as his single translation from the *Inferno*. This did not, however, prevent him from having strong views on Lord John Russell's translation of the Paolo and Francesca episode, published in the *Literary Souvenir* for 1844.

Gladstone's views were expressed in a 7,000-word article, originally published anonymously in the *English Review* of April 1844, provided by him as a gesture of goodwill for the magazine's inaugural issue. It was a unique situation when one future British prime minister published a passage from Dante and was harshly reviewed by another. Whether the quality of Gladstone's own translations entitled him to be so harsh with Russell's efforts is discussed by Mark Davie and Valerio Lucchesi. Nevertheless, Gladstone was insistent that he owed it to Dante to protect his reputation from spurious renditions:

> We trust that no apology will be required from us for bestowing a somewhat detailed notice upon a translation of sixty-nine lines, made from an original of about the same number; when it is considered that the subject in question is one of the most celebrated passages in the stupendous work of Dante. In the interest, not only of literature but of religion, we are persuaded that the study of the works of that master-poet and rare Christian philosopher is of an importance not to be over-rated.[26]

Dante, writes Gladstone, created the national poetry of his country. He was of all Italian writers the most unquestionably original. Gladstone compares him favourably with Virgil who was the Italian poet's own leader or 'dottore', as Gladstone claims Dante to be in his own life's journey. Dante's style, he continues, was central to his work and there was never a poet in whose case language and metre were 'more exclusively the handmaids of thought. To put the ideas of Dante into a tongue different from his own is like dividing bone and marrow'.[27] Gladstone goes on to list the approaches adopted by other earlier Dante translators, before turning specifically to Russell. He begins by welcoming Russell's translation as evidence that 'the man is not absorbed in the party-man, or even in the statesman; and that a taste may remain for what is beautiful and incorrupt, even after a long immersion in public affairs'.[28] But after a few sentences of faint praise, he confronts Russell for the shallowness of his Dante scholarship and the variability of his translation:

[26] Gladstone, 'Lord John Russell's translation', 1.
[27] Ibid. 2.
[28] Ibid.

Of all authors, Dante most demands, we apprehend, a continuous study. It requires the greatest mental effort to reach his level; and the temperament of the reader, much more of the translator, cannot again and again be lowered and raised at will . . . Mr Sydney Smith has told us that Lord John Russell would (amongst other things), with or without ten minutes' notice, assume the command of the Channel fleet; and it appears to us he has at ten minutes' notice sat down to translate Dante – an exploit, in its own way, quite as venturesome as the former. The translator of Dante must imbue and saturate himself with the spirit of Dante. Unless his intellectual being be in great part absorbed in that of his original, he must, we believe, fail in his task, whatever be his native powers.[29]

Gladstone concentrates on close analysis and demolition of specific textual extracts to illustrate 'how Lord John Russell forgot that the one most marked and prominent characteristic of Dante is compression, concentration, intensity'.[30] He does so with justification; in many instances Russell expands dramatically on the Italian, with loose and verbose additions that do nothing to enhance the original. Having dismantled Russell's version of Paolo and Francesca, Gladstone closes on a conciliatory note admitting that other translators, given the enormous task of rendering Dante in English, may have done little better – himself included:

But we are anxious to see a far higher conception of Dante spread abroad among our countrymen; and we are sure that if they are to advance in their moral health and intellectual vigour, he must advance in their estimation. For this end we desire that every thing which professes to represent him, should be strictly and minutely canvassed, lest he should be degraded by counterfeits and caricatures. As for *him*, no examination can be too severe and searching. He should be viewed both in the magnificence of his outline, and in the precision of his detail. . . . It is no slight matter, to transfer into a language other than his own, any one passage of his book. It is not an after-dinner relaxation. If we show that Lord John Russell has not adequately bent the bow of Ulysses, we have given a useful warning to weaker men. Dante was not made for annuals in silk covers. He is not to be the plaything of the butterflies of literature.[31]

There is no record of any response from Russell. And while Gladstone displayed no butterfly tendencies in his approach to the study of Dante, he was perhaps correct to include himself among the list of translators who sometimes failed to do justice to the original. Certainly, to the modern reader, Gladstone's English version of the Dante passages lack a certain magic and lightness of touch. Take, for example, the first three *terzine* of Dante's expanded Lord's Prayer which opens *Purgatorio*, canto 11. The version quoted

29 Ibid. 3.
30 Ibid.
31 Ibid. 15–16.

below is from the edition of the *Commedia* approved by the Società Dantesca Italiana, and used by Sinclair in the Penguin dual-text translation. Gladstone, in the *Translations*, uses a more recent Italian version for his parallel Italian text and begins each line, rather than each sentence as in Sinclair, with a capital letter. Dante wrote:

> O Padre nostro, che ne' cieli stai,
> non circonscritto, ma per più amore
> ch'ai primi effetti di là su tu hai,
> laudato sia 'l tuo nome e'l tuo valore
> da ogni creatura, com'è degno
> di render grazie al tuo dolce vapore.
> Vegna ver noi la pace del tuo regno,
> chè noi ad essa non potem da noi,
> s'ella non vien, con tutto nostro ingegno.

Sinclair's prose translation of 1939 reads as follows:

> Our Father which art in heaven, not circumscribed but by the greater love Thou hast for Thy first works on high. Praised be Thy name and power by every creature as it is meet to give thanks for Thy sweet effluence; May the peace of Thy kingdom come to us, for we cannot reach it of ourselves, if it come not, with all our striving.

Gladstone's verse translation is dated 1835, when he was twenty-five years old and had been intimately acquainted with Dante for just a couple of years. Since it was not published until 1861, he could – and may – have modified it prior to publication. The verse observes the aba/bcb system of the *terza rima*, but replaces Dante's hendecasyllabic lines with iambic pentameters:

> O Father ours, that dwellest in the sky,
> Not circumscribed, but for Thy love intense
> To Thy first emanations there on high;
> Let each and every creature that hath sense
> Praise Thee, Thy name, Thy goodness, as 'tis fit
> They render thanks for Thy warm effluence.
> Thy Kingdom come; Thy peace too come with it,
> Which, if it come not by Thy gift divine,
> Comes not to us by strength of human wit.[32]

Compare this with the blank verse version of the same passage by Cary, who was the first to publish a complete translation of the *Commedia* into English in the early years of the nineteenth century and whose work was a runaway success:

---

[32] Gladstone and Lyttelton, *Translations*, 163.

> O Thou Almighty Father! Who dost make
> The heavens thy dwelling, not in bounds confined,
> But that, with love intenser, there thou view'st
> Thy primal effluence; hallow'd be thy name:
> Join, each created being, to extol
> Thy might; for worthy humblest thanks and praise
> Is thy blest Spirit. May thy kingdom's peace
> Come unto us; for we, unless it come,
> With all our striving, thither tend in vain.[33]

A more recent translation by Singleton makes no concessions to either the rhyme or rhythm of the original but, by doing so, perhaps renders more faithfully its meaning:

> Our Father, who art in heaven, not circumscribed, but through the greater love Thou hast for Thy first works on high,
> Praisèd be Thy name and Thy worth by every creature, as it is meet to render thanks to Thy sweet effluence.
> May the peace of Thy kingdom come to us, for we cannot reach it ourselves, if it come not, for all our striving.[34]

Dante's Lord's Prayer is clearly a difficult passage to translate with elegance and meaning while staying close to the rhyme and rhythm structure of the original. But whereas translators of the complete *Commedia* had no choice but to tackle it, Gladstone actively chose to do so and therefore invites criticism. Some lines are clumsy: 'Thy kingdom come; Thy peace too come with it.' Others are wilfully eccentric, such as the translation of 'cieli' as 'sky' rather than simply 'heaven' or even 'heavens' (since there were ten heavens in Dante's system of paradise). Yet overall Gladstone has succeeded to some degree in capturing the Dantean cadence which, after his imagery, is one of the poet's most remarkable technical qualities.

Davie addresses primarily Dante's use of language, while Gladstone's Russell review and own translations provide a framework within which to consider the challenges faced by translators. But there are some interesting insights into Gladstone's linguistic approach, too. Davie echoes Gladstone's view of the ultimate impossibility of adequately rendering Dante in English at all, and highlights the sort of resulting creative tension that is exemplified in the Gladstone–Russell disagreement. Even for Dante's contemporaries, the *Commedia* was, and was meant to be, a disconcerting and shocking work, precisely because it violated the canons of literary style at the same time as it claimed the status of a classic:

> The poem's very forthrightness is part of a highly rhetorical strategy which embraces extremes of inventiveness and abstraction on the one hand, and

33 *The vision of Purgatory and Paradise*, trans. and comm. Henry Francis Cary, London 1893.
34 *The Divine Comedy*, trans. and comm. Charles Singleton, Princeton 1973.

downright crudeness on the other; Dante exploits the latitude offered by the comic style and pursues it to unprecedented lengths, redefining the whole hierarchy of styles in the process. His ability to hold these opposing extremes in balance is a measure of his uniqueness, and a wise translator will acknowledge that the achievement is unrepeatable; but the tension can and should be a creative one, for Dante's translators as it was for the poet himself.[35]

Davie finds Gladstone less unequal to the task than Russell and endorses Gladstone's 'merciless' criticism of the translation of the Francesca da Rimini episode with its 'leisurely expansiveness, its proliferation of adverbs and adjectives',[36] many of which he shows to be redundant. Where Dante's lines are succinct and relentless, Russell's efforts are diluted by superfluous verbiage and arbitrary alteration of the line structure:

> What has been lost in Russell's misty soft-focus is the whole force of the episode, which derives from Dante's ability to convey simultaneously both the romantic beauty and the adulterous reality of Francesca's love. Russell's indifferent verse and approximate understanding of Dante's text are an easy target.[37]

Davie reinforces Gladstone's indignation at the apparent insouciance with which Russell undertook his task. But how does Gladstone measure up to his own exacting standard as a translator? Gladstone was confident enough in his understanding of the original of the three texts he translated not to follow Dante slavishly. Nevertheless, there are 'indications of unease' in various unnatural forms of speech adopted by Gladstone. In the translation of the Ugolino episode there is a 'most dramatic lapse of tone' in the occasional 'pseudo-Shakespearean line'[38] where Dante's original had the rhythm of perfectly natural speech. Elsewhere, there is 'a measure of rhetorical heightening' which compromises the quality of the original, while some phrases 'continue to test Gladstone's ability to find a suitable stylistic level'.[39] But the translation improves as it progresses:

> By the end of the story, his touch is more confident, as the relative absence of alterations in the manuscript confirms; the (final) lines follow Dante closely in their plain, matter-of-factness . . . it seems, then, that once he is sufficiently confident to cease striving for a self-consciously elevated style, Gladstone can convey something of the force of Dante's poetry in the *Inferno*.[40]

Gladstone was in any case always more comfortable with the latter two cantiche of the *Commedia* which

---

[35] Davie, 'Not an after-dinner relaxation', 386.
[36] Ibid. 387.
[37] Ibid.
[38] Ibid. 390.
[39] Ibid. 391.
[40] Ibid.

offer to view a far more surprising achievement of the human mind: and they impart a deeper insight and delight. This is not merely or mainly because the images of the *Inferno* belong to a painful class, and those of the *Purgatorio* frequently, of the *Paradiso* always, to one which is pleasurable, but it is in the sense of art, of that kind of delight which is derived from the intense, the profound, the sublime.[41]

Since Gladstone identifies more closely with the subject matter of the two more devotional cantiche, translating these seems to come more easily to him and Davie finds more to commend, particularly as regards Piccarda's speech. This contains the famous line – 'E'n la sua volontade è nostra pace' – translated by Gladstone as 'In His will is our peace', which he repeated frequently to his wife Catherine as the motto by which they should conduct their lives. It is, comments Davie in perhaps his warmest praise, 'quite different in sound from the Italian line, with every word a monosyllable; but in its own way, like Dante's line, it comes as the simple climax of a dense, closely-argued passage'.[42] In conclusion:

> Gladstone's achievement as a translator of Dante should not be exaggerated; even his best efforts are uneven. High-minded Victorian that he was, he was understandably ill at ease in translating *Inferno*, where Dante's defiance of literary convention is at its starkest. But prompted by the intellectual, aesthetic and spiritual challenge of the *Purgatorio* and *Paradiso*, he was able to grasp and even, in places, to reproduce, those qualities of compression, concentration, intensity.[43]

Valerio Lucchesi agrees that Gladstone's performance 'is a patchy one, a mixture of good and bad'. He points out several additions and elaborations made for the sake of rhyme, but also occasional 'gratuitous epithets' and lines 'too freely translated'. At times Gladstone's rendering is 'too verbose and obfuscates Dante's compressed but transparent image'. At others, there are omissions and even inaccuracies. However, 'various terzine in Canto 33 (the Ugolino episode) and most of the shorter passages are quite acceptable not only for their fidelity to the original but also for their English rendering'.[44]

There appears to be no substantial contemporary commentary on the quality of Gladstone's translation, comparable with that of Gladstone on Russell's. This may be explained again by the fact that, until the publication of the *Diaries* began, the extent of Gladstone's interest in Dante was not widely known. There is, however, a brief mention of the *Translations* in a biography by Wemyss Reid, published in 1899, the year after Gladstone's death and four years before the official biography. According to Wemyss

---

41 Ibid.
42 Ibid. 398.
43 Ibid. 400.
44 Personal communication from Dr Valerio Lucchesi, Corpus Christi College, Oxford.

Reid, while Lyttelton's contributions to the work, which were translations from English into Greek and Latin,

> show unquestionably the finer scholarship and the more ultimate grasp of Greek and Latin diction, Mr Gladstone's testify to a wider range of reading. The rendering from Italian and German are all in his portion of the book; and they serve to show that before he had long left University – for most of the pieces, though not published till 1861, date from the 'thirties' – Dante and Schiller were as familiar to him as Homer and Horace.[45]

Wemyss Reid quotes much of Gladstone's translation of the Piccarda piece from *Paradiso*, on the grounds that it was not readily available otherwise, thus reinforcing Quaritch's view that the *Translations* was a private publication not widely circulated. He continues:

> The book is now scarce, and many readers may not have access to it. Those who know the original lines in the third canto of the 'Paradise' will recognise the fidelity of the version, all the more remarkable from the additional burden which the translator has put on himself through adherence to the somewhat complicated measure of the original.[46]

Wemyss Reid also mentions another of Gladstone's contributions to the joint work, namely a rendering into rhymed Latin of Toplady's famous hymn *Rock of ages, cleft for me* 'in which he has aimed, not unsuccessfully, at catching the manner of the mediaeval hymn-writers'.[47] This hymn, which was Gladstone's favourite, was sung at his funeral and a copy of the Latin hangs in the nave in St Deiniol's Church. Nor was it the only hymn translation that Gladstone had published. A translation by him into Italian of an English hymn appeared as the first item in the September 1883 issue of *Nineteenth Century*. Gladstone had taken it upon himself to provide the Italian nation with a hymn whether they wanted one or not. Pointing out that there were no hymns in Italian because of the predominance of the Latin liturgy, Gladstone adds:

> Although the want has not been felt in Italy, the language in which Dante wrote cannot be incapable of the force and the compression, both in form and substance, proper to the Hymn. The circumstances may give a certain interest to this slight attempt at translating into Italian Cowper's well-known hymn, Since I have found to be the case on the part of Italian friends who, since the translation was written, have given me the benefit of their skilful counsel.[48]

---

[45] Wemyss Reid, *Gladstone*, i. 139. It was as a result of working on this biography that F. W. Hirst was chosen by Morley to work on his own biography of Gladstone. Wemyss Reid was also a friend and political associate of Gladstone's son, Herbert. My thanks to Mark Nixon for this information.

[46] Ibid.

[47] Ibid.

[48] 'Senti senti anima mia', *Nineteenth Century* (Sept. 1883), 1.

There follows a translation of *Hark! My soul*. The wider Italian response is not recorded. It would have been difficult for the editor of *Nineteenth Century* to turn down an offer from the prime minister of the day.[49]

There is one more, this time again specifically Dante-related, translation that Gladstone recorded in his diary that remains a mystery. In August 1879 he wrote four entries in one week, indicating that he was working on a translation 'of a bit of Dante'. Certainly there is no evidence that he ever had any more translations published. But the most intriguing entry is that for 11 August when he wrote: 'Also a little on Dante's Gate; what a snail's pace is alone possible'. The translation of the episode where Dante and Virgil enter the gates of Hell – with its dire warning that those who enter should abandon all hope (canto 3) – would appear to be a new exercise for him. He was not reworking an old translation. Nevertheless, this was a man who was virtually bilingual in Italian, had translated Farini's substantial work in the 1850s and had first tackled Dante over forty years before. Why, then, was only a 'snail's pace' possible, particularly since, having resigned his leadership of the Liberal Party and being in virtual retirement for the time being, he had fewer claims on his time than usual?

The answer could lie in his autumn holiday plans. In September and October 1879, shortly before embarking on the Midlothian campaign and then his second ministry, Gladstone and two of his children toured Bavaria and Italy. His specific objective in Bavaria was to visit von Döllinger. Three diary entries during his stay show that he was talking to von Döllinger about Dante. Possibly the reason his August translations were slow was that he was rendering the Gate of Hell not into English, but into German, prior to his discussions with his German host.

Did Dante study in Oxford?

> He did not go to saunter by the Isis . . . He went to refresh his thirst at a fast-swelling fountainhead of knowledge, and to imp the wings by which he was to mount, and mount so high that few have ever soared above him, into the Empyrean of celestial wisdom.[50]

The Empyrean is the highest of Dante's heavens, the tenth in his system of the universe. By this allusion, Gladstone implies that Dante's presumed visit to Oxford provided him with the inspiration for the *Paradiso* – the third, final and Gladstone's personal favourite cantica of the *Commedia*. It is a fanciful one. As Agatha Ramm has commented:

---

49 James Knowles, a good friend of Gladstone's, was editor and sole proprietor of the *Nineteenth Century*, which was noted for publishing only signed works. Gladstone contributed a total of fifty-five articles and reviews to the magazine.
50 W. Gladstone, 'Did Dante study at Oxford?', *Nineteenth Century* xxxi (June 1892), 1032–42.

It is a pity that his one piece of writing on Dante was a half-serious *jeu d'esprit* towards the end of his life. It is a wonderfully clever argument to prove that Dante visited Oxford. Part at least of its cleverness lay in leaving anything like a shred of evidence to the end when he appears to clinch a series of tendentious deductions from poetry.[51]

Nevertheless, the article reflects the importance for Gladstone of trying to ensure that his favourite poet received due recognition in his favourite context. Like his devotion to Dante, Gladstone's attachment to Oxford was passionate and life-long: as an undergraduate and president of the Oxford Union, as a supporter of the Oxford Movement, as a long-time MP for the university, as an honorary Doctor of Law and, while prime minister, as an instrument in its reforms. He dedicated *The State in its relations with the Church*, 'To the University of Oxford, tried and not found wanting'. He became an honorary Fellow of All Souls while Chancellor of the Exchequer in Palmerston's second administration. He was an honorary member of the university's prestigious Dante Society from 1876 onwards. In an autobiographical fragment, quoted by Tilney Bassett, Gladstone wrote:

> I do not hesitate to say Oxford . . . laid the foundations of my Liberalism . . . while in the arms of Oxford I was possessed through and through with a single-minded and passionate love of truth, so that, although I might be swathed in clouds of prejudice, there was something of an eye within that might gradually pierce them.[52]

It is unsurprising that, towards the end of his life, Gladstone aspired to bring two of his great loves – Oxford and Dante – together. In an article published in *Nineteenth Century*, he argues at some length – 5,000 words – for the case that Dante studied or taught in Oxford while in exile from Florence in the early fourteenth century.

Gladstone's own acquaintance with Oxford began in 1828 when he went up to Christ Church. In so doing he was fulfilling his father's ambition for him to follow in the footsteps of George Canning. John Gladstone had been Canning's agent when the latter was the young Tory MP for Liverpool in the second decade of the nineteenth century. Later Foreign Secretary, then prime minister, Canning died shortly before William went to Oxford.

For John Gladstone, Canning was an image of what he would have liked to have been, but could not be. Canning was a feasible model also for what John Gladstone's sons might be. An upstart of dubious origins in an intensely aristocratic social and political world, Canning exemplified what innate talent combined with the processing offered by Eton and Christ Church, Oxford, could achieve.[53]

[51] Ramm, 'Gladstone as man of letters', 10.
[52] *Gladstone papers*, 95.
[53] Shannon, *Gladstone: Peel's inheritor*, 5.

Christ Church failed to provide William with the volume or quality of enduring acquaintances that Eton had furnished; but it was not the school but the university that held pride of place in his affections. His eighteen years (1847–65) as one of two MPs for the university was the longest period he spent representing any constituency. When he lost the seat, he successfully sought a replacement, representing South Lancashire. But he told the audience at his first canvassing meeting at Manchester's Free Trade Hall that although he was now 'unmuzzled', and free to come among them, he had loved the University of Oxford with a deep and passionate love and would love it to the end. And so he did. Even in old age, the connection continued. Well into his eighties, he was still speaking at the Oxford Union – on Homer. In 1892, just six years before he died, he delivered the first Romanes Lecture – on medieval universities – in Oxford's Sheldonian Theatre.[54] Research for his lecture may have triggered the idea of writing a piece on Dante and Oxford.

Oxford was also the recipient of Gladstone's last public statement. Shortly before he died, he sent an elegant reply to the message of 'sorrow and affection' he had received from the vice-chancellor of the university on behalf of the Hebdomadal Council, established by his own Oxford Act of 1854. Dictated to his daughter Helen, Gladstone's reply read: 'There is no expression of sympathy that I value more than that of the ancient University of Oxford, the God-fearing and God-sustaining University of Oxford. I served her perhaps mistakenly, but to the best of my ability. My utmost earnest prayers are hers to the uttermost and the last.'[55]

When he died a few weeks later, he was laid out in the 'Temple of Peace' at Hawarden Castle, but not in the privy councillor's uniform to which he was entitled. As if for an academic occasion, he was dressed in the sub-fusc and scarlet robes of his Oxford doctorate of civil law, awarded to him in the Sheldonian in 1848, with his mortarboard on his chest. His daughter Mary said he looked exactly as he did when last he wore them to give the Romanes Lecture: 'The Privy Council uniform, with its implication that he was a mere politician, would have struck the wrong note. At a different level, the academical gown was a striking choice, for the whole of his life had been conducted as if sitting a series of tests and examinations set by his Maker.'[56]

Such, then, was Gladstone's relationship with Oxford University. As regards the possibility that Oxford had been graced by Dante's presence, Gladstone may have been prompted to revive the issue by a recent new work

---

[54] 'Romanes, a Darwinian physiologist of Canadian and Cambridge provenance, wanted to endow Oxford with a prestigious public lecture on the model of the Rede Lecture at Cambridge. Gladstone's theme would be, in effect, his love and pride in Oxford, offered in the form of a historical survey of the development of its academic spirit': idem, *Gladstone: heroic minister*, 526–7.

[55] Matthew, *Gladstone*, 633.

[56] Ibid. 635.

on Dante by the Italian scholar G. A. Scartazzini. For it was a revival: the question itself, unlike the treatment, was not new, despite Gladstone's comment that 'such an inquiry will be strange for many, as indeed it may be new for nearly all'.[57]

Scartazzini was based variously at Chur, Milan and Leipzig, and wrote in Italian and German, both of which Gladstone read. An English translation of his major German-language publication, the *Dante-Handbuch* (Leipzig 1892), was not available – as *A Companion to Dante*, translated by A. J. Butler – until 1893, a year after Gladstone published his article in *Nineteenth Century*. However, a three-volume Italian edition – similar but not identical to the German version – was being published in Leipzig between 1874 and 1890, prior to being published in one volume in Milan in 1892. Gladstone may have had access to Scartazzini's brief, if authoritative, comments on Dante's possible visit to Oxford through this edition, read during a period of convalescence in Italy in the winter of 1887–8.

Gladstone had travelled with a family party to Florence in December 1887, on the advice of his doctor, to recover from throat problems. He was under instructions not to talk, to improve the condition of his voice. During this enforced quiet period, he read Scartazzini's book 'and found it fervid, generally judicial and most unsparing in labour'.[58] The chapter, 'Student or teacher?', which mentions Dante's supposed visit to Oxford, occurs early in the second part of the work. It is known that the third part was not published until 1890, but it has not been possible to confirm the publication date of the second volume, since the work can now be traced only in the 1892 single volume version. Nevertheless it may have been out in 1887 and Gladstone may therefore have been able to read it then, and to be inspired by the references.

Though controversial, Scartazzini was well regarded. In its review of Butler's 1893 translation, the *Manchester Guardian* said it was 'with unqualified satisfaction that we welcome the appearance of this work'.[59] Scartazzini had, it said, 'done more than any living man – nay, more than all other living men together – to make a broad and accurate study of the *Commedia* possible'.[60] Apart from having read Scartazzini, Gladstone admits in the article in *Nineteenth Century* that the same proposition – that Dante studied at Oxford – had been put forward by Dr Plumptre, the late dean of Wells, in an article in the *Contemporary Review* of December 1881. He also recalls hearing a lecture some forty years earlier by James Lacaita in which he did Oxford the honour of numbering Dante among its students. However, on balance, it seems likely, given the contemporary publication by Scartazzini, that this book was the trigger for the Gladstone article.

---

[57] Gladstone, 'Did Dante study at Oxford', 1.
[58] Ibid.
[59] *Manchester Guardian*, 17 Oct. 1893.
[60] Ibid.

The arguments put forward by Gladstone in support of the view that Dante studied at Oxford are often tortuous. It should, however, be pointed out that Dante's own methods of identification for persons, places and events were also often astonishingly circuitous. In *Paradiso*, canto 9, for example, Marseilles is not identified by name but as the place on the shores of the great valley flooded with water (the Mediterranean Sea) between the Ebro and the Magra (a river in Spain and a river in Italy) and opposite Bugia (a city on the African coast). The geography of Europe's rivers is a major feature of Dante's erudition. That Gladstone found satisfaction following the course and significance of Dante's rivers is obvious from a diary entry for 10 April 1892: 'Worked on Dante rivers' and the annotations to his copy of Scartazzini. Gladstone's arguments in support of the hypothesis that Dante studied at Oxford are felt to be unconvincing. Even Paget Toynbee, who praised Gladstone as a more accomplished Dante scholar than most Italian *Dantisti*, thought it unlikely, although he concedes the possibility in a poetic paraphrase of Boccaccio's letter to Petrarch:

> Thou know'st perchance how Phoebus self did guide
> Our Tuscan DANTE up the lofty side
> Of snow-clad Cyrrha; how our Poet won
> Parnassus' peak, and founts of Helicon;
> How, with Apollo, ranging wide, he sped
> Through Nature's whole domain, and visited
> Imperial Rome, and Paris, and so passed
> O'erseas to Britain's distant shores at last.[61]

Toynbee left open a small window of possibility that Dante visited Oxford; Italian Dante scholar Agostino Bartolini accommodated no such possibility. Whether he was right or wrong, Gladstone's textual knowledge of the *Commedia* is remarkable, as is his understanding of its context, allusions and the debate surrounding its interpretation. His level of scholarship is matched only by his enthusiasm for its author. Yet it is not perfect. Toynbee points out that 'Gladstone makes the extraordinary blunder of putting into the mouth of Sordello the speech of Nessus in *Inferno*, x canto 12, 119–20'.[62] On the other hand, one could argue that if this was the only fault he found, the rest must bear scrutiny. Gladstone begins by claiming as 'an admitted fact' that Dante studied in Paris, 800 miles from Florence but only 300 from Oxford. He quotes as evidence a reference to Dante's stay at Paris in a biography of the poet by Giovanni Boccaccio (1313–75). It was during this French trip, Gladstone insists, that Dante's Oxford visit took place. That this was the case he bases on the argument that 'not only do the grounds of general probability

---

61 Toynbee, *Britain's tribute to Dante*, verso of title page.
62 Idem, 'Oxford and Dante', in A. Cippico, H. E. Goad, E. C. Gardner W. P. Ker and W. Seton (eds), *Dante: essays in commemoration, 1321–1921*, London 1921, 67n.

supply no presumption against this extension of the exile's travel, but they tend to support it'.[63]

As supporting evidence, Gladstone emphasises the 'sisterhood of universities' established in the Middle Ages. He points to the steady stream of English students leaving the University of Paris at the time for Oxford, the two institutions being 'beyond doubt the two first and the two oldest of the European universities equipped with all the four faculties of Theology, Law, Medicine and Arts'.[64]

Gladstone continues by noting Dante's interest in describing the places he visited. He quotes specific Parisian scenes and people from all three cantiche of the *Commedia*, insisting that Dante only described places or events experienced at first hand. 'It is thus that we can commonly trace, when he is abroad, the limits of his travelling experience by his local allusions.' This last point becomes crucial in his defence of Dante's visit to England and to Oxford since 'Dante's local allusions outside of his own country are supplied by his experience in travel, and consequently enable us to trace his personal movements.'[65]

To corroborate this approach, Gladstone moves on to discuss events described in the *Commedia* that take place in Flanders. 'In connection with contemporary history, Dante mentions only seven towns outside Italy. Four of these are in Flanders . . . of itself a significant fact; for what had Dante to do with Flanders?' The towns are Douay, Lille, Ghent and Bruges. 'But why these? . . . Douay, at least, has only been known to us as an inconsiderable place.'[66] There is only one possible answer, Gladstone says. Dante named them because he had been there. It follows, then, that if Dante had been as far north as the North Sea coastal town of Bruges, he was well on the way to England.

Gladstone's arguments now take a constructional turn. In the fifteenth canto of the *Inferno*, he points out, Dante described how he and Virgil found a roadway on the edge of the burning sand where they were protected from falling flakes of fire:

> This roadway he compares to sea walls, such as beat off tide and storm along the coast between Bruges and place he calls Guizzante, which is now interpreted, by ruling authority, to be Wissant. The place appears to have been . . . in ancient times the port, or a port, of departure for England . . . I therefore do not see how the inference can be avoided, that Dante had himself sailed along the coast of Flanders between Bruges and Wissant. He must have had an aim in his voyage; this was not his route homewards; England, on the other hand, was before him. This England was indeed, in many senses, a remote and iso-

---

63 Gladstone, 'Did Dante study at Oxford?', 2.
64 Ibid.
65 Ibid. 4.
66 Ibid.

lated object, but not in an academical sense, and Dante's journey was academ-ical.[67]

It seems likely then, Gladstone maintains, that Dante sailed to England by an ordinary and well-established route. Having arrived, 'the most straightfor-ward supposition is that he may have sailed up the Thames'.[68]

Gladstone supports this supposition by drawing on references in the *Inferno* that imply that Dante had intimate knowledge of current or recent events in England. England was a country unlikely to attract his interest unless he had been there, since it lay 'outside the grand central movements of the continent, which had the German or Western Empire for their pole'.[69] Reiterating that Dante never described places of which he had no experi-ence, Gladstone quotes a number of references to recent or contemporary events in English history – involving Henry III, Edward I, Guy de Montfort and the river Thames which were 'not world-historic; they were purely local'. It was very improbable, he insists, that Dante would have been aware of this local history at all, 'far removed as it was from the circle familiar to his ideas', unless he had seen it as a visitor to England, and then taken advantage of it among his illustrations. For example:

> The mere mention of the Thames by Dante is a notable fact; for nowhere else, outside of Italy, does he name a river theretofore so unknown and of such sec-ondary importance, unless in connection with his own travels. Except in this case, the rivers named by him and unconnected with his personal knowledge are either great waterways or streams historically famous . . . The introduction of the Thames, and its association with a local contemporary incident, crowns the presumptive evidence derivable from his other references to England, all coloured with local interest, and all of them contemporary with his own life.[70]

Gladstone waits until nearly the end of the article before playing his two trump cards. These are the testimonials of two external witnesses. One is Boccaccio who puts Dante in Britain without mentioning Oxford; while the second witness, although writing a hundred years later, explicitly asserts that Dante went to Oxford. While Boccaccio's biography made no mention of either Oxford or England (only Paris), Gladstone quotes a letter in Latin from Boccaccio to Petrarch, whose father settled in Arezzo after being exiled from Florence in 1302 along with Dante. In this letter, Boccaccio specifically refers to Dante visiting the 'Parisians and then the far Britons'.[71] It seems unlikely he would risk making a dubious claim to a family who might well have known otherwise. Gladstone's second direct witness is Giovanni of

---

67 Ibid. 5.
68 Ibid. 6.
69 Ibid.
70 Ibid. 7–8.
71 'Parisios dudum extremosque Britannos': ibid. 9.

Serravalle, bishop and prince of Fermo who translated the *Commedia* into Latin in the early fifteenth century. The manuscript of this translation, which is in the Vatican Library, includes a preface in which Bishop Serravalle states categorically that Dante studied first at Paris, then at Oxford.[72] Gladstone points out that Saravalle was asked, while at the Council of Constance (1414–18), to carry out the translation by three fellow-delegates – an Italian cardinal plus the English bishops of Salisbury and Bath:[73]

> As to the value of the citation from Bishop Serravalle, we are certainly con-fronted by the interval of a full century from the date of the occurrence. But, on the other hand, the request to him from two English Bishops that he would undertake the labour of the translation can hardly imply less than that there was at the time a still surviving tradition in England which connected Dante personally with the country; or, in other words, which asserted his having been a student of Oxford.[74]

At no point in the article does Gladstone claim that Dante ever alluded to Oxford directly. But he adds: 'The fact that he does not name the University of Oxford in no way detracts from it; for neither does he anywhere name the University of Paris, where we know that he studied, and perhaps studied long.'[75]

The Paris angle is the first aspect of Gladstone's discussion to be attacked in a response by the Italian scholar Agostino Bartolini published in the Italian periodical *L'Arcadia* in 1894.[76] Bartolini was prompted to write the article by a letter Gladstone had sent to another illustrious Italian scholar, David Farabulini, in which he drew the latter's attention to his own article in *Nineteenth Century*. Gladstone's letter had been published in May 1894 in the Rome newspaper *La Voce*. In a piece only slightly shorter than Gladstone's, Bartolini acknowledges the exceptional and enduring[77] interest in Dante at

---

[72] 'Dilexit Theologiam Sacram, in qua diu studuit, tam in Oxoniis in regno Angliae, quam Parisiis in regno Franciae. Dantes se in juventute dedit omnibus artibus liberalibus, studens eas Paduae, Bononiae, demum Oxoniis et Parisiis, ubi fecit multos actus mirabiles; in tantum quod aliquibus dicebatur magnus Philosophus, ab aliquibus magnus Theologus, ab aliquibus magnus Poeta' ('He chose Sacred Theology, in which he was a student for a long time, at Oxford in the kingdom of England as well as at Paris in the kingdom of France. In his youth Dante devoted himself to all the liberal arts, studying these in Padua and finally at Oxford and Paris, where he performed many marvellous acts; to such an extent that he was called by some a great Philosopher, by some a great Theologian and by others a great Poet'): ibid. 10. It is not clear what is understood by 'actus' – probably lectures, writings and debates rather than miracles.

[73] See p. 27 above.

[74] Gladstone, 'Did Dante study at Oxford', 10.

[75] Ibid. 6.

[76] Agostino Bartolini, 'Il viaggio di Dante a Oxford: a proposito d'un articolo di Gladstone', *L'Arcadia* vii/3, Rome 1894.

[77] This may be a subtle pun on Bartolini's part. Dante is short for Durante, which means 'the enduring', and is what Dante was called by the family in his early years.

Oxford which might be seen by some to imply a sort of genetic memory of the poet's stay there. Or it would do, he says, were it not for the fact that many other places make similar, and demonstrably unfounded, claims. So, notwithstanding Gladstone's 'ingenious arguments', Bartolini is not inclined to accommodate the idea of Dante's visiting Oxford:

> On the one hand, it is very gratifying, this rivalry amongst foreigners to share in the glory of our poet . . . The cult of Dante in Oxford, and Gladstone's fine article, flatter our amour propre; we feel sincerely grateful towards all students of our great man. In honouring him, they do us great honour as well. But this is not about poetry and affection, but about historical fact.[78]

Then, item-by-item, Bartolini systematically demolishes Gladstone's argument. Much of the article comprises straight paraphrases of sections of the Gladstone piece, followed by straight contradictions. Bartolini dismisses Boccaccio as unreliable; he expresses doubts as to whether Dante even went to Paris, insisting that what he writes about the city could easily be second-hand. He emphasises Dante's extreme poverty in exile, which made even travelling around Italy difficult. In this connection, however, he makes no mention of Scartazzini's proposition, which he must have known of if Gladstone did, that Dante travelled through Europe not as a student but a teacher, and therefore earning his living. Bartolini maintains that Serravalle, who states categorically that Dante studied at Oxford, was simply trying to humour the English bishops at the Council of Constance who had asked him to carry out the translation into Latin. Dante was interested in all mankind, but that did not mean he experienced everything he wrote about. While accepting Gladstone's understanding and fair presentation of the basic background facts of the period, the conclusion he drew about Dante at Oxford was, says Bartolini, 'pure conjecture'. However, he concludes graciously,

> Those countries which cannot boast of having had Dante as a citizen, desire at least to have welcomed him as a visitor. . . . Ingenious efforts to show that Dante travelled to England and attended the University of Oxford, only serve to increase . . . our gratitude to all those outside our borders . . . who by showing their appreciation of our poet and by their longing to make him their own . . . do us a great honour as well.[79]

---

[78] 'Da un lato ci piace assai questo gara degli stranieri per la gloria del nostro poeta . . . Il culto di Dante in Oxford, il bell'articolo di Gladstone, toccano soavemente il nostro amore proprio, onde sentiamo riconoscenza vivissima verso tutti gli studiosi delle opere del nostro grande, che nell'onoranza che fanno a lui, ci onorano grademente; ma non è questione qui di poesia e d'affetto, ma di storia e critica': Bartoline, Il viaggio, 4.

[79] 'Quei paesi che non possono vantare d'averlo cittadino lo desiderano almeno viandante o visitatore. Gli sforzi dell'ingegno . . . che cercano di mostrare che Dante viagiasse in Inghilterra e frequentasse l'Università di Oxford, debbono crescere nel nostro petto . . . la riconoscenza verso tutti coloro . . . che, apprezzando il nostro poeta, e bramando congiungere al suo nome le patrie memorie, ci si mostrano cortesi a ci fanno onore': ibid. 18.

Despite Bartolini's dismissal of Gladstone's arguments for Dante at Oxford, the fact remains that the breadth of Gladstone's erudition in the subject was truly remarkable. It justifiably earned him the compliment from Paget Toynbee that, as regards Dante, 'few, even of Italians, were so well versed as he'.[80]

There is one interesting omission from Gladstone's evidence in support of Dante's presence in Oxford. Gladstone makes no mention of the inclusion by Dante in *Inferno* 25, with the sodomites, of Francesco d'Accorso, who is known to have taught at Oxford in the late thirteenth century. Born in Florence in 1225, the son of an eminent jurist, he was himself a celebrated lawyer. He was professor of civil law at Bologna and, in 1273, when Edward I of England passed through the city on his way home from Palestine, he decided, at Edward's invitation, to accompany him to England, where he lectured for some time at Oxford. In 1281 he returned to Bologna, where he died in 1293.[81] Gladstone said that Dante wrote only about people who were important, or people he had known about. Dante may have included d'Accorso because he heard talk of the lawyer when he was himself at Oxford. Gladstone may have omitted this possible evidence on grounds of delicacy, given the sexual nature of d'Accorso's sin.

The reaction of the loyal Wemyss Reid to the Dante-at-Oxford hypothesis is respectful but lukewarm, although he remains impressed by the scholarship:

> The evidence for this visit is not, it must be confessed, very strong, and it may be doubted if Mr Gladstone's arguments, some of which tempt the reader to record Dante's own line, 'Affection bends the judgement to her ply' induced many persons to accept it as proved. Indeed, we do not feel sure that they had that effect on himself; at any rate, in the lecture above referred to,[82] which was delivered shortly after the publication of the article, there is no hint that Dante may have been among the eminent men whom the growing fame of Oxford attracted from foreign parts. The article is, however, interesting as a good presentment of such evidence as there is in favour of the tale, reinforced by certain collateral considerations.[83]

Among the eminent men from overseas who taught at Oxford in the four-teenth century, there were many Italian nationals. There were also several Englishmen who studied in Italy, mainly at Padua and Bologna. By and large their special subject was Greek, which Dante did not have: he was therefore

---

80 Toynbee, *Dante in English literature*, 601.
81 Idem, *Concise Dante dictionary*, Oxford 1924, 3.
82 Wemyss Reid is referring to the Romanes Lecture.
83 Wemyss Reid, *Gladstone*, 51–2. Wemyss Reid was a former editor of the *Leeds Mercury*. His biography predates even that of Morley. Referring specifically to him, Asa Briggs has observed that 'biographies written immediately after the death of a public figure often reveal aspects of his life and influence subsequently forgotten': 'Victorian images of Gladstone', in Peter Jagger (ed.), *Gladstone*, London 1998, 36.

unable therefore to read much Homer, so dear to both Virgil and Gladstone, because in his time only a few extracts were available in Latin. Catto and Evans, in their history of Oxford University, list Angelo Poliziano, Pompononio Leto and Niccolò Leonico Tomeo amongst Italian-born lecturers in Greek at Oxford in the late Middle Ages, alongside a number of English scholars who went to Padua and Florence to learn Greek and then came back to Oxford to teach it.

The predominance of Greek would not automatically have excluded Dante from teaching at Oxford. Having studied the trivium and quadrivium, and having attended the University of Bologna, he was proficient to teaching level in theology and philosophy at least, and possibly also law, as well as Latin. Moreover, there was a considerable amount of movement between disciplines at the time. Catto and Evans quote the example of the thirteenth-century Englishman Nicholas of Farham who was a theological student at Paris, studied and practised medicine at Bologna, and then taught logic and natural philosophy at both Oxford and Cambridge.[84] C. Mallet, in his history of the university, emphasises the importance of medieval Oxford as a centre of learning for the whole of Europe:

> With the close of the Barons' War and the foundation of the earliest Colleges, a new period of prosperity for the University began. Oxford had taken her place beside Paris among the most famous seats of Western learning. She claimed indeed with superb assumption that Paris was an imitator if not a daughter of her own. Students flowed to her from every quarter. The tireless scholars of the Middle Ages were not content to study at a single University. They travelled far afield in search of teachers . . . They relied upon the comradeship of learners. They were franked by the common language of educated men. The Schoolmen of Oxford in the early fourteenth century became the leaders of European thought. Dante himself, it has been asserted, listened to her lecturers and wandered in her streets.[85]

Mallet draws attention to the evidence of Serravalle, outlined above by Gladstone, to reinforce the Dante-at-Oxford hypothesis, admitting that 'the tradition has some support'. But he adds that he was told personally by Toynbee that he did not accept it.[86] The fact remains that if Dante did visit Oxford – either to study or to teach – he would not have been out of place, or without compatriots, in the medieval university. My own view, originally sceptical, is now that Dante may well have visited Oxford at some time during his lengthy exile. It is a powerful tradition to have evolved at such an early date, had there been no foundation for it. What was appropriate and

---

[84] J. I. Catto and Ralph Evans (eds), *The history of the University of Oxford*, II: *Late mediaeval Oxford*, Oxford 1992, i. 380.
[85] C. Mallet, *A history of the University of Oxford*, I: *The mediaeval university and the colleges founded in the Middle Ages*, London 1968, 121.
[86] Ibid.

possible for Francesco d'Accorso of Bologna University was surely also appropriate and possible for Dante Alighieri, also of Bologna. Dante came to Oxford, if he did, with references from some of the great families of Italy who protected him during his exile. And there was the Franciscan dimension. As Lonsdale Wragg observed:

> It is in England, above all, that Franciscanism is identified with learning and speculation. All Europe flocked to Oxford to sit at the feet of those great Franciscan teachers . . . the English Fransciscans became the most learned body in Christendom, a character which they never lost till the suppression of the monasteries in the sixteenth century swept them out of the land.[87]

A period in Oxford could look like a sensible career move for a scholar – like Dante – with Franciscan connections. Mallet reinforces the idea of the growing importance and influence of the Franciscans in late medieval Oxford. Tradition has it that Dante's first vocation was to become a Franciscan friar. He was buried at the Franciscan monastery in Ravenna, the city that provided his final refuge. After enjoying the patronage of Can Grande della Scala in Verona in the early years of exile, Dante's later years were spent in Ravenna under the protection of Guido Novello da Polenta, the nephew of Francesca da Rimini. The Ravenna Franciscans set great store by Dante. Having buried him within their walls, they refused for centuries to return any part of him to that Florence of which Dante claimed, at the very start of the Commedia, he was a citizen 'by birth, not by morals'.[88] The Oxford Franciscans, who valued poverty, may also have provided him with a home, poor exile though he was.

---

[87] Lonsdale Wragg, *Dante and his Italy*, London 1907, 96.
[88] This original inscription is usually missing from later editions of the *Commedia*.

7

Understanding the Inner Man

Human beings live a double life on earth: an outer one and an inner one. Each influences the other; each informs the other; but the two are in no way interchangeable. External life experiences are one thing; the experiences of the heart and soul are quite another . . . the biography of an important person must aim to embrace not only the outer life but the inner life as well.[1]

With these words, it was the life of Dante that Scartazzini was addressing. Gladstone marked the paragraph with a double line in the margin of his German-language copy of Scartazzini, implying that it expressed sentiments with which he identified. The sentiments could be equally applied to the importance of including Dante in the equation when studying the life of Gladstone.

As a means of understanding the inner man, an analysis of Gladstone's relationship with Dante offers several important clues. His study of the *Commedia* was, for Gladstone, a 'vigorous discipline for the heart, the intellect, the whole man'.[2] Dante the person he described as 'the great Christian philosopher . . . who was like the ancient Egyptians of whom it was said they wrought upon the scale of giants with the nicety of jewellers'.[3] But there was more to Gladstone's appreciation of the Florentine poet, important though these attributes were, than objective approval of Dante's disciplined intellect, Christianity, philosophy, grandeur of scale and compactness of style. Gladstone's relationship with Dante was also a very personal one and many parallels can be drawn between their lives, temperaments, attitudes and aspirations, despite the half millennium that divides them. The scope for Britain's great Christian statesman of the nineteenth century to identify with, and draw strength from, Italy's great Christian philosopher of the Middle Ages – and as a private man not an institution – was considerable.

Dante saw his thoughts mirrored in Virgil's: 'S'io fossi di piombo vetro,/ l'imagine di fuor tua non trarrei/ più tosto a me, che quella d'entro impetro./

---

1 'Der Mensch lebt auf Erden ein Doppelleben: ein äusseres und ein inneres. Beide beeinflussen, bedingen einander, sind auf's Innigste miteinander verbunden, können aber durchaus nicht miteinander verwechselt werden. Ein Anderes sind die Erlebnisse des Herzens, des Gemüths. Ein Anderes sind die Erfahrungen, die wir äusserlich, – ein Anderes die, welche wir innerlich machen . . . die Biographie eines bedeutenden Menschen [muss] nicht allein das äussere, sondern das innere Leben desselben in den Kreis ihren Darstellung zu ziehen habe[n]': Scartazzini, *Dante*, 217.
2 Morley, *Gladstone*, i. 151.
3 Gladstone, 'Lord John Russell's translation', 16.

Pur mo venìeno i tuo' pensier tra' miei,/ con simile atto e con simile faccia,/ sì che d'entrambi un sol consiglio fei' ('Were I of leaded glass, I should not draw to me thy outward semblance sooner than I receive thy inward; just now thy thoughts joined with mine, being alike in action and aspect, so that of both I have made one sole counsel').[4] Gladstone may well have felt the same about Dante.

Both men originally had a religious vocation but gave it up to enter politics.[5] Dante remained close to the Franciscan movement all his life, as did Gladstone to High Anglicanism, whose values were expressed by the Oxford Movement to which he gave conditional support as a young man.[6] Dante died on Holy Cross Day 1321 and was buried in the Franciscan church at Ravenna,[7] wearing the habit of the order he loved. Gladstone died on Ascension Day 1898; he was buried in Westminster Abbey wearing, at his own request, the robes of a doctor of civil law[8] of the University of Oxford where he liked to think Dante had studied.[9]

Both men lived at an important transitional time. Dante bridged the Middle Ages and the Renaissance. Gladstone, whose life was half as long again, spanned a period from the beginning of the industrial age to the beginning of the modern. Both men combined the role of statesman with that of theologian and scholar. Dante was prior of Florence before his exile from the city, and afterwards acted as occasional ambassador for certain of his patrons; Gladstone was sixty-four years in parliament, spent thirty-one years as a government minister and thirteen years as prime minister. Both married above themselves socially and were indebted to their wives who, defying stereotypical medieval or Victorian roles, kept their families going during their husbands' absence.[10] Neither man was immune to the attractions of

---

4   DC, Inferno, canto 23, 25–30.

5   'The desire of my youth was to be a clergyman. My mental life (ill represented in the moral being) was concentrated in the Church understood after the narrowest fashion that of the Evangelical school': Gladstone, Autobiographica, 1871–2, 148.

6   One should not, however, ignore the enduring influence on Gladstone of the Evangelicalism of his early years, particularly as regards personal accountability to God, and the importance of virtue and good works. The latter fit neatly into the Aristotelian element of Dante's Commedia, as demonstrated in Limbo, from which Gladstone derives his idea of four 'doctors' leading him through life.

7   Dante's remains were found in a hidden cavity within the mausoleum in 1865 by plumbers involved in refurbishment work prior to Ravenna's 600th anniversary celebrations.

8   As a former prime minister, Gladstone was entitled to wear the robes of a privy councillor.

9   The statue of Gladstone in Westminster Abbey also depicts him wearing the robes of a Doctor of Civil Law, in marked contrast to those of Peel and Disraeli beside him, who are wearing classical togas.

10   Monna Alighieri, who was entitled to remain in Florence on the grounds of her own personal status, may have died in 1308, after which Dante's children joined him in exile, as they were required to do in any case on reaching their majority. There is, however, some debate about the year of her death.

other women. Yet, however they chose to express their affections, there is no evidence to suggest marital infidelity on the part of either.[11] Whatever tender sentiments they felt for the opposite sex seem to have fitted comfortably into the medieval matrix of courtly love or, to use T. S. Eliot's word in describing Dante's love of Beatrice, to have been 'sublimated'[12] into something that was, superficially at least, more spiritual.[13]

For both men, too, fame was a spur. Tilney Bassett wrote: 'One more selection from his literary jottings may be given – Mr Gladstone's choice of what, to his mind, were the finest lines in poetry.'[14] He lists lines from the fifteenth-century Florentine poet Pulci, from Milton, Wordsworth, Shelley, Homer – and Dante, from whom the chosen line is Dante's comment to his old teacher Brunetto Latini: 'm'insegnavate come l'uom s'etterna' ('you taught me how one makes oneself immortal').[15] Dante returns to the theme later in hell, when he has Virgil goad him to take action if he wants to make something of himself, because 'seggendo in piume, in fama non si vien, nè sotto coltre' ('sitting on down or under blankets none comes to fame').[16]

As for the personal characteristics they shared, an interesting insight is provided by other Gladstonian annotations on Scartazzini's *Dante*. The index to the *Diaries* does not mention Gladstone reading this book, which was published in 1869. But it does mention three other works by the same scholar that Gladstone was reading between December 1887 and February 1888. So Gladstone may have been reading the work in question too around the same time. The marks in the margin highlight well-established areas of common interest – for example, the Church and State issue, and the question whether Dante studied at Oxford. What is interesting is that the most heavily marked chapter is that where Scartazzini describes Dante's character. Gladstone marked the sort of characteristics the two men shared. They include being serious and thoughtful, caring for others sometimes at the expense of family,[17] being orderly, liking solitude, pondering at length before responding in a

---

11 For Dante's fidelity record see Federn, *Dante and his time*. For Gladstone's see *Gladstone diaries*, xiii. According to Butler, Boccaccio's biography of Dante records many love affairs in the poet's life (one possible explanation of his need for the refining fire to purify him in Purgatory). It is a charge against which Federn defends him. Gladstone, towards the end of his life, left a 'Declaration' in a note dated 7 December 1896, to his son and pastor Stephen Gladstone (not to be opened until after his death), testifying that 'at no period in my life have I been guilty of the act which is known of that of infidelity to the marriage bed'.

12 Eliot, *Dante*, 48.

13 Many of Gladstone's early letters to his friend, the reformed courtesan Laura Thistlethwayte, are addressed 'Dear Spirit'. A selection of his letters to her is included in the appendix to *Gladstone diaries*, viii. Gladstone burned her letters to him on 25 February 1893, lest they be misunderstood by posterity.

14 *Gladstone papers*, 46–7.

15 DC, *Inferno*, canto 15, 85.

16 Ibid. canto 24, 47–8.

17 'My country is my first wife' Gladstone wrote to Laura Thistlethwayte from Hawarden Castle on 22 Oct. 1869: *Gladstone diaries*, viii. 568.

finished manner, loving honour, tending to impatience in political matters, having a soft heart for women. But they also include being proud, sometimes arrogant and capable of great self-loathing.[18]

In religious matters, both Gladstone and Dante hated the papacy as it was in their own times, though for different reasons. But they loved God and their country, and recognised the importance of achieving some working accommodation between Church and State for the sake of the nation. They also operated in politics strictly according to their consciences, a characteristic that often manifested itself in stubbornness. Each was his own man, answerable to none but God in doing what he thought was right. This was one reason for Gladstone's intense dislike of Roman Catholic hegemony and the doctrine of papal infallibility. In Dante's case it meant remaining in exile, much as he craved a return to office, power and his family, rather than compromise his principles by admitting a guilt he did not accept and professing allegiances he did not share. Like Gladstone, who changed parties from Conservative to Liberal, Dante, though a member of the pro-pope Guelph party, aligned himself with the pro-imperialist Ghibellines when he deemed that to be in Italy's best interest. David Williamson could be describing Dante when he wrote of Gladstone in an appreciation published in the year of his death: 'All through his career he was courageous, never espousing a cause because it was likely to be successful; never hesitating, even with the certainty of losing power and prestige, to lead his party into the lobby where it would be outnumbered . . . His religious faith sustained his physical endurance when all his political hopes were shattered.'[19] Or, as Dante's revered forefather Cacciaguida consoled him when predicting his future political isolation on grounds of principle: 'a te fia bello/ averti fatta parte per stesso' ('it shall be to thine honour to have made a party by thyself').[20]

Williamson's appraisal is of particular interest since it engages with the psychology of Gladstone in a way that was ahead of its time. Even after making allowances for the hagiographic Victorian approach to biography – particularly in the case of great men recently deceased – Williamson's comment holds true for Gladstone, as it would have done for Dante.[21]

Like Willamson's, other biographies published soon after Gladstone's death tended towards adulation. They also focused mainly on his public

---

[18] Scartazzini, *Dante*, 435–45

[19] Williamson, *Gladstone*, p. xvi.

[20] *DC, Inferno*, canto 17, 68–9.

[21] In his parliamentary speech 'On the Bulgarian horrors', London 1876, 40–3, Gladstone calls the pursuit of prestige in politics 'the bane of all upright policies'. In the same speech Gladstone denigrates the claim of then prime minister, Benjamin Disraeli, that the British fleet was in the east 'for the support of British interests', adding: 'I object to this constant system of appeal to our selfish leanings. It sets up false lights – it hides the truth; it disturbs the world.'

life.[22] This was partly convention, but it is also because, until the publication of the *Diaries*, there was little first-hand insight into the psychology of the private man. The availability of the diaries coincided, moreover, with a changing fashion in life-writing which placed greater emphasis on the psychological profile of subjects alongside their achievements. It follows, therefore, that early interpretations differ widely from more recent ones that return often to the anxieties, excitability, tension and restlessness to which Gladstone was prone.

Travis Crosby takes this psychological analysis a step further to explain how Gladstone developed what are sometimes referred to today as 'coping mechanisms' to deal with stress. Dante could be described as one of those mechanisms. The strategies that Crosby lists range from Gladstone's famous tree-felling sessions to his rescue work with prostitutes and his enthusiastic collecting and cataloguing of books, letters, pictures and pottery. This compulsion to create order is perhaps most clearly expressed in the diaries, his account to God for the use of his time: 'By sorting and setting down his daily activities, Gladstone could impose order on the events that crowded in on him in his impossibly busy life . . . The diary taken as a whole is a monument to his determination to control the events of his life.'[23]

Gladstone agreed that imposing order was a way of getting more done in the time available. 'Doch Ordnung lehrt Euch Zeit gewinnen' ('Order teaches you to win time'), he wrote at the start of his diary for 1864, quoting Goethe.[24] Crosby quotes Wemyss Reid as saying that, for Gladstone, each minute 'had its employment, each book (of the many he read in the day) its appointed hour, each paper, letter and document its proper place!'[25]

His reading of Dante could be interpreted as another of Gladstone's ways of handling stress. Certainly in one diary entry he records, after a particularly trying day in parliament: 'Read a little Dante for quiet'.[26] And his frequent quotation of his canon for living, 'In la sua volontade è nostra pace' ('In his will is our peace'), gives it almost the quality of a mantra that accompanied him on his journey through life. Moreover, with his intense need for the comfort of orderliness, the very structured form of Dante's work must have added to the appeal of its content. In the field of poetry, few works have a more ordered structure than the *Commedia*. 'The poem is one great hymn to the spiritual and moral order of the universe', *The Times* newspaper commented on the 600th anniversary of Dante's death.[27]

---

22 See Briggs, 'Victorian images of Gladstone', 36. The problems of reconciling the private and the public man, and the question as to whether a biography should be written immediately after death (while 'the ashes of controversy are still hot') or later (when there is the danger of the detail being forgotten) are also dealt with in Morley, *Gladstone*, i. 1.
23 Crosby, *The two Mr Gladstones*, 10.
24 *Gladstone diaries*, vi. Matthew's footnote identifies the quote as from Goethe, *Faust*, pt 1.
25 Crosby, *The two Mr Gladstones*, quoting Wemyss Reid, *Gladstone*, ii. 601.
26 *Gladstone diaries*, ii, entry for 3 Apr. 1837.
27 *The Times*, Dante supplement, 14 Sept. 1921, ii.

The orderliness of the Middle Ages was an important attraction for the nineteenth, a period of enormous, rapid and unnerving change. It was a time when the moral authority of the Church in Britain was seriously under siege, and even factions in the art world felt threatened by the emphasis on neo-classical precedents. As a result, many people – including the Pre-Raphaelite brotherhood in art, and the neo-Gothicists in architecture, as well as the Oxford Movement in religion – longed for the perceived certainties of an earlier, but simpler, time. As such, medievalism would have been part of Gladstone's intellectual heritage.

One way in which the medieval preoccupation with order expressed itself was in a close interest in the mystical significance attributed to numbers and this is expressed fully in the arrangement of Dante's poem. The *Commedia* is centred on a series of symbolic numbers: three, nine, thirty-three, seven, ten and one hundred. Three is a symbol of the Holy Trinity; nine is three times three; thirty-three is a multiple of three and also Christ's age at his death; ten was considered in the Middle Ages as a symbol of perfection; one hundred is ten times ten. The *Commedia* has three cantiche, each of thirty-three cantos, totalling ninety-nine. The introductory canto of *Inferno* makes one hundred cantos in all. The poem is written in *terza rima*, a verse form of three-line stanzas, written in hendecasyllables producing, therefore, thirty-three syllables per *terzina* (tercet). *Inferno* is divided into nine circles in three divisions, the Vestibule making the tenth. *Purgatorio* is separated into nine levels, the Terrestrial Paradise making ten. *Paradiso* is formed by nine Heavens, plus the Empyrean. Sinners, penitents and the blessed are all arranged according to a three-fold structure. If Gladstone were looking for a work of literature that would satisfy his need for a sense of order, he need look no further than Dante.

The affinities continue. If Williamson's evaluation of Gladstone suggests a character that closely matches Dante, Karl Federn's study of Dante provides a cameo that could equally well describe Gladstone. Of the public man he wrote: 'He was proud and self-conscious in his behaviour, yet of the finest manners, but not adapted to society; of an unyielding temper, often abstracted and lost in thought.'[28] Of the private man, Federn added, 'That Dante was of a loving and fiery disposition, passionate as few men ever were, is evident in every line he wrote. That, on the other side, his character was severe and pure, that he certainly was . . . not a man of brutal sensuality, is likewise evident.'[29] Of the romantic man, he commented that 'a man who borrows all his similes from love, and in these similes speaks a lover's language with such a fire of life that nobody will believe them to be mere allegories – a man who could write the story of Paolo and Francesca must have known

---

[28] Federn, *Dante and his time*, 258.
[29] Ibid.

woman and loved well, and must have devoted to them a good part of his life'.[30]

Gladstone's acknowledgement of the importance of women in his life was simple: 'Friendships with women have constituted no small part of my existence', he told his 'Dear Spirit', Laura Thistlethwayte, in a letter written from Hawarden Castle on 25 October 1869.[31] That he, too, was affected by Francesca da Rimini's story as told by Dante is evident from the Munro sculpture he commissioned,[32] and from the plaque on his memorial.

Among other values that Gladstone may have felt reinforced by his reading of Dante was a sense of hope and justice. Morley related a conversation he had with Gladstone in Pau in January 1892:

> At tea time a good little discussion raised by a protest against Dante's being praised for a complete survey of human nature and the many phases of human lot. Intensity he has, but insight over the whole field of character and life? Mr G. did not make any stand against this, and made the curious admission that Dante was too optimistic to be placed on a level with Shakespeare, or even with Homer.[33]

Owen Chadwick has interpreted this as 'the single criticism of Dante to be found from Gladstone's mouth or pen. It is so untypical that it should be suspect'.[34] Its substantial authenticity, he continued, is only guaranteed 'by the appearance of the favourite Gladstonian word *intensity* and then by Morley's surprise at what he heard, which he marks by the phrase "curious admission" '.[35]

But is it so strange that Gladstone should claim that Dante's 'optimism' set him apart from writers like Homer and Shakespeare, whose breadth of work covered all types and outcomes of the human condition, tragic and comic? Dante's fame, by contrast, rests mainly on one big story and one small book of poetry.[36] And both have happy endings. As Dante explained in a letter to Can Grande della Scala,[37] one of the reasons that his allegorical tale of the soul's journey after death is called a comedy is because justice and love triumph in the end. Even the sign over the Gate of Hell proclaims: 'Jiustizia mosse il mio alto fattore:/ fecemi la divina potestate,/ la somma sapienza e 'l primo amore' ('Justice moved my Maker on high,/ Divine Power made me and Supreme Wisdom and Primal Love').[38] Moreover, just six months after

---

30 Ibid. 259.
31 *Gladstone diaries*, viii. 570.
32 See pp. 36–8 above.
33 Morley, *Gladstone*, ii. 545.
34 Chadwick, 'Young Gladstone', 258.
35 Ibid.
36 See introduction above for Dante's other works.
37 Dante, 'Letter to Can Grande della Scala'.
38 'Giustizia mosse il mio alto fattore:/ Fecemi la divina potestate,/ La somma sapienza e'l primo amore': *DC, Inferno*, canto 3, 4–6.

the Pau conversation with Morley, the periodical *Nineteenth Century* published Gladstone's article, 'Did Dante study at Oxford?'. This was his major tribute to Dante, his only sustained piece of Dante scholarship and, apart from a mention in his tribute to Arthur Hallam in 1898,[39] his last word on Dante before he died. It is likely to have been in preparation at the time of the Morley interview. It gives no indication that Gladstone had changed his mind about Dante's greatness.

Finally, would the path of Gladstone's life have been any different without Dante, given the importance of the Florentine's place in Gladstone's intellectual furniture? While there is no suggestion that Dante provides some hidden key to unlock all the mysteries of Gladstone's psyche, the evidence is strong that the *Commedia* reinforced and authenticated the beliefs he developed independently through experience. And it was, of course, through experience that Dante's own views were forged.

John Hammond sensed that it was the influence of Dante and Homer that set Gladstone apart from other contemporary politicians. Hammond may, of course, have taken this view, where other writers of the time did not, because he was given secret access to a copy of Gladstone's diaries decades before they were published. Other commentators could have had no concept of the scale of Dante's influence on Gladstone and could not therefore have included him in the equation as Hammond could. Discussing Gladstone's popular appeal compared with that of his contemporaries Shaftesbury and Chamberlain, Hammond wrote:

> It is easy to understand how Shaftesbury gained a great place in the affection and respect of the poor. He gave up his life to crusade for the rescue of the weak. It is easy to understand how Chamberlain set on fire the enthusiasm of the working class. He preached a class war . . . With neither is there any mystery about his popularity or his place in the emotions . . . Yet [Gladstone] held in the affections of the working-classes a place deeper and higher than either Shaftesbury or Chamberlain. It is safe to say that for one portrait of anybody else in working-class houses in the 'eighties of the last [nineteenth] century, there were ten of Gladstone.[40]

Hammond added that, to a modern age more alive to the importance of the social questions that Gladstone neglected, this is 'a mystery so strange' that superficial critics call Gladstone an impostor 'who by his immense power of oratory gained an ascendancy that he did not deserve'.[41] However, 'the key to his conquest of the esteem and affection of the English workman [is that] . . . both alike were the result of ideas that distinguished him from other public

---

[39] The article appeared in both the *Youth's Companion* (1898) and the *Daily Telegraph*, 25 Jan. 1898.

[40] Hammond, *Gladstone and the Irish*, 688–9.

[41] Ibid.

men . . . They reflect ultimately the influence on his mind of Homer and Dante'.[42]

Hammond saw Dante's influence on Gladstone as manifesting itself in a feeling for the unity of mankind, a sense of the world as common exile, his faith in democracy and his belief in the principles of nationhood and progress. And despite his learning, he did not patronise: 'His liberal views were not a body of truth acquired from the study of masters like Locke, Bentham and Mill; they were the effect of experience on a mind nursed on Aristotle, Augustine, Dante and Butler.'[43] This echoes the letter mentioned earlier which Gladstone wrote in 1880 to his old school friend Sir Francis Doyle, that his life had been 'remarkable for the mass of searching experience it has brought me ever since I began to pass out of boyhood; owing little to living teachers, but enormously to four dead men . . . It has been experience which has altered my politics'.[44]

Would Gladstone's politics have been significantly different had he not read Dante? Would he have been any less 'The People's William' who could show them 'a world in a grain of sand . . . and Eternity in an hour'?[45] Probably not. His reading of Dante was not his only anchoring-point; Homer, too, was a major influence.[46] And it was, as Gladstone said, experience that altered his politics, albeit experience 'nursed on Dante'. But the inner man might have sensed a lack. Hammond said Dante was the making of Gladstone as a politician. If so, it was because Dante's universality conditioned Gladstone's attitude to life, and Gladstone's attitude to life conditioned his approach to politics.

During the Midlothian campaign, Gladstone addressed a women's meeting at Dalkeith. It has been quoted often in recent years.[47] Discussing the plight of the Afghans, he said:

Do not suffer appeals to national pride to blind you to the dictates of justice. Remember the rights of the savage, as we call him. Remember that the happiness of his humble home, remember that the sanctity of life in the hill village of Afghanistan among the winter snows, is as inviolable in the eye of the Almighty God as can be your own. Remember that He who has united you together as human beings as the same blood and flesh, has bound you by the law of mutual love; that mutual love is not limited by the shores of this island, is not limited by the boundaries of Christian civilisation; that it passes over

42 Ibid.
43 Ibid. 535.
44 Morley, Gladstone, i. 154.
45 Gladstone diaries, i, p. xxvii.
46 See Bebbington, Mind of Gladstone.
47 Quoted in The Times, 20 Sept. 2001, 18. Also interesting in the context of Victorian gender role stereotyping is that Gladstone begins his speech with the words: 'I speak to you, ladies, as women'.

the whole surface of the earth, and embraces the meanest along with the greatest in its unmeasured scope.[48]

Few statements could be more universal. The sentiment could have come straight from *Paradiso*, and chimes with a comment by John Sinclair that 'the only justice for men – this was Dante's lesson – is justice for all men, and the only peace for men on earth is peace with God'.[49] 'We are every one citizens of one true city' ('ciascuna è cittadina d'una vera città'), Dante wrote.[50]

In his literary reviews, articles and addresses, Dante is the poet that Gladstone quotes most often, together with Virgil and Shakespeare. And, as Agatha Ramm has observed in her essay on Gladstone as a man of letters,

> the quotations bear a personal stamp . . . This is caused by their being called up by some association of ideas personal to himself. One can show that they *are* called from memory because the *Diaries* notice when he read the works from which they come. They do not come from what he is reading when he is writing, but from something read long before or some time before. The quotations are lines that *he* has remembered, because they chime with some thought of *his own*, not because they are especially poetic, not because they are especially important in conveying the meaning of the poet who has written them. Dante's 'in sua voluntade è nostra pace', 'in God's will is our peace' he quotes several times either alone or with neigh-bouring lines and he seldom uses a quotation more than once. It tells us more about Gladstone than about Dante.[51]

Gladstone was a private, enclosed man. In his private, enclosed world, Dante could provide him with the kind of support, validation and endorsement of his beliefs and aspirations that he may have felt too reserved to seek from friends or colleagues. Few people will ever have had the pattern of their outward lives changed directly and dramatically by a single book. Gladstone himself conceded that, as a general rule, 'it is but rarely that we can trace the influence exercised by particular books upon particular minds'.[52] But many may have had their inner lives quietly fashioned, nourished or reinforced – and thereby had their outward lives subtly and indirectly influenced – by a work whose values and perhaps even certain prejudices coincided with their own. So it was for Gladstone with Dante.

The universalism of Dante and his *Commedia* meant that Gladstone had no need to reject his 'dottore' when his own political allegiance changed. As a New Tory, he could admire certain aspects of Dante's medievalism – its certainties, its belief in an established hierarchy, its lack of liberalism with a

---

48 Ibid.
49 DC, *Paradiso*, 100.
50 Ibid. canto 13, 94–5.
51 Ramm, 'Gladstone as man of letters', 20, 21.
52 Gladstone, *Bishop Butler*, 132.

small 'l' – together with Dante's own brand of anti-papism. Later, the Liberal Gladstone could admire Dante's pan-Europeanism, his concept of the community of Christian states, his internationalism even, which sought the greater good of Italy within the Holy Roman Empire. Like all supporters of the Risorgimento, Gladstone had in Dante an earlier champion of Italian nationhood to fall back on. Gladstone the statesman could commend above all Dante's sense of civic duty, the arena where the personal and the political are perhaps most difficult to negotiate.

The poetic side of Gladstone could be charmed by the magic of Dante's art, pioneering and democratic as it was in medieval Europe in using the vernacular. The man of passion could be roused by Dante's righteous indignation at cases of injustice whenever and wherever in the world they occurred, and doubtless take some satisfaction from the perpetrators' relegation to the lower regions. The lover, courtly or otherwise, could identify with the Florentine's tender appreciation of women, and not only of virtuous ones. The Evangelical turned High Anglican could find in Dante's Christianised Aristotelianism the concept of human perfectibility before death, the belief that an honourable and a dutiful life is as important as faith in securing salvation, and that whether the one will succeed without the other is debatable. Gladstone the pilgrim found in Dante a guide and companion on his journey back to God, just as Dante found a guide of his own first in Virgil, and then in Beatrice.[53]

And the idealist in Gladstone, who struggled all his life, as his diaries show, to submit his own personal will to what he perceived to be God's purpose for him on earth, would have shared Dante's joy in the finale of *Paradiso*. Here the struggle ends. Here desire and will are brought together by the power of divine love. Here the pilgrim at last sees the face of God. Dante wrote: 'But now my desire and will, like a wheel that spins with even motions, were revolved by the Love that moves the sun and other stars.'[54] This is so close as to be almost indistinguishable from what Gladstone wrote to his wife Catherine on 21 January 1844. He began by quoting yet again that 'rare gem', Piccarda's line from *Paradiso*: 'In la sua volontade è nostra pace'. After which he explained:

> The final state which we are to contemplate with hope, and to seek by discipline, is that in which our will shall be *one* with the will of God; not merely shall submit to it, not merely shall follow after it, but shall live and move

---

53 Virgil, symbolising human reason, could only take Dante as far as the earthly paradise, where Beatrice took over as a symbol of divine grace. Gladstone needs as his guide only Dante who, as both philosopher and Christian, can be his guide through the entire journey of life.

54 'ma già volgeva il mio disio e 'l velle/ sì come rota ch'ugualmente è mossa/ l'amor che move il sole e l'altre stelle': DC, *Paradiso*, canto 33, 143–6. So ends the *Commedia*.

with it, even as the pulse of the blood in the extremities acts with the central movement of the heart.[55]

Statesman and scholar, politician and poet, lover, man of conscience, idealist, spiritual pilgrim: many sides of Gladstone had their counterpart in Dante, many facets of nineteenth-century Britain's Grand Old Man were mirrored in the life and thoughts of medieval Europe's greatest poet. It is unlikely that, without Dante, Gladstone's contribution to public life would have been any different or any less. But without Dante as a personal inspiration, as a provider of coherence and order who articulated many of his innermost beliefs, it is hard to imagine that Gladstone as a private man would not have felt a desiderium. As an article in *The Times* of 16 January 1883, entitled 'Mr Gladstone and Dante' commented:

> There is no reason why our Premiers should continue to be students of Dante and Homer, and we do not predict any very disastrous results if they cease to do so; but all the same a little sweetness and light will have gone out of public life and a precious element will have been lost when our chief statesmen scorn poetry and stick to Blue Books.[56]

---

[55] Morley, *Gladstone*, i.161.

[56] *The Times*, 16 Jan. 1883, 8. The article would appear to have been written in response to Gladstone's letter to his Italian friend Giuliani, published in *The Standard* a week earlier, as it begins with a reference to Gladstone's recent 'interesting letter to the author of a commentary on the great Florentine'.

APPENDIX

Gladstone's Marginalia on the Commedia

Hand-written notes to Gladstone's own copy of the *Commedia* (Minerva Press, Padua 1822, edited and annotated by Baldassare Lombardi). Reduced in size to reproduce original page layout.

Inferno

[Inside front cover]

Diff.	14. 34.	Popes	3. 60.	
	20. 11–15.		7. 47.	
	24. 125.		19. 46. espy.	90–3.
				115–17.
			27.70. Bonif. XVIII, 85.	
			Celestine 104.	

Good citizens, bad men 6. 81.		Florence	6. 61.
Epicurus 10. 13.			10. 26.
Art & nature 11. 99.			13. 143.
Popes etc. 7. 46.			15. 61.
Trust reposed 15. 118			16. 9. 73.
Carrara m. 20. 49.			19. 17.
Michael Scott 20. 115.			22. 95.
Fame 24. 47			26. 1.
Philosophy, phys. 25. 82&49.			
Ulysses 26. 55.		Pisa	33. 79.
History 28. 7.		Genoa	33. 151.
Mahomet 28. 22.			
Alchymy 29. 118.			
French char. 29. 122, 3.		Similes	24. 1–15.
Siennese 29. 122, 134.			106. Phoenix
Brutus & Cassius 34. 64.			112.
Gravitation 34. 110.			25. 64.
			79.
			26. 25.
			34.
			27. 7.
			94 x.
			31. 54.
			32. 25. 31.130.

Gate
Ugolino
Lucifer

[Inside back cover]

Words It. & Germ.   landa 14. 8

se, impr. 29. 105. 30.34.
31. 83 al trar d'un balestro

Purgatorio

[Inside front cover: no notes]

[Inside back cover]

VI. XI.XIV (Flor.) 16–66. XVI. 58–132. XVII. 85 ad fin (phil.)
XVIII. 1–75. Phil. XXII. Virgil & Statius

p. 109.   Death with the name of Mary spoken
  125.   Italy apostrophised
  236.   Merit (good)
  256,7. Chr. & pagan mixed. 592.
  603.   protest aft. (abt.?) popular opinion of poets
  702,3. modesty
  732.   Beatrice. mystical or real?
  771.   La puttana

Paradiso

[Inside front cover]

              Giù per lo mondo senza fine amaro (Inf.)
              E per lo monte, del cui bel cacume (Purg.)
(xvii. 112)   Gli occhi della mia Donna mi levaso
to
(xxi. 59)   La dolce sinfonia di Paradiso (Parad.)

Summary of the seven heavens XXII. 139–150.

[Inside back cover, over two pages]

I. 103–42, III. 46–90.
III–IV from 64. VII from 61. XII (San Domenico). XIV. XVII. XIX.
XX, I, II, III, IV, V, VI, VII to 66. IX 85–128 on the preachers, XX, I, III
V 1–12.

VI. 112. 124
IX. 133. Decretals. X. 103
XIII. 52. Platonism. & segg. 112. 118. Wise

XV. 40. Heaven why unintelligible
     79. Motto for a great subject
XVI. 1. foreknowledge (51. Rome)
                         (18. 121)
XXI. 52. mercede e merito
XXIV. 100. Evidence of miracles
XXVI. 64. The measure of human loves
XXVII. 19 & segg. &n. on 25 ref to Petrarch & Boccaccio

an imp. not a Ghib.
a RC not a pap.

High doctrine. n 805, 6, on 32. 67
Scholastic def. Of substance, self-subsistence stop 832
IV. 41 Nihil in intellectute

Bibliography

Unpublished primary sources

Hawarden, St Deiniol's Library
Glynne-Gladstone MSS

Liverpool, Central Record Office
Liverpool Dante Society records

Liverpool University, Sydney Jones Library
Liverpool Dante Society records

Manchester, Central Archive Office
Manchester Dante Society records

Manchester, Central Language and Literature Library
Manchester Dante Society records

Oxford, Taylor Institute
Oxford Dante Society records.

Printed primary sources: W. E. Gladstone

Gladstone, W. E., *The State in its relations with the Church*, London 1841
――― 'Lord John Russell's translation of Dante's Francesca da Rimini', *English Review* (Apr. 1844), 1–16
――― 'Works and life of Giacomo Leopardi', *Quarterly Review* (Mar.1850), 293–336.
――― *The Vatican decrees in their bearing on civil allegiance: a political expostulation*, London 1874
――― 'Italy and her Church', *Church Quarterly Review* i (1875), 1–35.
――― 'On the Bulgarian horrors', speech delivered to parliament, London 1876
――― *Gleanings of past years, 1843–78*, London 1879
――― 'Senti senti anima mia', *Nineteenth Century* (Sept.1883), 357–60
――― 'Did Dante study at Oxford', *Nineteenth Century* xxxi (June 1892), 1032–42
――― *Studies subsidiary to the works of Bishop Butler*, Oxford 1896
――― *Later gleanings*, London 1897

—— 'Arthur Henry Hallam', *Youth's Companion* (Jan. 1898)

—— 'Personal recollections of Arthur H. Hallam', *Daily Telegraph*, 5 June 1898

—— *Diaries*, ed. M. R. D. Foot (vols i–ii) and H. C. G. Matthew (vols iii–xiv), Oxford 1968–94

—— *Autobiographica, 1871–2*, ed. John Brooke and Mary Sorensen, London 1981

—— and Lord Lyttelton, *Translations*, London 1861

The Gladstone papers, London 1930, ed. A. Tilney Bassett

Printed primary sources: Dante Alighieri

Dante Alighieri, *Opere di Dante*, Padua 1822.

—— *The vision of Purgatory and Paradise*, trans. and comm. Henry Cary, London 1893

—— *Divine Comedy: Inferno, Purgatorio and Paradiso*, original text with English trans. by John Sinclair (1939), New York 1961

—— *La vita nuova (Poems of youth)*, trans. and intro. Barbara Reynolds, London 1969

—— *The Divine Comedy*, trans. and comm. Charles Singleton, Princeton 1973

—— *The Divine Comedy: Hell*, trans. and intro. Dorothy Sayers, Harmondsworth 1987

Printed primary sources: other

Gladstone, Mary, *Mary Gladstone: her diaries and letters, 1870–1886*, ed. Lucy Masterman, New York 1930

The letters of Arthur Henry Hallam, ed. Jack Kolb, Columbus 1981

Ruskin, John, *Works*, ed. E. T. Cook and Alexander Wedderburn, London 1912

The writings of Arthur Hallam, ed. T. H. Vail Motter, London 1943

Newspapers

The Daily Telegraph
The Manchester Guardian
The Standard
The Times

Contemporary books and articles

Ampère, Jean-Jacques, 'Voyage Dantesque', in *La Grèce, Rome et Dante*, Paris 1848

Apjohn, Lewis, *W. E. Gladstone: his life and times*, London 1899

Barnett Smith, G., *Life of Gladstone*, London n.d.

Bartolini, Agostino, 'Il viaggio di Dante a Oxford: a proposito d'un articolo di Gladstone', *Arcadia* vii/3 (1894), 1–18

Bassett, A. Tilney, *Gladstone to his wife*, London 1936

Beerbohm, Max, *The poet's corner*, London 1904

Bryce, James, *The Holy Roman Empire* (1864), London 1925

Bunyan, John, *The pilgrim's progress*, ed. Roger Sharrock, London 1987

Caetani, Michelangelo, *Tre chiose . . . nella Divina Commedia di Dante Alighieri: Three explanatory notes . . . in the Divine Comedy of Dante Alighieri*, n.p 1876

——— *La materia della Divina Commedia*, Florence 1894

Carlyle, Thomas, *Past and present*, London 1845

Carmichael, Charles H. E., *Dante and the thirteenth century*, London 1877

Cornoldi, G. M., *La Divina Commedia: a commentary*, n.p. 1887

Croce, Enrico, *Carta d'Italia illustrativa della Divina Commedia di Dante*, Genoa 1875

Drew, Mary, *Catherine Gladstone*, London 1920

Federn, Karl, *Dante and his time*, trans. A. J. Butler, London 1872

Gosse, Edmund, *Father and son* (1907), London 1989

——— *Some diversions of a man of letters*, London 1919

Gurney, Emilia Russel, *Dante's pilgrim's progress; or, the passage of the blessed soul from the slavery of the present corruption to the liberty of eternal glory*, London 1897

Hallam, Arthur, *Remains in verse and prose*, Boston 1863

Macaulay, T. B., 'Gladstone on Church and State', in *Critical and historical essays*, London 1907

Morley, John, *Life of Gladstone*, London 1908

Plumptre, Henry, *Commedia and canzoniere*, London 1886

Ruskin, John, *Pre-Raphaelitism*, New York 1886

——— *Sesame and lilies*, Orpington 1894

Scartazzini, G. A., *Dante: seine Zeit, sein Leben und seine Werke*, Biel 1869

——— *A companion to Dante*, London 1893

Schooling, J. Holt, 'The handwriting of Mr Gladstone from March 1822 to March 1894', *Strand Magazine* viii (1894), 73–89

Sermatelli, Bartolomeo, *Discorso sopra la prima cantica del divinissimo theologo Dante d'Alighieri, del bello nobilissimo fiorentino, intitolata Commedia*, n.p.n.d.

Smith, Samuel, *My life-work*, London 1902

Symonds, J. A., *An introduction to the study of Dante*, London 1872

Tennyson, Alfred, *Selected poems*, London 1991

Tennyson, Hallam, *Alfred, Lord Tennyson: a memoir*, London 1851

Toynbee, Paget, *Dante studies and researches*, London 1902

——— *Dante in English literature from Chaucer to Cary*, London 1909

——— *Life of Dante*, London 1910

——— *Britain's tribute to Dante in art and literature*, Oxford 1921

——— 'Oxford and Dante', in A. Cippico, H. E. Goad, E. C. Gardner W. P. Ker and W. Seton (eds), *Dante: essays in commemoration, 1321–1921*, London 1921

——— *Concise Dante dictionary*, Oxford 1924

Tozer, H. F., *An English commentary on Dante's Divina Commedia*, Oxford 1901

Wemyss Reid, T., *The life of William Ewart Gladstone*, London 1899

Williamson, David, *William Ewart Gladstone: statesman and scholar*, London 1898

Secondary sources

Altick, Richard D., *Victorian people and ideas*, London 1974

Anderson, William, *Dante the maker*, London 1980

Baldassari, Stefano Ugo and Arielle Saiber (eds), *Images of quattrocento Florence*, London 2000

Battiscombe, Georgina, *Mrs Gladstone*, London 1956

Beales, D. E. D., *England and Italy, 1859–60*, London 1961

—— *The Risorgimento and the unification of Italy*, London 1981

—— 'Garibaldi in England: the politics of Italian enthusiasm', in John Davis and Paul Ginsborg (eds), *Society and politics in the age of Risorgimento*, Cambridge 1991, 184–216

—— 'Gladstone and Garibaldi', in Peter Jagger (ed.), *Gladstone*, London 1998, 137–56

Bebbington, David, *The mind of Gladstone: religion, Homer and politics*, Oxford 2004

Biagini, Eugenio, *Gladstone*, Basingstoke 2000

Bowler, Peter J., *The invention of progress: the Victorians and the past*, Oxford 1989

Boyde, Patrick, *Human vices and human worth in Dante's 'comedy'*, Cambridge 2000

Briggs, Asa, 'Victorian images of Gladstone', in Peter Jagger (ed.), *Gladstone*, London 1998, 33–50

Butler, Perry, *Gladstone: Church, State and Tractarianism*, Oxford 1982

Caesar, Michael (ed.), *Dante: the critical heritage*, London 1988

Catto, J. I. and Ralph Evans (eds), *The history of the University of Oxford*, II: *Late mediaeval Oxford*, Oxford 1992

Chadwick, Owen, 'Young Gladstone and Italy', *Journal of Ecclesiastical History* xxx (1979), 245–59

Chandler, Alice, *A dream of order: the mediaeval ideal in nineteenth century English literature*, London 1971

Checkland. S. G., *The Gladstones: a family biography, 1764–1851*, Cambridge 1971

Crosby, Travis, *The two Mr Gladstones: a study in psychology and history*, New Haven–London 1997

Cunningham, Gilbert, *The Divine Comedy in English: a critical bibliography, 1782–1900*, London 1965

Davie, Mark, 'Not an after-dinner relaxation: Gladstone on translating Dante', *Journal of European Studies* xxiv (1994), 386–400

Davies, W. W., *Gladstone and the unification of Italy*, Oxford 1918

Davis, Charles T., *Dante's Italy and other essays*, Philadelphia 1984

Deacon, Richard, *The private life of Mr Gladstone*, London 1965

Eliot, T. S., *Dante*, London 1929

Farnell, Stewart, *The political ideas of the Divine Comedy: an introduction*, Maryland 1985

Ferrante, Joan, *Woman as image in mediaeval literature: from the twelfth century to Dante*, New York 1975

Feuchtwanger, E. J., *Gladstone*, London 1975

Foot, M. D., 'Gladstone and Panizzi', *British Library Journal* v (1979), 48–56

Foster, Kenelm, *The two Dantes*, London 1977

Gardiner, John, *The Victorians: an age in retrospect*, London 2002

Ginsberg, Warren, *Dante's aesthetics of being*, Ann Arbor 1999

Gissing, George, *Born in exile*, London 1993

Gombrich, E. H., *Gombrich on the Renaissance*, London 1998

Hale, John, *England and the Italian Renaissance*, London 1996

Hammond, J. L., *Gladstone and the Irish nation*, London 1938

—— and M. R. D. Foot, *Gladstone and liberalism*, London 1952

d'Haussy, Christiane, 'Gladstone, France and his French contemporaries', in Peter Francis (ed.), *The Gladstone umbrella*, Hawarden 2001, 115–36

Havely, Nick (ed.), *Dante's modern afterlife: reception and response from Blake to Heaney*, Basingstoke 1998

Helmstadter, Richard J., 'Conscience and politics: Gladstone's first book', in Bruce Kinzer (ed.), *The Gladstonian turn of mind*, Toronto 1985, 3–42

Holmes, George, 'Dante and the popes', in Cecil Grayson (ed.), *The world of Dante*, Oxford 1980, 18–43

Hughes, Kathryn, *George Eliot: the last Victorian*, London 1998

Jackson, H. J., *Marginalia: readers writing in books*, London 2001

Jenkins, Roy, *Gladstone*, London 1995

Laski, Marghanita, *George Eliot and her world*, Norwich 1978

Lewis, R. W. B., *Dante*, London 2001

McDougall, Stuart Y., *Dante among the moderns*, Chapel Hill–London 1985

McGann, Jerome, *Dante Gabriel Rossetti and the game that must be lost*, New Haven 2000

Magnus, Philip, *Gladstone: a biography*, London 1954

Mallet, Charles Edward, *A history of the University of Oxford*, I: *The mediaeval university and the colleges founded in the Middle Ages*, London 1968

Marlow, Joyce, *Mr and Mrs Gladstone: an intimate biography*, London 1977

Matthew, H. C. G., *Gladstone*, Oxford 1997.

—— 'Gladstone and the University of Oxford', a lecture given in Christ Church Hall, 18 May 1998, published in the College's *Annual Report* for 1998 and reprinted in the *Oxford Magazine* clxx, Oxford 1999.

Milbank, Alison, *Dante and the Victorians*, Manchester 1998

—— 'Moral luck in the second circle: Dante and the Victorian fate of tragedy', in Havely, *Dante's modern afterlife*, 73–89

Miller, Edward, 'Antonio Panizzi and the British Museum', *British Library Journal* v (1979), 37–46

Newsome, David, *The parting of friends*, London 1966

—— *The Victorian world picture*, London 1998

Nuttall, Geoffrey N., *The faith of Dante Alighieri*, London 1969

Pite, Ralph, *The circle of our vision: Dante's presence in English romantic poetry*, Oxford 1994

Pointon, Marcia, 'Gladstone as art patron and collector', *Victorian Studies* xix (1974), 73–98

Powell, Geoffrey, *Hell and the Victorians*, Oxford 1974

Powell, John, 'Small marks and instinctual responses: a study in the uses of Gladstone's marginalia', *Nineteenth Century Prose*, special issue xix/3 (1992), 1–17

Ramm, Agatha, 'Gladstone as man of letters', *Nineteenth Century Prose* xvii (1989–90), 1–29

Reynolds, Simon, *William Blake Richmond: an artist's life*, Norwich 1995

Sandiford, K. A. P., 'Gladstone and Europe', in Bruce Kinzer (ed.), *The Gladstonian turn of mind*, Toronto 1985, 177–96

Schreuder, D. M., 'Gladstone and Italian unification 1848–70: the making of a Liberal', *English Historical Review* lxxxv (1970), 475–501

Scott, John A., *Dante's political purgatory*, Philadelphia 1996

Shannon Richard, *Gladstone: Peel's inheritor, 1809–1865*, London 1999

—— *Gladstone: heroic minister, 1865–1898*, London 1999

Shapiro, Marianne, *Woman, earthly and divine, in the 'Comedy' of Dante*, Ann Arbor 1995

Southern, R. W., *The making of the Middle Ages*, London 1970

Steiner, George, *Grammars of creation*, London 2001

Strachey, Lytton, *Eminent Victorians*, London 1986

Thompson, Andrew, *George Eliot and Italy: literary, cultural and political influences from Dante to the Risorgimento*, Basingstoke 1998

The Victorian vision of Italy (exhibition catalogue), Leicester Museums and Art Gallery, Leicester 1969

Wertheim, Margaret, *The pearly gates of cyberspace: a history of space from Dante to the internet*, New York 1999

Wheeler, Michael, *English fiction of the Victorian period*, London 1994

Withey, Lynne, *Grand tours and Cook's tours: a history of leisure travel, 1750–1915*, London 1998

Woodhouse, John (ed.), *Dante and governance*, Oxford 1997

Wragg, Lonsdale, *Dante and his Italy*, London 1907

Wright, Herbert G., *Boccaccio in England from Chaucer to Tennyson*, London 1957

Index

(Entries in **bold** indicate illustrations)